Wireless Game Development in Java™ with MIDP 2.0

Ralph Barbagallo

Wordware Publishing, Inc.

Library of Congress Cataloging-in-Publication Data

Barbagallo, Ralph.
  Wireless game development in Java with MIDP 2.0 / by Ralph Barbagallo.
    p. cm.
  Includes index.
  ISBN 1-55622-998-4 (pbk.)
  1. Computer games—Programming. 2. Java (Computer program language) 3.
  Wireless communication systems—Programming. I. Title.
  QA76.76.C672B365 2004
  794.8'1526—dc22   2004013484
                                                          CIP

ISBN 1-55622-998-4

10 9 8 7 6 5 4 3 2 1
0604

All inquiries for volume purchases of this book should be addressed to Wordware
Publishing, Inc., at the above address. Telephone inquiries may be made by calling:

(972) 423-0090

To Ralph, Marie, and Anne Marie!

Contents

Foreword

Not too long ago — I believe it was at the end of 1999 — a press release was put out by Motorola and Sun Microsystems. They announced kJava, a version of Java for limited devices such as mobile phones, which would allow application downloads onto the device. At that time I don't think anyone in the mobile industry quite understood what that would mean to all of us and I don't think the game developer community understood the impact Java would have as a platform to build games on. In early 2001 a mobile phone was still either a closed closet full of proprietary software or it was a big old "communicator" with some early-days open OS, such as EPOC (which later evolved into Symbian OS). Since then a lot has happened, both on the technology side and with Java on mobile phones.

Today, just a few years later, Java for mobile phones (or rather J2ME MIDP CLDC — what's with these acronyms anyway?) is the key technology for allowing games to be added to mobile phones after they ship. All major manufacturers of mobile phones (with a few exceptions) are currently behind it; most mobile operators require J2ME MIDP in phones, and in the end consumers are able to enjoy it. Also, Java MIDP has now evolved into its second iteration. What's great for game developers is that the major enhancements in MIDP 2.0 focus on dedicated game APIs, such as sprite management and improved bitmap control. This shows the importance of and the focus on games based on MIDP 2.0 for mobile phones. With the components we are building into the mobile phones today, the performance of MIDP 2.0 lets you create amazing games.

But even running MIDP 2.0, mobile phones have inherent limitations such as smaller screen size, refresh rate, a portrait aspect ratio, etc. In my opinion, the most limiting factor when creating an awesome game experience today is the input method offered: usually a joystick and a couple of programmable buttons. The need for a game design that takes this into account is essential — if I hear another pitch on bringing retro games onto mobile phones I don't know what I'll do! ;-). At this point we are still waiting for the first super-hit game. I think that game will be designed to deliver an extraordinary game experience using the capabilities of MIDP 2.0 and at the same time turning the input limitations into an advantage.

I have known the author of this book, Ralph Barbagallo, for a couple of years now. We actually met at GDC when I demoed one of our first Java-capable phones to him. Ralph had just gotten out of the PC gaming business and was looking for something to use his gaming skills on. I was given the second degree on our strategy on Java and how we were going to support and evolve Java in future products. I told him that Java would be as important to mobile gaming as DirectX has been to PC gaming, and Ralph argued that the sheer number of phones in the coming years combined with the lesser effort of actually creating the games made Java a really interesting platform to try out. And here we are today. We can now say that, in the end, we both underestimated how Java has been embraced by the mobile industry, game developers, and customers alike.

I could go on about this for a long time, but instead I will stop here and encourage you to indulge yourself in the good stuff that Ralph has put together for you. You've come to the right place for some insight into MIDP 2.0 game development and I'm excited that you picked this book up and decided to get jiggy with mobile gaming. I can't wait to try out your new games.

Signing off...

Mikael Nerde
Head of Sony Ericsson Developer Program
Stockholm, Sweden

Acknowledgments

In the year or so between the completion of this book and the release of my first book, *Wireless Game Development in C/C++ with BREW*, we have all witnessed the rapid development of tools, technologies, products, and business models in the wireless gaming industry. This book covers some of these new developments with the introduction of MIDP 2.0. However, with the industry growing so fast, a number of different books could be written on many different facets of wireless programming. They are beginning to fill the shelves at your local bookstore as we speak.

Anyway, many people helped me out in the course of this book's development. This includes Wes Beckwith and Jim Hill at Wordware who put up with my somewhat erratic schedule. Also David Sowsy at Savaje and Tom Park at Acroband, who heroically tech-checked this work. A big thanks goes out to Mikael Nerde and Jens Greve at Sony Ericsson who kept me up to date with the latest handsets as well as fine imported Swedish Viol-flavored candy. (Which next to Princess Cake is probably the greatest contribution to human society the Vikings ever gave us.)

Oh yeah, of course there are my parents — we can't forget the obligatory parental acknowledgment. As I said last time, without them I'd probably be a random assortment of molecules in a tube of toothpaste or a can of baked beans or something. Sure, I used that schtick last book, but it's all true!

A lot of other people helped out on this book including getting pictures of applications, providing technical information, and other forms of moral support. These include Oliver Miao at Centerscore, John Szeder at Digital Chocolate, John Chasey at Iomo, Kristian Segerstråle at Macrospace, and Roger Seto for providing some of the graphics used in this book. I can't forget the crew at *Game Developer Magazine*, such as the recently departed Jennifer Olsen and Peter K. Sheerin who continually allow me to publish articles and sneak plugs for my company and my books in my craftily written byline. Oh yeah, and the trusty crew at the Valencia Town Center Coffee Bean & Tea Leaf for providing plenty of fine caffeinated beverages. I'll pour a little Moroccan Mint Latte out on the concrete for my baristas that ain't here.

Since writing my first book, lots of different people from around the world have written me or otherwise hunted me down like a dog for various reasons. Some people are just fans, others shower me with gifts and cash. Sadly, all the groupies have been male so far. We games programmers still have a lot to learn from our rock star cousins. Anyway, thanks to all the folks who contacted me about my first book with praise, jeers, bug fixes, business proposals, free lunches, and trips to foreign lands.

Oh yeah, I almost forgot. I have to list all the music I've been listening to during the creation of this book. Let's see....Gang Starr, M.F. Doom/King Gheedorah/Viktor Vaughn/MADVILLAIN, Ghostface Killah, The Notorious B.I.G., Jay-Z, Kurious/Biollante, Kool Keith, People Under The Stairs, De La Soul, Willie Hutch, Diamond D, John Carpenter, Z-Man/Gingerbread Man, Chris Lowe, Wu Tang Clan, 7L & Esoteric, Intelligent Hoodlum/Tragedy, Non Phixion, Jedi Mind Tricks, Wyclef, Del The Funky Homosapien, Powerule, Large Professor, Main Source, Al Tariq, James Brown, Monsta Island Czars, MC Ren, EPMD, Pete Rock/INI, Ron Grainer (The Omega Man!), and probably a bunch of other stuff I totally forgot to list! Go to your local record shop now!

Chapter 1

Introduction

The Story So Far...

By the time this book is on store shelves, wireless gaming will be in full swing. What started as a few primitive blocks chasing dots around a screen on an unwieldy little monochrome handset has matured to lush gaming experiences complete with full-color graphics, animation, and multi-track musical scores. In some cases, these games are running on "handsets" that look more like a Nintendo GameBoy Advance than something you make phone calls with.

The ever-growing catalog of wireless games is astounding. Now, there are all kinds of games running on mobile phones. Sports games, card games, puzzle games, action games, games based on movies, games advertising popular consumer products, games tied in with major console and PC releases, and just about every other genre you can think of are now available on handsets worldwide.

The wireless gaming industry is finally at the point where it is possible to get a return on your development investment. This is not just in Japan and South Korea, where the mobile gaming market is arguably the most robust, but all over the planet. Carriers, handset manufacturers, and publishers have developed a business model that, while not perfect, at the very least is able to generate revenue from paying customers.

We mobile gaming developers had to suffer through years of feeble APIs, a myriad of so-called "platforms," half-baked distribution systems, and a host of other growing pains as the industry matured. Many of these issues are still here, but we are leaps and bounds from the humble beginnings of monochrome text-based WAP pages and simplistic embedded games.

Sun Microsystems was one of the first companies to recognize mobile phones as a potentially lucrative new avenue for data services and applications. Sun's Java platform was slimmed down for smaller devices including mobile phones in the form of Java 2 Micro Edition (J2ME). Sun further catered their platform specifically to handsets using the CLDC/MIDP profile and configuration. These confusing acronyms defined a series of features and packages specifically designed for the restrictive environment of cell phones.

The first version of MIDP, MIDP 1.0, didn't do very much. It had lacking graphics functionality, virtually no sound support, a highly inflexible GUI, limited input capabilities, few network communications options, and a lot of other hurdles for game development. Despite the MIDP standard's stagnation over the years, Java handset manufacturers began releasing phones with full-color graphics, multiple channel sound, and console-style control pads. As a result, many wireless phone manufacturers and carriers began to include their own custom packages in the firmware. Motorola, Siemens, Sony Ericsson, SprintPCS, Nokia, and many other firms created custom SDKs to address their handsets' capabilities that were not accessible in the plain-vanilla MIDP 1.0 specification.

For a while, Sun had been forming a new MIDP revision to address many of these concerns. Finally, Sun has released the long-awaited MIDP 2.0 to the world. This major upgrade not only includes many other general enhancements to the Micro Java platform, but also a game API dedicated to the needs of wireless game developers. Built-in support for tiles, sprites, animation, and MIDI music are now part of the MIDP 2.0 standard. This book will guide you through these new features, as well as other major handset-specific SDKs and third-party packages useful to game developers.

Just Who Do You Think You Are?

My name is Ralph Barbagallo, and I am a professional game developer. In the past, I have worked for such companies as Ion Storm, Neversoft, and Papyrus/Sierra On-Line on a variety of platforms and genres. Since my days working on so-called "real games" for both PCs and consoles, I have struck out on my own — forming my own game development company, Flarb LLC (www.flarb.com). One of the main focuses of Flarb has been the development of wireless games. Flarb produced some of the earliest BREW games for Verizon Wireless' network, as well as both Java and BREW mobile games for carriers all over the planet. My first book, *Wireless Game Development in C/C++ with BREW*, was a success — so naturally a book on J2ME would be the obvious follow-up. Well...here it is!

Who Is This Book For?

This is not a book designed to teach you general programming, or even general game programming for that matter. This book is intended for those who already have some familiarity with game programming and want to get acquainted with the relevant features of the MIDP 2.0 API. With the glut of game development books out right now, I really don't see the point in writing a 1200-page tome covering every possible aspect of game programming. These days there are books out on just about every aspect of game development. Books on general game programming that include information on AI, collision, physics, data structures, and such convey concepts that are applicable to any language and API.

Thus, this book is focused squarely on using J2ME to create games — and essentially learning how to use MIDP to apply your game programming knowledge to the platform. I also expect you to have at least some knowledge of Java; however, I do from time to time explain a few basic Java concepts.

How Do I Use This Book?

Every major block of functionality relevant to game programming is covered in this book. Although some sections may seem highly reference-oriented, this is not a general MIDP 2.0 reference. There are plenty of other books and web sites out there for that purpose. Instead, this book walks you through the game-related functionality of J2ME/MIDP with some basic examples and detailed instructions. If you want to know every tiny detail, method, and field of each class, check the official documentation.

Coding Conventions

Much to the chagrin of some programmers out there, I am a fan of Hungarian notation. However, my Java-weenie friends contest that this is a no-no in Java style. Thus, I am going to adhere (at least somewhat) to the Java style standards as detailed on Sun's own web site (java.sun.com/docs/codeconv/html/CodeConvTOC .doc.html) as well as the Java community recommendations listed at geosoft.no/javastyle.html. Personally, I'm not a huge fan of this coding style — but in the interest of keeping it simple, I won't expose you to my Hungarian madness for the time being. Rather, I will continue to use it in my personal projects. And I don't care what you say, I think suffixing private class variables with an underscore is silly. But I'll do it. It doesn't mean I have to like it, though.

How Do I Use the Companion Files?

Even if not directly referenced in the text, most chapters in this book have at least one example MIDlet that shows basic usage of the major concepts. The companion files are available at www.wordware.com/files/wireless2. There is a folder in these files for each chapter that contains the source code. These are all stored in the directory structure required by Sun's KToolbar, as that is the primary IDE for this book. Simply copy the folders underneath the chapter folder to the apps folder in your KToolbar installation. When you run KToolbar next, you should be able to choose between your new projects to run, package, or compile.

Because the usage examples are rather basic, discussing them in addition to the API would be somewhat redundant. Which is why not every chapter goes line by line through the example code as the fragments discussed in the chapter already give the details. The example MIDlet projects show how the concepts discussed work in the context of a functioning MIDlet and will make sense after you have read their respective chapters.

Conclusion

Well, there really isn't much to conclude here. I have just finished outlining what this book is about, who it is for, and how you should use it. Hopefully I have justified why so many trees bravely gave their lives for this book to sit around on your shelf. Read on to start developing mobile games with Java.

Chapter 2

A Crash Course in J2ME

Introduction

A few short years ago, wireless gaming was the realm of simplistic text games and primitive monochrome graphics. With the relentless pace of progress in both handset hardware and mobile application APIs, we now are seeing wireless games with not just high bit-depth color and digital sound, but full 3D graphics and massively multiplayer gaming. With that said, wireless still has a long way to go before the market rivals that of the GameBoy Advance or other long-standing gaming markets. However, Sun Microsystems' J2ME standard for mobile devices is doing much to close the gap. This chapter will guide you through a brief tour of what J2ME is, what it can do, and how it is used in today's mobile gaming market.

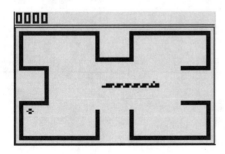

Figure 2-1: Nokia's Snake — a smash hit in the pre-history of wireless games

J2ME in Short

Before the J2ME standard was even created, Japanese carriers such as NTT DoCoMo and J-Phone sold handsets with their own custom Java virtual machines with great success. Naturally, games and entertainment applications became the most popular uses for these handsets. American and European carriers were slow to notice this; however, we are finally seeing some robust handsets over here that rival Japanese hardware in features and performance. As gaming revenue drives customer growth and data service revenue, carriers are destined to focus on selling handsets with even more powerful gaming capabilities.

Being very early to recognize a massive new market for their technology, Sun shortly provided their own slimmed-down version of Java. This is part of Sun's family of Java platforms that includes Java 2 Standard Edition (J2SE) for desktop applications, Java 2 Enterprise Edition (J2EE) for server applications, and Java 2 Micro Edition (J2ME) for cell phones and other small devices.

J2ME is not just for cell phones. It is designed for a wide range of small consumer electronics that may not have the available memory or CPU horsepower to run a full J2SE implementation. Its small execution footprint and code size has also lent itself to other uses such as a convenient scripting language inside larger desktop PC games such as Nihlistic's Vampire: The Masquerade. However, within the category of small devices, there still is a wide range of platforms to support. For this reason, J2ME is further broken down into configurations and profiles.

Configurations

A configuration defines a basic set of language features, hardware capabilities, and Java packages for a slightly narrower range of devices. The two most commonly referred to configurations are the Connected Device Configuration (CDC) and the Connected Limited Device Configuration (CLDC). The CDC defines a basic platform for high-bandwidth devices with relatively large amounts of memory. CLDC is what we are interested in. It is a configuration for low-end hardware with tiny amounts of memory, small screens, and unreliable, low-bandwidth network connectivity. The CLDC specification identifies these machines as things like wireless phones, two-way pagers, and smart set-top boxes.

Currently, there are two versions of CLDC: 1.0 and 1.1. The 1.1 version is largely the same as 1.0, aside from a few minor and some major changes. These changes include things like support for floating-point math, a few new method additions to existing classes, and a slight increase in the memory budget from 160K to 192K. Even though 1.1 includes floating-point math operations, it is still most likely not fast enough on current hardware for our purposes.

Profiles

The range of devices a configuration targets is still rather broad. Sun narrows this category down even further with the concept of the profile. A profile further hones the target by detailing an API for a very specific kind of device. In this case, we are interested in the Mobile Information Device Profile (MIDP). MIDP defines a set of packages specifically designed for the constraints of mobile phones, even though MIDP is supported on a variety of other devices, including PalmOS PDAs.

The first version of MIDP, MIDP 1.0, was a sparse array of features that made developing any kind of modern game an arduous task. MIDP 1.0 featured a rather inflexible GUI, very limited support for bitmap graphics, and virtually no sound functionality at all. Network communication was constrained by the Generic Connection Framework, which only supported the HTTP protocol.

As more advanced handsets appeared supporting music, color graphics, and various other advanced features, hardware companies and even individual carriers began creating custom Java extension classes to support handset functionality that went beyond the limited scope of MIDP 1.0. Sony Ericsson, Nokia, Siemens, Motorola, and many other companies released their own SDKs, making Java a dizzying array of unique platforms instead of one cohesive standard. Compounding this problem were the various bugs and operational nuances of each manufacturer's virtual machines, forcing developers to customize their game for each platform even if the MIDP 1.0 specification was strictly adhered to.

Granted, the "write once, run anywhere" mantra Sun has been pushing with Java since its inception has largely been a myth. J2ME is no exception to this, as even if handsets all strictly adhered to MIDP 1.0, you have radical changes in processor speed, screen resolutions, and button layouts that make customizing your code for at least some handsets inevitable. Of course, Java's lack of a preprocessor and other build management features you may be used to from C/C++'s preprocessor make maintaining multiple builds something of an annoyance.

Regardless of MIDP 1.0's shortcomings, Sun's J2ME standard shipped on tens of millions of devices. Sun's open-standard philosophy got free SDKs and tools into the hands of any interested programmer ranging from the highly paid corporate software engineer to your average spare-bedroom hobbyist. Those who were familiar with J2SE easily moved their skills over to this new standard, and those new to the technology could quickly learn from a large supply of documentation, free sample code, and help from an eager programming community. Games based on MIDP 1.0 and its various manufacturer-specific flavors quickly multiplied, both on pay-for-play carrier portals and free Internet web sites.

Figure 2-2: Flarb LLC's DangerDrop is an example of early MIDP 1.0 gaming.

To combat the plague of splintering custom Java standards and fulfill the needs of mobile application developers everywhere, Sun recently released the MIDP 2.0 standard. This release has many major updates, including an all-new game API dedicated to the needs of mobile game developers. These updates include native support for sprites, tiles, animation, and background scrolling, not to mention leaps in networking support and media playback. MIDP 2.0 will be the core of this book, along with my coverage of additional SDKs and notes on MIDP 1.0 development.

J2ME in Action

Over the past few years many great games have been released for Java handsets. In this section we will look at some examples of wireless Java games in a variety of genres. Perhaps after reading this section you will get some ideas for your own games and applications.

Action/Arcade Games

With the advent of color handsets and beefier CPU and memory specifications on new Java handsets, action games are coming into their own. Back in the plinkety-plink monochrome MIDP 1.0 days, action games were pretty basic. But now we are seeing a lot of great new titles.

Pursuit Squad

Pursuit Squad is a 3D chase-view racing game from one of the UK's leading developers, IOMO. Harkening back to the days of Chase HQ, Pursuit Squad puts you in the seat of a supercar police vehicle chasing down criminals in the continuing war against organized crime.

Figure 2-3: Pursuit Squad has graphics reminiscent of '80s pseudo-3D racing games. Game and images copyright IOMO.

Sports Games

Sports has been a popular genre for wireless games since the advent of cell phone games. The next generation of sports games feature 3D graphics, network play, and all sorts of bells and whistles. Most major sports are represented, such as football, soccer, and baseball — but even some niche sports like cricket and horse-racing are getting the mobile treatment.

3D Golf

IOMO has developed a proprietary 3D engine for J2ME that has been used in this impressive golf title. As you can see from the screen shots, the course can be viewed from a number of different vantage points. This includes a bird's-eye overview and an on-the-green first-person perspective. Featuring varying weather conditions and a variety of clubs and holes, 3D Golf is one of the more impressive sports offerings available on Java phones.

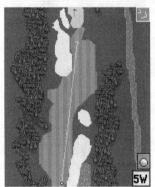

Figure 2-4: IOMO's 3D Golf packs a real 3D polygonal golf experience into a tiny Java MIDlet. Quite impressive. Game and images copyright IOMO.

Note   Instead of the typical name, applet, which is used in regular J2SE programming, J2ME MIDP applications are called MIDlets.

Strategy Games

Because of the limited interface and system resource constraints of the average handset, strategy games have become a popular genre of wireless game. On J2ME they have been a staple since the very beginning.

Ancient Empires

Macrospace's Ancient Empires is a turn-based strategy game akin to the Advance Wars series on the GameBoy Advance. In Ancient Empires you command units of medieval armies across various fantasy landscapes. You can occupy buildings, purchase units, and of course attack hordes of invading monsters on a variety of terrain. With vivid graphics and deep gameplay, Ancient Empires is a good example of where mobile gaming is going in the near future.

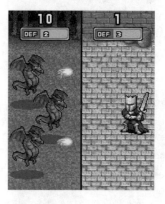

Figure 2-5: Macrospace's Ancient Empires is similar to games such as Fire Emblem and Advance Wars on the GameBoy Advance. Game and images copyright Macrospace Ltd. 2003-2004.

Card/Puzzle Games

Card and puzzle games are a natural fit for the constrained interface and paltry performance of many common handsets. Also, it just so happens that for the casual gaming audience that dominates mobile games, card and puzzle games are a good fit. That's why you'll find so many of them in MIDlet catalogs worldwide.

Poker Solitaire

This game from Flarb LLC is a simple but highly addictive card game. Just place cards in a 5 x 5 grid to form high-ranking poker hands horizontally, vertically, and diagonally. Sure, this isn't going to tax the abilities of your brand new color MIDP 2.0 handset — but it is surprisingly fun. This is a good example of how the wireless platform is well suited for simple puzzle and card games. Oh, and of course since I wrote this game, this is an entirely unbiased and objective description.

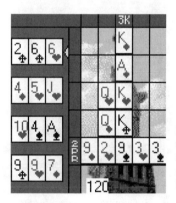

Figure 2-6: Obviously the pinnacle of wireless game technology, Poker Solitaire remains at the bleeding edge of innovation. Oh yeah, copyright Flarb LLC!

Multiplayer Games

Considering the fact that every single wireless phone has at least some kind of connection to the Internet (whether it be via TCP/IP or WAP), wireless is a prime platform for multiplayer games. However, because eating up network traffic playing networked games can be expensive, users are somewhat cautious about which multiplayer games they choose.

SHADE

Cosmic Infinity's SHADE is one of the more impressive multiplayer offerings out there. Building on their earlier WAP games, the J2ME version of SHADE is a 2D massively multiplayer role-playing game with many features you may be accustomed to on such PC titles as EverQuest or Ultima Online. This includes sprawling terrain, hordes of monsters, and various other live players wandering through the world to team up with or fight.

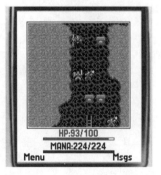

Figure 2-7: Cosmic Infinity's SHADE is one of the very first massively multiplayer mobile games.
Game and images copyright 2004 Cosmic Infinity.

The Handsets

At the time of publication, there are precious few MIDP 2.0 handsets on the market. For the purposes of this book, we will describe several of the current and near-future handsets that may be fairly easy for the average developer or hobbyist to acquire. Although the code in this book may cater to the particular SDKs or device specifications of the handsets listed in this section, the code should run on or at least be easily portable to many current J2ME phones.

Sony Ericsson P900

Sony Ericsson's P900 is the successor to the dazzling P800. Featuring support for both Symbian and MIDP 2.0, the P900 is one monster of a smartphone. The P900 is more akin to a PDA than a phone, with a large color screen and stylus in addition to a flip-up keypad for punching in phone numbers. The MIDP 2.0 performance on this device is blindingly fast, and Sony Ericsson provides an excellent suite of tools and documentation for programming the device. Other goodies on the P900 include MP3 playback, memory stick compatibility, and a camera that can record MPEG4 video and audio. Being the monster that it is, the P900 has a hefty price tag.

Figure 2-8: Sony Ericsson's 900-pound gorilla, the P900. Image copyright Sony Ericsson.

Sony Ericsson Z1010

The Z1010 is Sony Ericsson's second device supporting MIDP 2.0. This resembles more of a traditional phone, with a flip-up design and small form factor. The Z1010 is an impressive device that supports the Mobile Media API for playback of sound and video. The Mobile Media API also allows the viewing of photos and videos taken with the Z1010's built-in digital camera. In this respect, the Z1010 actually has an advantage over the P900 as the P900 does not support the full Mobile Media API and thus cannot play back video clips via MIDP 2.0. The Z1010 is sure to make waves as a cutting-edge MIDP device for both consumers and developers worldwide.

Figure 2-9: More suited for the traditional handset consumer, the Z1010 brings MIDP 2.0 back down to size.
Image copyright Sony Ericsson.

Sony Ericsson K700

Sony Ericsson's K700 is a snazzy new consumer-level MIDP 2.0 camera phone that includes Java 3D graphics, as well as the proprietary Mascot engine for the display and animation of 3D characters. This killer new device has a vibrant 16-bit 126 x 220 TFT screen, and great audio capabilities featuring 40-note polyphonic voices and full Mobile Media API support. Much like the Z1010, this is aimed at the consumer markets and is sure to be priced accordingly.

Figure 2-10: Sony Ericsson's K700 offers full Mobile Media API support. Image copyright Sony Ericsson.

Motorola i730

The i730 is a handset produced by Motorola that is designed specifically for their iDEN network. This means you can mainly find this device for Nextel in the United States. It is a full-color flip-phone handset with a full implementation of MIDP 2.0. This includes the Mobile Media API, OTA provisioning, and push architecture.

Figure 2-11: One of the earliest MIDP 2.0 handsets available in the U.S., the Motorola i730. Image copyright Motorola.

Featuring well over a megabyte of RAM and plenty of space for application storage, the i730 also has several device-specific APIs for dealing with Motorola's custom hardware features and Nextel's network. Particularly of interest for game developers is Motorola's Micro3D API.

Conclusion

If you go by the sheer number of devices in the market, J2ME is the overwhelming champion in the mobile gaming market. Of course, with MIDP 2.0 being in such an early state, it will take a while for the new standard to become economically viable. However, with J2ME as a whole, the ability to generate money from this huge customer base is a whole other story. Regardless, the appeal of J2ME to game programmers is there, and after reading this chapter you perhaps have a better idea of what J2ME is and what kinds of games are possible with the technology.

Chapter 3

Introduction to MIDP 2.0

Introduction

If you are already familiar with J2SE programming, using
CLDC/MIDP may seem similar. However, there are a number of
critical differences both in basic virtual machine (VM) functionality
as well as the included packages and classes. In some cases, familiar old J2ME classes have been modified to suit the limited size
and memory footprint of mobile devices, while in other cases they
have been altogether removed or replaced with new packages and
interfaces. This chapter will give a rundown on the basic features
of CLDC/MIDP 2.0.

The Basic Requirements of CLDC

Not only do CLDC and MIDP define packages and language features for their respective APIs, but they also define basic
hardware requirements that the platforms they run on must have.
Starting with the base of CLDC, we have the following hardware
requirements from Sun's own documentation:

- At least 160 kilobytes of non-volatile memory available for the
  virtual machine and CLDC libraries
- At least 32 kilobytes of volatile memory available for the virtual machine runtime

As you can see, these are very basic requirements. It is the job of the profile to get more specific on hardware features. CLDC also defines various features of the software platform, including general behaviors of the VM as well as specific packages. As for behaviors, Sun's CLDC documentation goes into explicit detail about all of these matters. We will just highlight a few:

- Class loader can only load classes from its own JAR.
- No native libraries can be downloaded that provide native access aside from the CLDC and manufacturer-specific classes.
- CLDC has eliminated several basic virtual machine features including user-defined class loaders, thread groups and daemon threads, finalization of class instances, and asynchronous exceptions.

CLDC defines a series of classes that are available from J2SE, as well as a number of new classes created specifically for the CLDC standard. The CLDC documentation goes into extensive detail on the available classes. Throughout this book I will highlight instances of critical classes that are omitted or new classes that you may need to use. In the case of CLDC, there is only one CLDC-specific class, the Generic Connection Framework.

The Generic Connection Framework (GCF) is a networking class that is a simplified way to define network communication with a variety of protocols including HTTP, TCP/IP, and even serial connections. The thing is, although the GCF allows for a variety of protocols, it does not require any protocols to be present in the CLDC implementation. It is, after all, a framework. This means it specifies a hierarchy and interface organization in which others can implement their own communication protocols. Device manufacturers and OS vendors are free to include the protocols and connection types that they want. Until MIDP 2.0, this has meant that many handsets only supported HTTP connections. As we will see in Chapter 13, "Wireless Networking with HTTP," there are new developments that bring robust networking support to mobile phones.

The Basic Requirements of MIDP 2.0

Now that we have seen how CLDC is implemented, it is time to focus on MIDP 2.0. MIDP further defines packages and classes that are built on top of CLDC to address the needs of a more specific class of device. In this case, the class includes devices such as wireless phones and other low-end mobile data terminal type platforms such as the RIM Blackberry and such.

Much like CLDC, MIDP defines a minimum set of hardware requirements that must be present to implement the profile. In this case, the requirements as defined in Sun's own documentation are:

- At least a 96x54 resolution, 1-bit color screen with a square pixel shape
- Support for at least a one-handed keyboard, two-handed keyboard, or touch-screen for input
- 256 kilobytes of non-volatile memory for the MIDP implementation
- 8 kilobytes of non-volatile memory for application-created persistent data
- 128 kilobytes of volatile memory for the Java runtime
- Two-way wireless networking with possibly intermittent connections and limited bandwidth
- The ability to play tones via software or dedicated hardware

If a handset were to actually come out with just these basic features, it would be rather pathetic. For old-school mobile game developers such as myself, this was state-of-the-art in the U.S. a few years back. Thankfully, the vast majority of Java handsets go well above and beyond these basic requirements.

Now that we are past the hardware platform specifications, it is time to delve into the software requirements of MIDP 2.0. MIDP makes a few basic assumptions about the hardware it is running on:

- A minimal kernel to manage hardware (interrupts, exceptions, and scheduling)
- A mechanism to read and write from non-volatile memory
- Read and write access to wireless networking

- A mechanism to provide a time base for time-stamping records written to persistent storage as well as the Timer API
- Minimal capability to write bitmap graphics to a display
- A mechanism to capture input from at least one of the defined input methods
- A mechanism for managing the life cycle of the device

These are very basic requirements that are generally meaningless to you as the software developer. All you need to know is that every MIDP device will have wireless networking, bitmap graphics, and some form of persistent memory I/O. MIDP also specifies a number of features required by the device's suite of classes and packages. Not all of these are required. In fact, Sun prefixes their requirements with either MUST, MAY, SHOULD, or SHOULD NOT in their documentation. The difference between MAY and SHOULD is really unknown. Anyway, straight out of the MIDP 2.0 documentation comes this list of software requirements:

- MUST support MIDP 1.0 and MIDP 2.0 MIDlets and MIDlet suites
- MUST include all packages, classes, and interfaces described in this specification
- MUST implement the OTA User Initiated Provisioning specification
- MAY incorporate zero or more supported protocols for push
- MUST give the user a visual indication of network usage generated when using the mechanisms indicated in this specification
- MAY provide support for accessing any available serial ports on their devices through the CommConnection interface
- MUST provide support for accessing HTTP 1.1 servers and services either directly, or by using gateway services such as provided by WAP or i-mode
- MUST provide support for secure HTTP connections either directly or by using gateway services such as provided by WAP or i-mode
- SHOULD provide support for datagram connections

- SHOULD provide support for server socket stream connections

- SHOULD provide support for socket stream connections

- SHOULD provide support for secure socket stream connections

- MUST support PNG image transparency

- MAY include support for additional image formats

- MUST support Tone Generation in the media package

- MUST support 8-bit, 8 KHz, mono linear PCM .wav format IF any sampled sound support is provided

- MAY include support for additional sampled sound formats

- MUST support Scalable Polyphony MIDI (SP-MIDI) and SP-MIDI Device 5-to-24 Note Profile IF any synthetic sound support is provided

- MAY include support for additional MIDI formats

- MUST implement the mechanisms needed to support "Untrusted MIDlet Suites"

- MUST implement "Trusted MIDlet Suite Security" unless the device security policy does not permit or support trusted applications

- MUST implement "Trusted MIDlet Suites Using X.509 PKI" to recognize signed MIDlet suites as trusted unless PKI is not used by the device for signing applications

- MUST implement "MIDP x.509 Certificate Profile" for certificate handling of HTTPs and SecureConnections

- MUST enforce the same security requirements for I/O access from the Media API as from the Generic Connection Framework, as specified in the package documentation for javax.microedition.io

- MUST support at least the UTF-8 character encoding for APIs that allow the application to define character encodings

- MAY support other character encodings

- SHOULD NOT allow copies to be made of any MIDlet suite unless the device implements a copy protection mechanism

As you can see, this list defines a number of properties about the MIDP software itself. A few tidbits relevant to game programmers are the requirement for PNG bitmap file support, 8-bit PCM .wav sound support (only if digital sound is supported), polyphonic MIDI support (if MIDI sound is supported), and the requirement for HTTP 1.1 network access. Of course, all those ifs give the OEMs plenty of room to weasel out of implementing features that we game programmers really need.

Interestingly, socket and stream I/O only gets a SHOULD, not a MUST. However, in contrast to most MIDP 1.0 devices, the vast majority of MIDP 2.0 handsets support TCP/IP sockets — or at least they are supposed to. We will detail this later when we get to wireless networking. It is also worth noting that a big SHOULD NOT is given to the ability to copy MIDlets. Piracy has become an issue in the mobile gaming world, and it is good to see Sun mandate that some form of copy protection is necessary — even if it will probably end up being totally ineffectual.

Keep in mind that with both CLDC and MIDP, the device manufacturers, or OEMs as they are usually called, are free to implement their own custom classes, packages, and hardware features — just as long as they adhere to the basic specification as outlined here and in Sun's documentation. This keeps the J2ME platform flexible and able to change with new hardware features that become popular (such as Bluetooth networking or built-in digital cameras). Of course, relying on hardware-specific features and APIs can make your code difficult to port to the wide variety of handsets out there.

Getting Started

Okay, so all of this is very interesting and everything, but how do you actually get started writing MIDlets and getting them running on handsets? The first thing you need to do is download the required tools and APIs from Sun's web site. The central repository for all things Java is Sun's site at http://java.sun.com. Here you can keep abreast of the latest news in the Java world, download the various SDKs and tools, peruse vast amounts of documentation on all facets of Java, and even participate in discussions on Sun's various forums. Keep in mind that Java provides tools that run on a variety of platforms, including Win32, Solaris, and Linux. I am a bit partial to Microsoft's Windows 2000 OS, so I am using it for the purposes of this book. If you plan on only using Sun's free tools and SDKs, then Linux or other alternative operating systems may suit you fine.

On the first page, you can see a number of links that direct you to the Enterprise Edition, Standard Edition, or Micro Edition sub-sites in addition to other Java products. What you need to do first is download the latest version of J2SE, if you do not already have it installed on your machine. Either click on the J2SE button, or go directly to http://java.sun.com/j2se for downloading instructions for the J2SE SDK. You will most likely have to go through the annoyance of registering to get a login for the site. Once you have downloaded J2SE, install it and reboot your machine if necessary.

Once you have installed the J2SE SDK, it is time to do the same for J2ME. Click on the J2ME button or head to http://java.sun.com/j2me to download the latest J2ME SDK and tools. What you need to get is the Sun J2ME Wireless Toolkit. This contains the CLDC and MIDP APIs for wireless development, as well as several handy tools including a free IDE for developing MIDlets.

The Wireless Toolkit

Now that you have the Wireless Toolkit, what is in it and how do you use it? Well, first we will go through each element of the toolkit and illustrate its purpose.

KToolbar

Aside from the MIDP and CLDC APIs and classes, one of the most important elements of the Wireless Toolkit is KToolbar. KToolbar is a free IDE Sun provides that contains basic resources for compiling, packaging, debugging, and running MIDlets. Sure, it is a little bare bones, but I have developed entire commercial games using only KToolbar.

Figure 3-1: KToolbar in action

Emulator

Sun also provides a basic emulator used to run your MIDlets on your host PC. This emulator is far more advanced than the one provided in earlier editions of the SDK.

The emulator features a host of new preference settings that can be used for debugging, performance emulation, memory monitoring, and other functions that greatly improve the ability to debug and otherwise examine your MIDlet's execution in a fully comprehensive manner. Aside from these new features, the emulator has all the standard attributes, including the ability to create custom "skins" to simulate the appearance and performance of any handset. The skins that come with the toolkit are all fictional phones; however, you can sometimes find emulators from OEMs that are designed for their various hardware platforms. The Sun emulator is rather generic and really does not accurately simulate a real handset of any kind, therefore handset manufacturers such as Motorola provide custom emulators for their own hardware. These will be discussed later when we address handset-specific issues.

Figure 3-2: The emulator up and running

Documentation

The J2ME Wireless Toolkit comes with extensive documentation in the form of HTML web pages and Adobe Acrobat PDF files. These pages and files detail every class, package, and method in MIDP, as well as how to use the included tools and demo MIDlets.

The Tools of the Trade

Although it is entirely possible to create J2ME games with just the Sun toolkit, you most likely will want to research a few other pieces of software that may make your development process go smoother. The following sections will detail a few of my favorite Win32 tools that I use when creating J2ME games.

TextPad

Every programmer needs a good text editor. Since the dawn of time programmers have argued about which editor is the best. From the heady days of VI vs. EMACS to the last remaining freaks who still demand Borland BRIEF emulation in any tool they use, everyone has his or her own preference. One of my recent favorites is Helios Software Solutions' TextPad. Available at www.textpad.com, TextPad is a fine shareware text editor that includes syntax highlighting for Java, as well as some nice search and macro capabilities. The price is low, the features are great, and it is very easy to use.

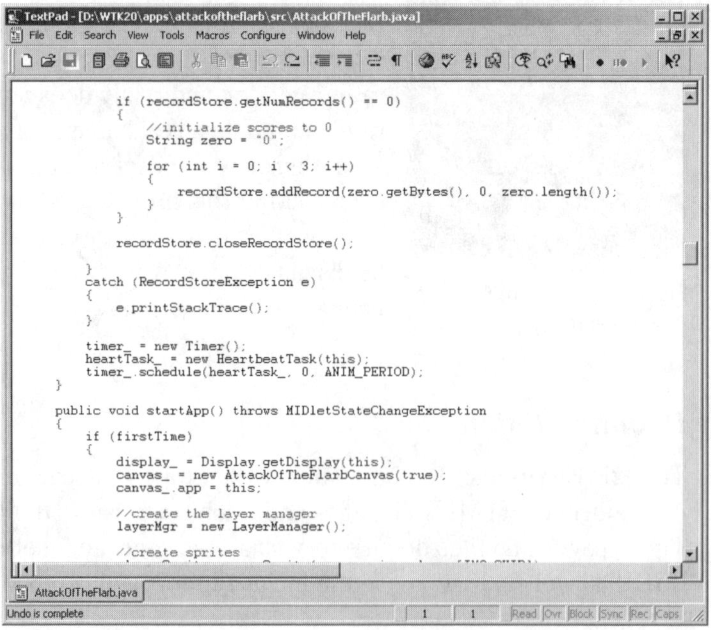

Figure 3-3: TextPad, a quality text editor with Java syntax highlighting

ProGuard

ProGuard is what is called an obfuscator. Obfuscators were originally designed to change all variable and method names to random unintelligible nonsense in an effort to make it hard for others to reverse-engineer your class files. One side effect of this process is a slight compression of your class file, sometimes in the 5-10% range. Now, obfuscators also advertise themselves as code "shrinkers" that remove unused classes and other extraneous information that leads to even greater compression factors.

Most IDEs including Sun's KToolbar include support for third-party obfuscators. ProGuard happens to be a free open-source tool that you can simply drop into KToolbar's bin folder for automatic obfuscating of your code upon packaging into a JAR (Java archive file). ProGuard is available at proguard.source-forge.net. Further discussion of obfuscators and other size economizing techniques will be discussed later in the book.

Cosmigo Pro Motion

Borrowing heavily from the late, great Deluxe Paint series from Electronic Arts, Cosmigo's Pro Motion is a fantastic bitmap drawing and animation package that my artists have nothing but praise for. For a seemingly arbitrary $58 you can have the full version. A trimmed down "lite" edition is also available for a mere $19.95. A trial version can be downloaded at www.cosmigo.com/promotion.

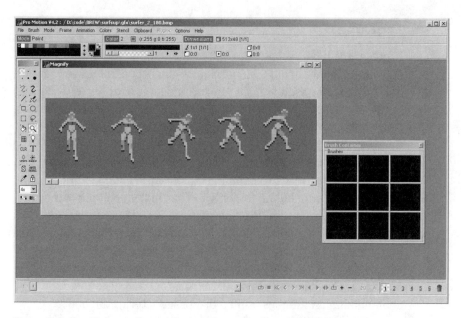

Figure 3-4: Pro Motion is the spiritual successor to the mighty, mighty DP.

Pngcrush

Portable Network Graphics (PNG) files are the standard file format for bitmap graphics in J2ME. Depending on the program you use to create and edit these files, there may be a lot of extraneous information stored in your PNGs that take up valuable space. When trying to fit your JAR into restrictive carrier size limitations and easing slow download times, every byte counts. Pngcrush is a free open-source tool that can potentially compress your PNGs by removing the useless information and trying various compression and filter methods to optimize your graphics files. The tool is available at pmt.sourceforge.net/pngcrush/.

CodeWarrior Wireless Studio

There are many J2ME-supporting integrated development environments (IDEs) on the market. One that I use often is Metrowerks' CodeWarrior Wireless Studio. This tool includes an editor, compiler, debugger, packager, obfuscation support, project management, and the ability to target multiple devices and integrate a multitude of J2ME SDKs into your project. It may be a little rough around the edges with some weird obfuscation issues, the occasional SDK install nightmare, and a rather slow debugger. It is, however, relatively cheap, allows you to easily switch from most any modern J2ME SDK, and supports on-device debugging on certain devices. Unfortunately, CodeWarrior Wireless Studio has all but disappeared with Metrowerks seemingly abandoning the product. You might think since this product is largely unsupported it doesn't deserve mention here. But since I have used it so much in the past, I figure it's worth a mention.

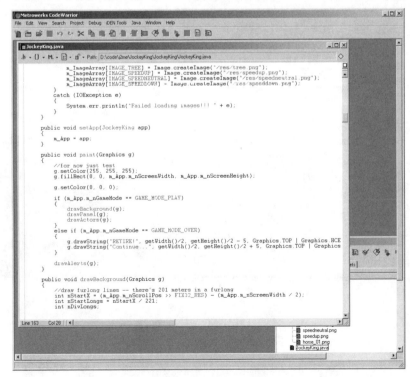

Figure 3-5: The poor abandoned CodeWarrior Wireless Studio

JBuilder Mobile Edition

Borland has brought its familiar JBuilder IDE to the mobile arena with JBuilder Mobile Edition. This has the same interface we all know and love with a product tailor-made for J2ME developers. This includes a neat UI tool that shows flowcharts of how your displayables link to each other and what controls are on each screen. JBuilder sports a snappy debugger, and at a price of around $350, JBuilder is amazingly cheap and quite versatile. It features the same JDK selection as CodeWarrior with the advantage that Borland actually continues to support this product. There is a free demo available at Borland's web site: www.borland.com.

Figure 3-6: JBuilder, the new king of the IDE heap

Other IDEs

There are a multitude of other J2ME IDEs you can use with J2ME, including Eclipse, IBM WebSphere, Whiteboard, and a number of others. Most have some kind of downloadable demo or free trial offer. I suggest trying out as many as you can before you decide on an IDE to use for all of your projects.

Other J2ME SDKs

Each handset manufacturer has its own custom J2ME SDKs. In fact, some carriers such as Bell Mobility and Sprint PCS have SDKs as well. Although plain-vanilla MIDP will work, in order to harness the special features of each manufacturer's handsets that are not necessarily supported by MIDP, you will have to use the SDK provided by the OEM or carrier. Tools such as CodeWarrior Wireless Studio allow for the easy integration of SDKs into the IDE. Alternatively, most of these custom SDKs come with their own version of KToolbar or can be integrated with Sun's free tools as well.

Using the Emulator

Now that we have described the various tools and toolkits needed for J2ME development, it's time we discussed how to use some of the basic tools that come with Sun's own Wireless Toolkit. First we will discuss how to use the emulator in order to show you a few MIDlets in action.

Running a MIDlet

If you chose the default install options of the J2ME 2.0 Wireless Toolkit, you should select **Start ▶ J2ME Wireless Toolkit 2.0 ▶ Run MIDP Application**. The result should be a file requester dialog like the one shown in Figure 3-7. From here, you must select the JAD (Java Application Descriptor) of the MIDlet you wish to run.

Figure 3-7: The Run dialog

Go to the folder WTK20\apps and you will see folders for all the MIDlet suites included with the toolkit. Proceed further to games\bin and select the games.jad file to execute. The JAD file is the Java Applet Descriptor that defines various settings and properties for the MIDlet that allow it to run in the emulator. In some cases it is also possible to execute from the JAR itself with no JAD. But for our purposes, we will stick with the JAD. The end result of this operation is a screen that looks like Figure 3-8.

The game's applet is actually a MIDlet suite, meaning there are multiple MIDlets in one JAR file. The first screen you are presented with gives you the ability to select between TilePuzzle, WormGame, and PushPuzzle. Use the keyboard or click on the buttons on the emulator skin to select WormGame. Note that the two words at the bottom of the screen are known as soft buttons. Soft buttons are

Figure 3-8: Executing the MIDlet in the emulator

labels that are changeable and describe the functionality of the two buttons underneath the screen. For instance, the soft button on the right is labeled "Launch" when selecting between MIDlets in the suite. By clicking the button underneath that word on the emulator skin, you run the currently highlighted MIDlet. The result is a screen that looks like Figure 3-9.

You probably already know this game — Worm was made famous by its inclusion on Nokia handsets for the past several years. Of course, in a long-lost era known as the 1980s, games like Worm were actually major releases stocked on the shelves of national retail outlets. Today it is but a quaint reminder of how starved we were for entertainment in the bygone era of goofy-looking Huffy Stu Thompson BMX bikes, Julian Lennon, and the constantly looming specter of total nuclear annihilation. Simply guide the worm around with the control pad, eating dots and trying not to collide with anything.

Figure 3-9: WormGame — games like this were the Doom IIIs and Grand Theft Autos of the early '80s!

Feel free to experiment with the other games in this suite. They are all of similar quality, but do serve as an example of an incredibly basic, sample J2ME game. Also, you might want to try running the other sample MIDlets included with the toolkit. These illustrate things such as networking, GUI controls, and other MIDP elements that may come in handy as you read further in this book.

Creating a Custom Device

Sometimes you are developing for a device that has no custom SDK or proper emulator skin in Sun's toolkit. In these cases, you need to create your own device profile for use with the emulator. These device profiles are simple text files that define various properties such as screen size, bit depth, and skin bitmaps for each device included with the SDK. You can switch between the devices in the emulator by running **Start ▸ J2ME Wireless Toolkit 2.0 ▸ Default Device Selection**. To start with, the toolkit comes with four profiles: DefaultColorPhone, DefaultGrayPhone, MediaControlSkin, and QwertyDevice. These are all fictional, and thus not representative of any real device. If you can find the precise specifications for the handset you want to use, you can create your own device configuration file with a simple text editor such as Notepad or the aforementioned TextPad.

Figure 3-10: Default device selection

These profiles are found in the folder WTK20\wtklib\devices. As you can see, there is a folder for each default profile. If you click on the DefaultColorPhone folder, you find the DefaultColor-Phone.properties file. This is a regular text file that you can edit. To make your own profile, copy and rename the directory and properties file to whatever you want and place it in the WTK20\wtklib\devices folder.

If you look at this properties file you will see that it is very large. However, it is also well commented. It should be a trivial matter for you to create your own custom settings. As a basic example, search for the property "screen.width" or "screen.height." You will find the following settings:

```
screen.width=180
screen.height=208
```

As you can see, a property is a simple key/value pair, with the key on the left and the value on the right of the equals sign. Simply change these numbers around to modify the screen resolution to match your target device. The rest of the properties are similar. Read the comments and examine the differences between properties files if you want to fully understand this process.

Conclusion

Although brief, this chapter has given you an introduction to what MIDP is, as well as the tools you need to create and run MIDlets including demonstrating a few simple MIDP games in action. Now you are ready to begin the process of creating your first MIDlet.

Chapter 4

Getting Started with MIDP 2.0

Introduction

Now that we've gone over what J2ME and MIDP are and what tools you need, it's high time we got started writing a MIDlet. In this example and for the rest of the book we will use KToolbar to create our code, along with a common text editor. All of these examples can be moved into your IDE of choice later on. For this chapter, we will create everyone's favorite example, "Hello World."

Creating a New Project in KToolbar

The first step in creating the HelloWorld MIDlet is to create a new project in KToolbar. This process is pretty straightforward. First, click on the KToolbar icon to get it started. You should be presented with the KToolbar GUI as shown in Figure 4-1. Then click on **File ▶ New Project**. The result is a dialog that looks like Figure 4-2. This dialog has two fields: Project Name and MIDlet Class Name. The Project Name will be the name of the directory the project is placed in under the apps folder in KToolbar's hierarchy. The MIDlet Class Name is the name of the main class in this MIDlet. This one you should be careful about, as it should fall in line with your own naming conventions. In our case, we will use "helloworld" as the Project Name and "HelloWorld" as the Class Name. Fill out the fields as shown in Figure 4-3.

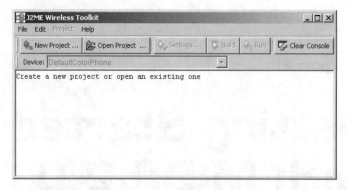

Figure 4-1: The KToolbar interface

Figure 4-2: The New Project dialog

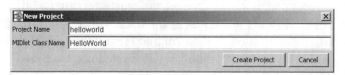

Figure 4-3: Filling out the dialog

After you click the Create Project button, KToolbar will display some information in the console window telling you about the file structure of the project. As with all projects in KToolbar, there are several subdirectories under the project folder (in this case apps\helloworld). The folders we are concerned with are src, res, and lib. The src folder is where we will put all of our .java source files. The res folder is where we will place all resource files we wish to include in our project's JAR. These resources include but are not limited to things like PNGs, MIDI files, and custom binary data. Just about anything can be put in here and it will be automatically packaged in the resultant JAR. Finally, there is the lib folder. This is where you put any classes you wish to use as a library. For instance, you may have a game engine class that you want to reuse or a carrier-specific API that needs to be placed in this folder so you can import its packages. The lib folder is where you would put those relevant class files. Although not mentioned in KToolbar's output, the bin folder is where the resultant JAD and JAR files will be once you've compiled and packaged your MIDlet.

So, now the first thing we need to do is create a source file inside the src file with the same name as our main class. In this case, we need to create a .java file called HelloWorld.java. Remember, Java class names are case sensitive, and thus the file name has to reflect this. If you look at Listing 4-1, you can see what our source looks like for the complete HelloWorld MIDlet.

Listing 4-1: The HelloWorld MIDlet

```java
import javax.microedition.midlet.*;
import javax.microedition.lcdui.*;

class HelloCanvas extends Canvas
{
    public HelloCanvas()
    {
    }

    public void paint(Graphics g)
    {
        g.setColor(255, 255, 255);
        g.fillRect(0, 0, getWidth(), getHeight());
        g.setColor(0, 0, 0);

        g.drawString("Hello World!", 0, 0, Graphics.LEFT | Graphics.TOP);
    }
}

public class HelloWorld extends MIDlet implements CommandListener
{
    private HelloCanvas canvas_;
    private Display display_;

    public HelloWorld()
    {
        canvas_ = new HelloCanvas();
    }

    public void startApp()
    {
        display_ = Display.getDisplay(this);
        display_.setCurrent(canvas_);
        canvas_.repaint();
    }
```

```
public void pauseApp()
{
}

public void destroyApp(boolean unconditional)
{
}

public void commandAction(Command c, Displayable s)
{
}
}
```

As you can see in Listing 4-1, this applet is fairly simple. Perhaps slightly more complicated than most HelloWorld MIDlets as I am using a Canvas class, but this will help ease you into game development with MIDP.

The first thing you'll notice is the packages we import are javax.microedition.midlet.* and javax.microedition.lcdui.*. Obviously, we need to import the MIDlet classes because we are writing a MIDlet. But what exactly is lcdui? The lcdui package is a collection of GUI classes that replace the AWT system from J2SE. These are new GUI elements that are designed with the constraints of mobile phones in mind. Although we use no GUI components in this example, the lcdui package also contains the Canvas and Graphics classes for J2ME. Thus, if we intend to do any kind of drawing or text display, we need to import this package.

Now we'll examine the class definition of the MIDlet itself. As you can see, the MIDlet is declared like so:

```
public class HelloWorld extends MIDlet implements CommandListener
```

Of course, this class is public. Although there are multiple classes in this example, only one public class is allowed per file. We extend the MIDlet class, which has a number of functions that we must implement to support the device's application management system. Finally, we implement the CommandListener interface, which is the key to MIDP's GUI interactions.

The only two members of our HelloWorld MIDlet class are the following:

```
private HelloCanvas canvas_;
private Display display_;
```

The HelloCanvas class will be discussed later. This is what is used to draw the text on the screen. The Display object is part of the aforementioned lcdui package. This class manages the display of the device, allowing for the display of different screens, retrieving the properties of the display, and even vibrating the phone. I guess they had no place to put that functionality other than in Display, despite it not really being a display operation. In our case, we will use the Display object to set our custom Canvas to be what is currently on the screen.

The MIDlet class itself requires each MIDlet to have a few different abstract functions defined. These are startApp, pauseApp, and destroyApp, as well as a constructor. In the constructor there is not much you can do. I usually use this space to initialize any variables, arrays, objects, and other data global to the MIDlet. A number of methods relating to displays and other system resources have undefined behaviors in the constructor, therefore it is a good idea to push as much startup functionality as you can into the startApp method. In our constructor, we simply create the objects that we will use throughout the life cycle of the MIDlet. In this case, we construct our custom HelloCanvas class to be used later on.

The startApp method is called when the MIDlet is put into an active state. The tricky thing here is this happens when the MIDlet is first created, as well as when it is resumed from a suspension (such as when the user suspends the game to take a phone call). Therefore, in a real MIDlet you want to make a distinction between which startApp functionality should be called upon the initial MIDlet creation and what should be called upon a normal resume. In this case, we make no distinction since in any instance we want to grab the current display and perform a repaint.

Next up is pauseApp. This function is called when the MIDlet is put into the paused state, obviously. This happens for a number of reasons, the most common of which are when the user gets a phone call or text message in the middle of using your MIDlet, or hits the disconnect button to forcibly quit or suspend the MIDlet. For most games, this may involve doing things like saving the state of the game, doing some thread management, or dealing with any timed or ongoing tasks. In our case, we do not have any of these concerns with a simple HelloWorld MIDlet, so we do nothing in this function. It is also possible to force the MIDlet to pause itself by calling the notifyPaused method in the MIDlet class. Note that when the MIDlet enters the active state from being paused, startApp is called again.

The final abstract function of the MIDlet class that we define is destroyApp. This method is called when the MIDlet is in the destroyed state, and thus is in the process of being terminated by the phone's application manager. This is where you might do any final cleanup such as releasing resources, tearing down net connections, saving game data, and performing any other housekeeping duties. It is also possible to force the MIDlet to destroy itself by calling the notifyDestroyed method in the MIDlet class itself.

The next method is inherited by the CommandListener interface, commandAction. This method is used to parse input from the user. We will go into detail on this when we discuss input and the GUI later on in the book. For now, be aware that this is a standard issue method for most MIDlets.

Now, let's look at our Canvas. Above the MIDlet, we have HelloCanvas. This class is defined like so:

```
class HelloCanvas extends Canvas
```

This class is derived from Canvas. Canvas is found in the lcdui package, and is used for low-level graphics operations such as drawing text, bitmaps, and geometric shapes. The Canvas is also used to parse input from the keypad as well as issue commands via the commandListener interface in the MIDlet to which the Canvas belongs. This weird amalgam of input and rendering leads to some strange code architecture, but alas, we have to deal with it. The Canvas has a lot of functionality built into it, but for our purposes we are only concerned with clearing the screen and drawing text, which is exactly what we do in HelloCanvas' paint method:

```
public void paint(Graphics g)
{
    g.setColor(255, 255, 255);
    g.fillRect(0, 0, getWidth(), getHeight());
    g.setColor(0, 0, 0);

    g.drawString("Hello World!", 0, 0, Graphics.LEFT | Graphics.TOP);
}
```

As you can see, we use the Graphics object passed to the function to draw on the screen. For those of you versed in J2SE programming, the Graphics object pretty much behaves in the same way it does in regular Java. In the case of J2ME, Graphics is found in the lcdui package and is a slimmed-down and changed version of the one you may be used to. However, it should be easy to get the hang of it.

What we do is set the color to white via a call to setColor. Then we fill a rectangle with white that is as large as the screen by using the Canvas class's inherent getWidth and getHeight methods. Finally, we set the color to black and then use draw-String to display the text. If you are confused as to what exactly we are doing with these operations, we will describe the graphics operations in depth in a later chapter. Right now, this is just a basic overview.

Compiling and Packaging

Okay, now the code is written. How do you get it compiled? Although there is a detailed command-line process for this, KToolbar simplifies this tremendously. Simply click the Build button on the toolbar and you should see a display such as in Figure 4-4. With the message, "Build complete," we know that the code has been compiled successfully.

Now we have to build a JAR that can be used in the emulator. To do this we click **Project** ▶ **Package** ▶ **Create Package** from the menu bar. You actually don't need to click Build and Create Package, because as you can see from the KToolbar console in Figure 4-4, the packaging function actually performs a build as well. The console output also tells us that JAR and JAD files have been created for us. Later on we will discuss how to edit the JAD, but for now the automatically generated one is fine.

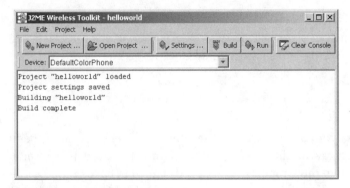

Figure 4-4: The build results

Running the MIDlet

Now that we have a JAR and JAD, how do we run it? This is even easier. First, open the Device pull-down menu as seen in Figure 4-5. This determines which emulator device configuration we are going to run the MIDlet in. It doesn't really matter in this case since all we are doing is displaying text, but I like to use DefaultColorPhone and will throughout this book's examples. By clicking on the arrow on the pull-down menu, you can pick from any of the available device configurations as described in Chapter 3.

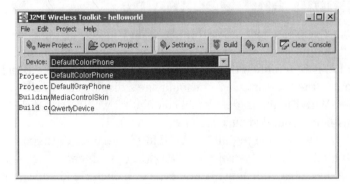

Figure 4-5: The device configuration options

Now, click **Run** from the toolbar. The result should be an emulator
window that looks like Figure 4-6. From here you select the
MIDlet to launch. It may seem silly as there is only one MIDlet
available, but remember you can have more than one MIDlet per
JAR as seen with the game MIDlet Suite in Chapter 3. Click the
Launch soft button on the right to begin our HelloWorld MIDlet.
The result is a screen that looks like Figure 4-7.

Figure 4-6: The emulator's
initial screen

Figure 4-7: HelloWorld in
action!

Congratulations! You have created, packaged, and run your very
own MIDlet. Okay, it doesn't do much, but this could be the beginning of an empire — or perhaps just a mildly interesting hobby.
Regardless, you have taken the basic steps to creating your first
killer J2ME game. Now it is time to talk about general MIDlet programming in more detail.

The JAD and Manifest in Detail

We sort of glossed over what the JAD is in the previous example. It is important to know what the JAD is for and how it works. Here we will give a brief rundown of the JAD and its related file, the Manifest.

The JAD

We have seen that KToolbar generates what is known as a Java Application Descriptor (JAD) file. But what exactly is this file and how can you use it? The Java Application Descriptor provides the application manager with a description of the MIDlet, including what the main class is, where the icon file is, and such. Also, it is possible to use the JAD file to pass attributes to the MIDlet by including key/value pairs that can be pulled in from the MIDlet code itself. First, let's look at the JAD file KToolbar generates for our HelloWorld example.

Listing 4-2: The HelloWorld JAD

```
MIDlet-1: helloworld, helloworld.png, HelloWorld
MIDlet-Jar-Size: 1430
MIDlet-Jar-URL: helloworld.jar
MIDlet-Name: helloworld
MIDlet-Vendor: Sun Microsystems
MIDlet-Version: 1.0
MicroEdition-Configuration: CLDC-1.0
MicroEdition-Profile: MIDP-2.0
```

In Listing 4-2 you can see the basic format of the JAD. Each entry is a simple key/value pair with the key on the left and the value(s) on the right. The first entry we see is MIDlet-1. This is a required entry, as is any that begins with the text "MIDlet-." In this case, the field is known as MIDlet-<n>, and the number is used to identify successive MIDlets inside the JAR in the case of a MIDlet suite. We only have one MIDlet in this JAR, so we only fill out the MIDlet-1 field. The syntax for the value is:

```
MIDlet-<n>: (MIDlet name), (MIDlet icon), (MIDlet main class name)
```

The first argument is the MIDlet name. This is the name that will be displayed in the application manager when selecting the MIDlet to execute. The second is an optional argument that specifies where the PNG icon image is for this MIDlet. The icon is sometimes displayed in the menu of available MIDlets when scrolling though them on the phone's interface. Some phones support icons; others do not. And every phone seems to have its own restrictions on icon sizes and colors. In some cases, the icon will not display if it does not fall into the basic size and color guidelines for the device. Refer to the developer documentation for your device if you are having issues with this. This is an optional argument, so you can simply put a blank space after the comma here to omit the icon specification. Finally, there is the main class. This is the class the application manager will load when executing your MIDlet. In this case, obviously HelloWorld is our main class as it is the only public class in the code.

Note   As mentioned earlier, you can have custom key/value pairs in the JAD that can be retrieved from inside your MIDlet. Using this method, it is possible to use the JAD as a mini-resource file with strings and other data stored inside that are pulled in via code.

Next is the MIDlet-Jar-Size attribute. This is automatically set by the packager and therefore you don't have to worry about it. This is the size in bytes of the JAR containing the MIDlet and its associated files.

The MIDlet-Jar-URL attribute tells the device where the JAR is located. In this case we don't really care, but if you are deploying your MIDlet on a real device, this may be the URL of the web server you are distributing the JAR file for. Or, the carrier may require you to put a certain address in here as specified by their regulations. The emulator is rather cavalier about this, and thus you only need to type the JAR file name here. When uploading your JAR to a device, this field can cause a lot of headaches. We will discuss this when we get into running code on an actual device.

The MIDlet-Name attribute may seem redundant, but it only seems so because this is not a MIDlet suite. The MIDlet-<n> field determines (among other things) the name of each MIDlet inside the JAR. The MIDlet-Name attribute names the entire suite. Thus, in the case of the games suite in Chapter 3, this field may be set to "games," and there will be a MIDlet-<n> field for each game inside the suite, each with its own name (Snake, TilePuzzle, etc.).

The MIDlet-Vendor attribute is the name of the creator of the MIDlet. You could put your name here, or perhaps your company name. If your MIDlet is being distributed by an aggregator or publisher, they probably want their name here.

Obviously, MIDlet-Version represents the version number of the MIDlet suite. In the case of this and the MIDlet-Vendor attribute, this sort of data is displayed on a MIDlet info screen accessible via the handset's interface. Otherwise, it is not normally visible.

Finally we have the MicroEdition-Configuration and MicroEdition-Profile attributes. These entries tell the application manager which version of MIDP and CLDC you are using. As you can see here we are using CLDC 1.0 and MIDP 2.0. If these do not match what is currently installed on the handset, the application manager may not allow the execution of this MIDlet, as it is deemed incompatible. This is despite the fact that it is entirely possible to write MIDP 1.0-compliant code using the MIDP 2.0 libraries by not using any actual MIDP 2.0 features. In this case, you may have to manually edit the JAD to get it to run on MIDP 1.0 devices. Otherwise, MIDP 2.0 code is not backwardly compatible with MIDP 1.0.

The Manifest File

Each JAR has a Manifest (MF) file as well. If you look at the MF file generated for this JAR, it looks very similar to the JAD:

Listing 4-3: The HelloWorld Manifest

```
MIDlet-1: helloworld, helloworld.png, HelloWorld
MIDlet-Name: helloworld
MIDlet-Vendor: Sun Microsystems
MIDlet-Version: 1.0
MicroEdition-Configuration: CLDC-1.0
MicroEdition-Profile: MIDP-2.0
```

In fact, as evidenced by Listing 4-3, this is nearly identical to the JAD. Many emulators and devices will use the Manifest file to execute the MIDlet if the JAD is not available. We don't really need to mess with the Manifest file as it is automatically generated, and any settings we edit for the JAD in KToolbar are also reflected in the Manifest file.

Editing the JAD

So, how do we edit the JAD? After all, we might want to get rid of the Sun Microsystems Vendor attribute since we need to give credit where credit is due. You could always simply edit the field with a text editor, but the next time you package your MIDlet up, it will be overwritten with the old value. Thus, we need to use KToolbar's JAD settings interface. Simply click **Project ▸ Settings** and you will see an interface such as in Figure 4-8.

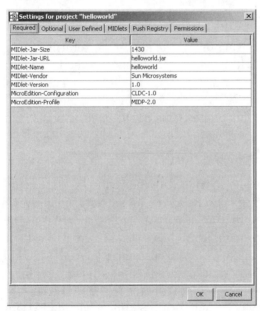

Figure 4-8: The settings window

The project settings window has several tabs. The first includes the previously discussed JAD entries, which are absolutely required by every MIDlet. If you click on the Value field for MIDlet-Vendor, you can change it to whatever you want. Now, whenever you package the MIDlet up, the JAD will have your new Vendor string instead of "Sun Microsystems."

As you explore the other options, you can see that there is a tab for optional keys. These attributes are not necessarily needed by the phone or the emulator; however, they may be nice to have. Here you can provide a short text description of the MIDlet, as well as strings that display upon the installation and removal of your MIDlet.

Perhaps the most interesting tab here is the User Defined tab. Here you can click the Add button to create your own key/value pairs. For instance, you might want to include the URL of your server from which the MIDlet will pull new levels or maps. Instead of hard-coding the server's address in the MIDlet code itself, you can create an optional key/value pair and then retrieve it inside the MIDlet using the getAppProperty method. The syntax is like so:

```
public final String getAppProperty(String key)
```

Here you pass a string that is the key, and it returns a string containing the value. If the key can't be found in the JAD or Manifest, it returns null. So, for instance, we might create an optional property called "MapURL" with the value "flarb.com/maps." Now, if we want to retrieve this property inside the code, we do something like this:

```
String m_sURL = getAppProperty("MapURL");
```

The result should be a string with the contents "flarb.com/maps." Unfortunately, many emulators do not support the getAppProperty function for some reason, despite it being standard issue on any phone VM I have seen. Regardless, this is a great way to provide non-programmers the ability to customize your MIDlet. For instance, you might want to encode things like the screen resolution or other device-specific attributes in the JAD so that a handset port may be as simple as creating a custom JAD instead of modifying and recompiling the game's source code.

More MIDlet Programming Details

Now that we have created our first MIDlet, we should probably go over the bland basics of MIDlet programming. I promise I'll keep it short; however, you need to know the basics on how a MIDlet works before you start any real game programming. So, here we go.

The MIDlet Life Cycle

Every J2ME device has what is known as an application manager. This is part of the OS that takes responsibility for the execution of MIDlets. The application manager will create, start, pause, and destroy MIDlets for a variety of reasons. For instance, if you select the MIDlet from the phone's menu, the application manager will create and start the MIDlet. If you get a phone call, the application manager will put the MIDlet into a paused state. You must handle these events in your MIDlet with the previously detailed abstract methods startApp, pauseApp, and destroyApp. Figure 4-9 shows how these states and methods interrelate.

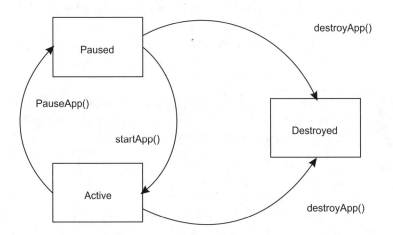

Figure 4-9: The MIDlet life cycle. The life cycle is actually a little more complicated in MIDP 2.0 as a MIDlet can be started via incoming messages, but this basic diagram still applies. In fact, this is pretty much the same one that's in Sun's MIDP documentation.

Event-Based Programming

Unlike Java applications that have a main loop, MIDlets are similar to Java applets in that they are strictly event-based. This means that there is no main loop, and that the code reacts to events sent to the MIDlet. That doesn't mean you can't have any autonomous activity such as animation, music, and other such things. MIDlets still allow the usage of threads and timers, which can be used to create continuous tasks for just such operations. So, instead of a main loop you might create a thread whose run member is the actual main loop. However, in the cases of user input and GUI interaction, you must deal with J2ME's events and commands.

Unlike Win32 or BREW programs, which have a massive event handler loop with a bunch of case statements for every conceivable message received, MIDlets rely on listeners and commands. For instance, our MIDlet extends the CommandListener interface. This requires us to define the commandAction method in our MIDlet that will receive commands from soft buttons on Displayable objects (like Canvases). In addition to the abstract functions for life cycle management and painting, this usually covers most of the events you will come into contact with while programming with MIDP. We will detail the listener and commandAction function when we get into the nuts and bolts of GUI programming.

Note   For J2SE folks, the commandAction and CommandListener concept works in much the same way as ActionListener and the actionPerformed method.

Conclusion

Now you know the basics of MIDlet development. You have created a simple MIDlet and are ready for the next step. It's a good
idea to keep this code around to use as a quick way to get started
with a framework for any MIDlet you may be writing. Now it's
time to start learning about the different packages and features of
J2ME and how they relate to developing wireless games.

Chapter 5

The Anatomy of MIDP 2.0

Introduction

Okay, you know how to write really simple MIDlets. Before we start going into detail on each major functional block (graphics, GUI, networking, etc.), we need a basic overview of all major MIDP packages and some of their major classes. This will be far from exhaustive, but will provide you with a handy road map when looking for specific functionality. For minute details, I suggest reading Sun's excellent documentation.

The MIDP Packages

There are 11 major packages in MIDP 2.0. Some of these are taken from J2SE, but modified and slimmed down. Others are totally new, and there are a few packages that serve as replacements for J2SE classes with completely different names.

java.io

As many familiar with J2SE may know, the java.io package has a number of classes that are used for stream input and output.

java.lang

Another old classic, java.lang contains the MIDP 2.0 Language
Classes from J2SE. These are the basic objects we are all familiar
with such as Boolean, Byte, Integer, etc. Without this, there is no
Java.

java.util

The java.util package should also be familiar to you. This includes
a bunch of handy utilities including collection classes, timers, and
random number generation. Although some warn of performance
issues with using Vectors and other such util classes, I have found
them to be quite useful and fast in commercial J2ME games.

javax.microedition.io

Updating the sparse networking support from MIDP 1.0, the io
class now includes socket, stream, UDP, datagram, and secure connections in addition to the familiar HTTP connection interface. It
also contains classes dealing with push connections, which will be
discussed later in this book.

javax.microedition.lcdui

This package replaces the AWT package from J2SE. Don't look for
anything even remotely similar to AWT's layouts and controls.
This is a GUI API designed for very small displays and restrictive
controls. In my opinion it's much too simplistic, but it gets the job
done and will be detailed in Chapter 8, "The Graphical User Interface." The kinds of GUI elements you can find in this package
include text boxes, scrolling tickers, lists, progress bars, and other
widgets.

javax.microedition.lcdui.game

This is a brand new package introduced with MIDP 2.0. It includes
all new classes that facilitate game graphics operations like scrolling tile maps and sprites. These objects include all kinds of
functionality such as collision, animation, and many other features.

Perhaps placing it under the lcdui hierarchy is a weird decision, but there seems to be nowhere else to put it.

javax.microedition.media

Another new entry for MIDP 2.0, the media package is based on the older Mobile Media API (JSR-135 if anyone cares to look it up). This package allows for the playback of sound, among other media types, and finally does away with the nuisance of custom sound APIs for every handset, which was commonplace in many MIDP 1.0 implementations.

javax.microedition.media.control

This package includes a few controls that are used for the playback and adjustment of playback of some media types. In this case, it includes a control for the playback of tones (such as simple ring tones) and a control for adjusting the audio volume of a regular Media Player object.

javax.microedition.midlet

We have already seen this in action with our HelloWorld example in Chapter 4. This defines MIDP itself, and includes the MIDlet class from which all J2ME MIDlets are extended.

javax.microedition.pki

This is a new class used for certificates with secure connections. Right now, the only type of certificate mandated is X.509; however, OEMs and OS vendors can provide their own custom certificate support if they choose.

javax.microedition.rms

The sandbox security model used in J2ME does not allow for writing to the file system; instead, there is what is known as record stores. A *record store* is basically a very simplistic database system that lets you create records as basic key/value pairs. In this case, the key is an automatically generated ID number for each entry in the database. The value can be anything from text to raw binary data, allowing for some flexibility in what you write to the system. The RMS package includes classes and interfaces used for creating, writing to, and reading from record stores.

Conclusion

Short, but sweet. This is an overview of each major package included in the MIDP 2.0 specification. Some of these we may not use at all, while others will be frequently used for the duration of this book. I suggest you read Sun's official documentation for more detail on each package.

Chapter 6

Bitmap Graphics

Introduction

With each new book I write, I find the task of providing a fresh new introduction to a chapter about bitmap graphics an increasingly difficult challenge. Surely there isn't a soul on the planet worth her salt in game programming who doesn't know about bitmap graphics. After all, they may be the most important factor in your game's success. The ability to amaze the player with glorious visuals has covered up many a title's painfully dull gameplay. Wireless games are no exception. In this chapter we will explore a few different ways to display bitmap graphics in MIDP 2.0. Also, for those bitmap-impaired folks out there, we will also give a brief tour of the bitmap concept itself.

The Bitmap

What is a bitmap, you may ask? If you didn't, feel free to skip this section. If you did, you might want to read this but pretend you never asked it. Sure, a stupid question is the one unasked, but you still might want to pretend that you actually know what you are talking about to avoid the shame and scorn of your similarly clueless peers.

A bitmap is a two-dimensional array of bits representing a picture or image. In computer science and also mathematical terms, two-dimensional data structures are usually referred to as maps. And this happens to be a map of bits. Get it? Bit-map? Ha! There are many different file formats for bitmaps such as BMP, PCX,

JPEG, and the like. J2ME only uses
the Portable Network Graphics
(PNG) format for its bitmap
operations.

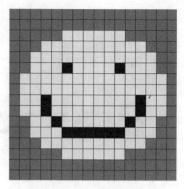

   While we are on the topic of
bits, how many bits are used for
each pixel in a bitmap determines
how many colors the bitmap uses.
This property is usually referred to
as the bit-depth of the image. For
instance, if you have 8 bits for each
pixel in the bitmap, then there are

Figure 6-1: A bitmap closeup as a
2D array of pixels

256 possible color choices for each
pixel, as the range of numbers represented by 8 bits is 0 to 255.
Thus, a bitmap with a bit-depth of 8 has 256 possible colors in the
entire image. Obviously, the more bits you use per pixel, the
larger the file is. It is recommended you keep the colors to a minimum in mobile applications, usually in the 4- or 8-bit range at
most.

PNG

The Portable Network Graphics file format was created in 1995 as
an alternative to CompuServe's Graphics Interchange Format
(GIF) standard. Back in the pre-JPEG days, GIF was the file format of choice for online applications. However, the GIF included
one fatal flaw, a patented compression algorithm known as LZW.
Unisys, the holders of the LZW patent, woke up one day in 1993
and figured they could make a bundle defending their patent by
suing a bunch of people who used GIFs in their products. The end
result was an agreement between Unisys and CompuServe in
1994 to collect royalties from everyone who used GIFs in their
programs. This outraged the Internet community and thus a loose
coalition headed by programmer Thomas Boutell was formed to
create an alternative and open graphics format free from any patented intellectual property.

Note   June 20, 2003, was celebrated as GIF Patent Expiration Day. That was the day that patent 4,558,302 for LZW compression expired. During the years LZW was locked up, PNG made huge leaps as an image file standard. Despite the new free status of GIF, PNG is now a ubiquitous and much more functional alternative.

Properties of the PNG

The end result is the Portable Network Graphics standard, or PNG for short. PNG is a very flexible and wide-ranging file format that has grown to encompass many features for applications never thought of during its genesis in the mid-'90s. PNG soars above and beyond the GIF standard to provide features that are not only handy for artists and web developers, but game programmers as well.

Going into the minute details of the PNG format is well beyond the scope of this book. In fact, entire books have been written about the PNG format itself. If you are really curious about the inner workings of PNG, I suggest starting at the official home page located at www.libpng.org/pub/png. Here you will find all sorts of documentation of features, the history of the file format, and links to useful code, libraries, and tools for the creation, manipulation, and editing of PNG images.

For our purposes, it is useful to know that PNGs are compressed images. This means they are shrunk in size from the raw bitmap data using a number of different compression filters. This does not save you any RAM, as they are uncompressed in memory when displayed, but it does reduce the file space taken up by all of your bitmap assets (which may be compressed in the JAR itself).

Pixel Transparency

PNG files support alpha transparency, meaning that you can have see-through pixels in your sprites and images by using this feature. See Figure 6-2 for pixel transparency in action. In the past, not all MIDP implementations have supported PNG's alpha transparency system, but these days it is becoming fairly standard. This is a critical feature for games, and you should check if your

handset supports this feature as soon
as possible. The lack of pixel transparency has wide-ranging
implications for how you code and
design your game.

While it depends on the graphics
package you use, most allow for the
setting of transparency in PNGs
despite it being a newer addition to
the standard. In my favorite paint program, Paint Shop Pro, the process is
simple. Paint Shop Pro allows you to
pick a color in the palette that will be
transparent. All pixels that are drawn
with this palette entry will be trans-

Figure 6-2: Pixel transparency
in action

parent in the resultant PNG. To do this, click **Colors ▸ Set
Palette Transparency**. The Set Palette Transparency dialog
should appear as in Figure 6-3. If you click the third radio button,
you can pick the color in the palette that will be regarded as transparent. Now, when you display this image in a MIDP 2.0 MIDlet,
the pixels of that color will be see-through.

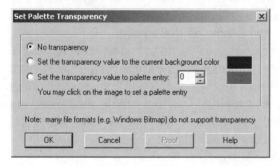

Figure 6-3: The Set Palette Transparency dialog in Paint Shop Pro

Note   For the curious, palette transparency is set using the tRNS block in the PNG spec. This block contains a single-byte alpha value for each color in the palette. So all the entries will be solid except for the corresponding tRNS entry for the color selected in the Set Palette Transparency dialog. You can have 256 levels of variable transparency (not just clear or solid) with tRNS, and some devices may support this in the future.

The Image Class

Found in the javax.microedition.lcdui package, the Image class is the oldest and easiest way to display PNGs in your MIDlet. Images can also be used within MIDP's GUI system for more complicated and modern-looking interfaces. With the advent of MIDP 2.0 we now have layers and sprites, which we will discuss later, but back in the MIDP 1.0 era this is all we had as far as bitmap graphics were concerned. It is still a very viable way to display, move, and animate bitmaps today and thus is worth going into in detail.

Creating an Image from a PNG File

By loading up a PNG and creating an Image out of it, you are creating what is called an immutable image. *Immutable* means it cannot be changed — you cannot alter the pixels or color palette inside the image. Creating an Image is as simple as using the createImage method. There are many overloaded versions of this method; however, the one we are interested in is defined like so:

```
static Image createImage(String name)
```

With this version, you pass the file name of the PNG and the end result is an Image object bearing your bitmap. Let's look at it in action:

```
Image monster;
monster = Image.createImage("monster.png");
```

As you can see, you simply pass the file name of the PNG to createImage and the end result is a valid Image containing the bitmap data in the PNG file. Be warned that this creation process takes time. In many cases, extensive decompression and format conversion operations are taking place behind the scenes. This is why many of the MIDP games you may have played on your mobile phone take so long to load. We will discuss ways to avoid this, as well as other techniques to mask or otherwise notify the user of the loading progress, later on in the book.

Where are these files coming from? In this case, the monster.png file must be placed in the res folder located in the project directory for KToolbar. When you package up your MIDlet, KToolbar will place the files in the JAR along with your classes and other files. In the end, the MIDlet is pulling this particular file out of the root level of the JAR. If you open up the JAR to most MIDP games you will probably find a bunch of PNG images scattered throughout.

Creating an Image from Raw Data

There is another way to create an Image that is brand new for MIDP 2.0. You can use an array of pixel values that MIDP will then use to create an Image. This method is createRGBImage:

```
Static Image createRGBImage(int[] rgb, int width, int height, Boolean processAlpha)
```

This method first takes an array of ARGB values in the format 0xAARRGGBB — this is your actual bitmap image. What this means is each pixel is represented by a 32-bit integer. The first 8 bits of the integer is the alpha (transparency) value, the second is the red component, the third is the green component, and the final byte is the blue component. Now, by having a 32-bit value for each pixel, you may think that the device is capable of 32-bit color depth graphics. While this may be true on some advanced machines, most current MIDP devices can only handle 16-bit color at most. What ends up happening is that this 32-bit color value will be mapped to the closest 16-bit color or the closest color in the handset's hard-coded palette. Each device seemingly has different screen properties, color palettes, and color conversion routines, so the same color on two different handsets may vary. Also, although there are 8 bits of alpha transparency in the pixel data, usually most handsets only have the capability for either fully opaque or fully transparent pixels. Thus, if your alpha value is 255 (0xFF) it will be totally opaque; any other value will be transparent.

Continuing on with the method declaration, the next two arguments are the width and height of this image. So, let's say you have an image that is 64 pixels wide by 64 pixels high. You will end up having an array of 4096 32-bit integer-sized pixels. That's 16K of data. As you can see, using raw data arrays to create images can eat up a lot of memory compared to compressed PNG files.

Finally, you pass a Boolean in the form of the processAlpha argument. This signifies whether or not the image has any transparent pixels. If true, your image's alpha channel (the first byte of the 32-bit pixel) will be considered; otherwise, it will be ignored. This may lead to better drawing performance if you turn alpha off when there aren't any clear pixels. This way, no special per-pixel processing must be done when the image is drawn. Therefore, it pays to make sure you only set this to true when the image data has an alpha channel component.

Creating Images from Streams

It is also possible to create images from streaming data in MIDP 2.0. This is useful if you want to stream new PNG images off a server via HTTP or other network protocols. See later chapters in this book for an explanation of streams and networking. However, for the sake of completeness, we will discuss this concept briefly here. There is an overloaded version of createImage for this:

```
static Image createImage(InputStream stream)
```

This function takes an InputStream of PNG (or any other supported image format) data, decodes it, and creates an Image object out of it. This method blocks until the entire stream is decoded, so if you have a slow net connection (which is usually the case with mobile phones), this may take a while. It may be a good idea to put this in a separate thread.

Drawing an Image

Now that you have an Image created, how do you draw it? This is also a fairly simple operation, requiring the use of the Graphics class, usually inside your Canvas object's paint() method. By using the drawImage() method of the Graphics class, you can paint the bitmap image directly on your Canvas. The drawImage method is defined like so:

```
public void drawImage(Image img, int x, int y, int anchor)
```

Here, we first pass a reference to our Image object. Then we pass the x and y location in pixels on the Canvas. Finally, we pass an anchor value, which is a combination of bit flags that determine which pixel the x and y location is relative to. For instance, if we wanted to draw the monster.png image we just created in the upper left-hand corner of the screen, we would do it like this inside the Canvas' paint method:

```
g.drawImage(monster, 0, 0, Graphics.TOP | Graphics.LEFT);
```

Here, we first pass the Image object itself, then the x and y location of 0, 0 — the upper left-hand corner. Finally, by ORing together the TOP and LEFT anchor flags, we tell the Graphics object to use the upper left-hand corner of the image as the origin. Thus, drawing the Image at 0, 0 puts it in the upper left-hand corner of the screen. You can use the anchor to reference different points of the image. For instance, in a platform game, it may be easier to reference the image at the bottom to ease the process of collision with the character's feet. If that's the case you might use the combination of BOTTOM and LEFT instead.

Mutable Images

What you have seen so far are immutable images. That is, images that cannot be changed once they are created. MIDP also supports the concept of mutable images. A mutable image is essentially a blank image you create that you can then draw on by getting its associated Graphics object and using it to perform drawing operations on the image. This image can then be drawn on a Canvas like any other normal immutable image loaded from a PNG or data stream. The way to create a blank immutable image is through the createImage method:

```
static Image createImage(int width, int height)
```

As you can see, you simply pass the width and height in pixels and the result is a blank (white) mutable image. How do you perform drawing operations on this image? Call getGraphics:

```
Graphics getGraphics()
```

This method will give you a Graphics object associated with the mutable image that you can use for drawing. This image can be drawn on the Canvas like any other immutable image. The only real difference between mutable and immutable is the ability to modify the contents of the Image itself.

A Simple Example

Now that we know how to create and draw images, it's time we saw a complete MIDlet that uses these techniques. This example is a very basic slide show that toggles between two images. The interesting thing is that this not only uses Canvas and Image objects, but Timer objects as well. If you are not familiar with Java threads and timers, this may serve as a good introduction to the concept. If you look at Figure 6-4 you will see this slide show in action. Impressive, eh? Okay, not really — but it serves its purpose to illustrate the concepts at the most basic level.

Figure 6-4: The slide show in action

Listing 6-1: The slide show MIDlet

```java
import javax.microedition.midlet.*;
import javax.microedition.lcdui.*;
import java.util.*;
import java.io.*;

interface Constants
{
    public static final byte MAX_IMAGES = 2;

    public static final byte IMAGE_1 = 0;
    public static final byte IMAGE_2 = 1;

    public static final short SLIDE_DELAY = 2000;
}

class SlideTask extends TimerTask
{
    private SlideCanvas canvas_;

    public SlideTask(SlideCanvas slideCanvas)
    {
        canvas_ = slideCanvas;
    }

    public void run()
    {
        canvas_.repaint();
    }
}

class SlideCanvas extends Canvas implements Constants
{
    private Image[] imageArray_;
    private int imageNo_;

    public SlideCanvas()
    {
        imageNo_ = 0;

        try
        {
            //Load up our images
            imageArray_ = new Image[MAX_IMAGES];
            imageArray_[IMAGE_1] = Image.createImage("/picture1.png");
            imageArray_[IMAGE_2] = Image.createImage("/picture2.png");
        }
```

```java
        catch (IOException e)
        {
            System.err.println("Failed loading images! " + e);
        }
    }

    public void paint(Graphics g)
    {
        //clear screen
        g.setColor(0, 0, 0);
        g.fillRect(0, 0, getWidth(), getHeight());

        //draw appropriate slide
        g.drawImage(imageArray_[imageNo_], getWidth() / 2, getHeight() / 2,
                Graphics.HCENTER | Graphics.VCENTER);

        //increment the image number for the next time around
        ++imageNo_;
        imageNo_ %= MAX_IMAGES;
    }
}

public class ImageSlideShow extends MIDlet implements CommandListener, Constants
{
    private Timer timer_;
    private SlideTask task_;
    private SlideCanvas canvas_;
    private Display display_;

    public ImageSlideShow()
    {
        canvas_ = new SlideCanvas();
    }

    public void startApp()
    {
        display_ = Display.getDisplay(this);
        display_.setCurrent(canvas_);
        canvas_.repaint();

        timer_ = new Timer();
        task_ = new SlideTask(canvas_);

        timer_.schedule(task_, 0, SLIDE_DELAY);
    }

    public void pauseApp()
    {
    }
```

```
public void destroyApp(boolean unconditional)
{
}

public void commandAction(Command c, Displayable s)
{
}
}
```

Listing 6-1 represents the entire MIDlet code. Not too complicated, eh? Let's break it down. The first thing you will notice is
our use of an interface. Interfaces in Java are a way to provide the
same functionality as C++'s multiple inheritance without the
messiness. Essentially, an interface is a way to force a class to
implement methods declared in that interface. So if you want more
than one base class to share a few methods, you can place those
methods in an interface and thus force those classes to implement
the methods in that interface. One handy thing about interfaces is
that you can declare public static final members such as the bytes
and shorts listed in our Constants interface. Thus, each class that
implements this interface will have those values available to it. I
frequently use this technique to simulate the #define functionality
of C/C++'s preprocessor. Unlike the preprocessor directive that
is just a text replace, interfaces consume memory as each method
and member is represented by a chunk of data. So you must be
careful in how large your interface is and, in the case of declaring
public static final variables, how large those variables are. Note
that I only use bytes when necessary and a short in the case of
SLIDE_DELAY to represent a value over 255.

Note   Some developers have written their own prepro-
cessors in PERL, or run GNU's C/C++ preprocessor over
J2ME code with a custom script. I still say it's about time Sun
made a standard preprocessor.

After the interface, we have our SlideTask class. This is extended
from MIDP's TimerTask object. A TimerTask is a task that can be
executed by the Timer at scheduled intervals. In this case, we use
the TimerTask to repaint the canvas and thus swap and draw the

slide images every time it is executed. The TimerTask object is defined like so:

```
class SlideTask extends TimerTask
{
    private SlideCanvas canvas_;

    public SlideTask(SlideCanvas slideCanvas)
    {
        canvas_ = slideCanvas;
    }

    public void run()
    {
        canvas_.repaint();
    }
}
```

First, we declare the private SlideCanvas reference, canvas_. This reference is initialized in the constructor below. Finally there is the run() method, which all TimerTasks must have. This is the method that gets called when the TimerTask is executed by the Timer after its scheduled interval is up. In this method we simply call the repaint() method through the SlideCanvas reference. This will cause the SlideCanvas to call its paint method and subsequently redraw the screen.

Speaking of SlideCanvas, let's look at that part of the code listing. The two private member variables are defined at the beginning of the class. The imageArray_ member is our array of Image objects that we will draw in the slide show. The imageNo_ integer keeps track of which image we are currently displaying.

```
public SlideCanvas()
{
    imageNo_ = 0;

    try
    {
        //Load up our images
        imageArray_ = new Image[MAX_IMAGES];
        imageArray_[IMAGE_1] = Image.createImage("/picture1.png");
        imageArray_[IMAGE_2] = Image.createImage("/picture2.png");
    }
    catch (IOException e)
    {
```

```
        System.err.println("Failed loading images! " + e);
    }
}
```

In the constructor, we initialize imageNo_ to 0, so we start with the first picture. Then we attempt to load up our PNG files. You will notice that the createImage calls are bracketed by try and catch blocks. This is because createImage throws an exception.

Exceptions are Java's way of handling errors and unexpected results. A function may "throw" an Exception object when it encounters an error. In this case, createImage will "throw" an Exception object if, for instance, the PNG file we are trying to load is not in the JAR. For methods that throw exceptions, we need to write exception handlers for the ones we want to catch. First, the function call that throws the exception must be placed in a try block. If you notice, we put all the createImage calls in one block. You don't need to bracket every single one. This try block must be followed by a catch block. We can write multiple catch blocks to catch different kinds of exceptions. In many cases a method may throw more than one kind of exception. Here we are only concerned with the IOException class, which is the kind of exception thrown if the file doesn't exist or something like that. When writing your own methods you can not only throw exceptions, but also create your own kinds of exception classes. That is a subject for another book, however. Anyway, in our catch block, we simply print out to the console that there has been an error. System output and error text can also be read with a terminal program on your PC to connect to some J2ME handsets. This is very useful for debugging on the device itself.

Finally we come to the paint method. This method must be overridden in every canvas. Paint does the heavy lifting here, swapping the images and drawing them to the screen. First, we clear the screen with fillRect after setting the color to white via a call to setColor. Then, we call drawImage on the image indexed into the array by imageNo_. We center this on the screen by using the HCENTER and VCENTER anchors as well as placing the image at a point in the middle of the screen computed by using the screen dimensions returned from getWidth and getHeight. We then increment the current slide number and then MOD it with the MAX_IMAGES value defined in our Constants interface. This makes the number flip back around to 0 when we hit the maximum number of slides — which is 2 in this MIDlet.

```
public void paint(Graphics g)
{
    //clear screen
    g.setColor(0, 0, 0);
    g.fillRect(0, 0, getWidth(), getHeight());

    //draw appropriate slide
    g.drawImage(imageArray_[imageNo_], getWidth() / 2, getHeight() / 2,
            Graphics.HCENTER | Graphics.VCENTER);

    //increment the image number for the next time around
    ++imageNo_;
    imageNo_ %= MAX_IMAGES;
}
```

Our last stop is the MIDlet class itself, ImageSlideShow. Here we have four private member variables. The Timer reference, timer_, is used to schedule our TimerTask for drawing and swapping the slide images. Obviously, task_ is the actual TimerTask that will be scheduled. SlideCanvas is the canvas we will be drawing the images on, and display_ is the Display object that is used for managing drawable objects such as Canvases and GUI objects. In this case, we are just going to use it to make our SlideCanvas the displayed object.

```
public ImageSlideShow()
{
    canvas_ = new SlideCanvas();
}
```

The constructor is pretty basic; here we create our SlideCanvas object. I tend to keep most startup processing in the startApp method because the MIDlet environment is not guaranteed to be properly initialized when the MIDlet's constructor is called.

```
public void startApp()
{
    display_ = Display.getDisplay(this);
    display_.setCurrent(canvas_);
    canvas_.repaint();

    timer_ = new Timer();
    task_ = new SlideTask(canvas_);
```

```
    timer_.schedule(task_, 0, SLIDE_DELAY);
}
```

The startApp method is where it all happens. First, we get the display from the system's Display object. We then call setCurrent in the Display object to make the SlideCanvas we created in the constructor the currently displayed object. If we don't do this, then we can invoke the paint method of the SlideCanvas all we want, but nothing will show up on the screen. Next we create the Timer object and the SlideTask itself. Finally, we call the schedule method inside of Timer. The schedule method that we are using is defined like so:

```
public void schedule(TimerTask task, long delay, long period)
```

The first argument is our TimerTask object that we want to execute. Obviously, here we pass in our task_ reference. Next up is the delay before executing the TimerTask. In our case, we want no delay so we pass 0. Finally, we need to pass in the period, which is the delay between each TimerTask execution. This, as well as the other delay argument, is specified in milliseconds. We pass it SLIDE_DELAY from our Constants interface, which is defined as 1500 milliseconds. This means the MIDlet will wait for a second and a half before flipping and redrawing our slides. With this call to schedule, the MIDlet goes on its merry way, switching slides and redrawing every second and a half.

So now you have seen your first bitmap-drawing MIDlet. This is a really basic example, and the code is really of no practical use, but at least you know how to draw bitmap images. However, there is one other subject we might as well discuss while we're down here.

And Now...A Word about Repaint

If you notice, we call repaint on the canvas to have it draw all the graphics to the screen. This operation, however, can be asynchronous. You can tell the Canvas to repaint, but the actual repaint may not happen until some other event processing is finished. So, the MIDlet may return from the Canvas' paint call and continue executing even though the screen has not been fully updated yet. If you want to make sure that the code is synchronized with the screen refresh, you can use the method serviceRepaints in the Canvas class:

```
public final void serviceRepaints()
```

This method blocks until all the repaint calls issued are finished executing. In some cases this may cause the screen repaint to occur faster, thus giving you some minor performance increases. So, in our previous example, we could change the paint code in our TimerTask to do something like this:

```
public void run()
{
    canvas_.repaint();
    canvas_.serviceRepaints();
}
```

One problem with this is that since the execution blocks until the paints are finished, you may end up with deadlocks if you are using threads that need critical resources inside your paint method. Be aware of this when wielding the power of serviceRepaint.

Animation

Animation is the display of images in rapid succession to give the illusion of movement. I'm sure I don't really need to tell you this, but it needed to be said. You could theoretically use the previous example to display animation by making every bitmap in the slide show another frame of, say, a character's walk cycle. But keeping each frame as a separate file can not only get a bit unwieldy, it also wastes a lot of memory and slows the startup time of your MIDlet because of the number of individual PNG files that must be loaded and unpacked.

The solution to this is to place all the frames of animation in one large image, and then display a portion of it for each frame. Back in the day, the problem was that MIDP 1.0 did not have a simple way to paint a sub-portion of an image to the Canvas. Never say die! The secret to old-school MIDP 1.0 animation is to use MIDP's clipping system. Sure, this is a stone-age technique, but it's still very common and thus worth discussing.

Note In many MIDP games, animation frames for every sprite and other graphics are put in a single large square bitmap. Sub-sections of this bitmap are drawn to the screen to display individual images and frames. The use of a giant square bitmap instead of a single strip of frames per sprite is frequently called "UV mapping."

Clipping Bitmaps

One method of the Graphics object is setClip. This method is defined like so:

```
void setClip(int x, int y, int width, int height)
```

This sets what is known as a clip rectangle. This is a rectangle outside of which no graphics can be drawn. By default, the clip rectangle is the entire screen — meaning you can draw anywhere on the screen. But let's say you wanted to limit the viewable window to a small box in the corner of the screen. You would do that like this:

```
g.setClip(0, 0, 20, 20);
```

Now, anything that is drawn outside of this 20-pixel square in the upper left-hand corner will be clipped out. If something is drawn inside this box but is large enough to go outside it, you will still only see a portion of it as shown in Figure 6-5.

Figure 6-5: The results of setClip. As you can see, the string "inside" is being clipped in the upper left-hand corner by a 20x20 clip rectangle.

Animating with Clip Rectangles

How can you use this to perform animation? Simple. Just create a strip of frames — let's say a horizontal strip of 32 x 32 animation frames. Then, set the clip rectangle when you draw the frame to clip out everything but the frame you want.

Figure 6-6: A bitmap strip of animation frames

For instance, let's say we are using a strip like in Figure 6-6. We also have an image, animationImage, and an integer that keeps track of our current frame called curFrame. Now, say we have two integers, x and y, that track the x and y location of the object. What we do is set the clip rectangle to be at this x and y location and at the width and height of our frame:

```
g.setClip(x, y, 32, 32);
```

Now, we have to draw our image, but offset it so that the frame we want fits perfectly in this clip window:

```
g.drawImage(animationImage, x - 32 * curFrame, y, Graphics.TOP | Graphics.LEFT);
```

So, with this call we of course first pass the reference to our animated image, animationImage. Next we have to move the image back by the Frame width multiplied by the current frame. This makes sure we position the image so that the current frame fits perfectly inside the clip window. The y value remains unchanged and we use TOP and LEFT as the anchor. Now, whenever you want to alter the frame of animation, just change curFrame and redraw.

If you want to really see this in action, try modifying the slide show example to use one large bitmap and clip rectangles instead of swapping between images. In fact, if you look at the image-slideshow2 example in the companion files, you can see how it's done. The code is nearly identical to the previous example aside from including code similar to the above in our paint method.

current frame

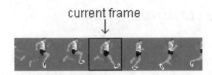

Figure 6-7: This is the area of the strip we are seeing with the clip rectangle set.

Animating with Regions

If using clip rectangles to draw portions of a bitmap seems silly to you, you are correct. But MIDP 1.0 provided no way to paint portions of a bitmap to a Canvas. In the stone age of MIDP 1.0, clip rectangles were all we had, and it is still a technique worth knowing. However, this has all changed in MIP 2.0.

Brand new for MIDP 2.0 is the drawRegion method of the Graphics class. This lets you draw a rectangular subsection of a method onto a Canvas. In the process, you can transform the graphic by rotating or mirroring the image before it is drawn on the Canvas. This is a fantastic way to save memory. For instance, you can store the frames of your character walking to the left, and when he turns around, you simply draw the same frames but apply a mirror transform to flip the image to face right before you paint it to the Canvas. The way you do this is with the new method drawRegion:

```
public void drawRegion(Image src, int x_src, int y_src, int width, int height,
        int transform, int x_dest, int y_dest, int anchor)
```

Here, the first method is a reference to the Image object we want to use. Next up is the x and y location inside the image of the region we want to draw. The width and height arguments specify the width and height of this source rectangle. The next argument, transform, specifies what kind of transformation you want to perform. These are actually part of the Sprite object that we will discuss in a later chapter; however, the Sprite transformation types are listed in Table 6-1. Next we pass in the x and y location on the Canvas we want to draw this Region via the x_dest and y_dest arguments. And finally we pass in the anchor type that we are familiar with from previous Graphics object operations. So, if we were to replace the clip rectangle version of animation code with drawRegion, we would do something like this:

```
g.drawRegion(animationImage, x - 32 * curFrame, 0, 32, 32, Sprite.TRANS_NONE, x, y,
    Graphics.TOP | Graphics.LEFT);
```

The end result is the same. If we wanted to flip or rotate the image, we could play around with the transform argument instead of simply passing it Sprite.TRANS_NONE.

Table 6-1: Sprite transform table

Transformation Type	Description
TRANS_NONE	The image is copied unchanged.
TRANS_ROT90	The image is rotated clockwise by 90 degrees.
TRANS_ROT180	The image is rotated clockwise by 180 degrees.
TRANS_ROT270	The image is rotated clockwise by 270 degrees.
TRANS_MIRROR	The image is reflected about its vertical axis (flipped horizontally).
TRANS_MIRROR_ROT90	The image is reflected about its vertical axis and then rotated 90 degrees clockwise.
TRANS_MIRROR_ROT180	The image is reflected about its vertical axis and then rotated 180 degrees clockwise (flipped vertically).
TRANS_MIRROR_ROT270	The image is reflected about its vertical axis and then rotated 270 degrees clockwise.

Figure 6-8: Flipping a bitmap can save memory by using the same frame for left and right facings.

Copying Bitmaps Over Themselves

MIDP 2.0 also has introduced the somewhat curious ability to
copy a block of a bitmap over itself. Through the use of the
copyArea method in the Graphics class, you can copy one area of
the Image to another. The method looks like this:

```
public void copyArea(int x_src, int y_src, int width, int height, int x_dest,
    int y_dest, int anchor)
```

As you can see, this looks almost identical to copyRegion, except
there is no transform argument, which sort of makes this a bit
useless as you can't do any neat mirroring effects with the screen
to simulate pools of water and things like that. But I digress.

The first group of arguments represent the x and y location of
the upper left-hand corner of the part of the screen we want to
copy, and the width and height of this portion. The next two arguments, x_dest and y_dest, specify where on the screen we want to
copy this area. Finally we pass in an anchor type that we are familiar with from other Graphics operations. One of the major
restrictions to this method is that it does not work on a Graphics
object associated with the screen. Regardless, I'm sure you can
come up with a creative use for this function.

Double Buffering

You may notice that on some devices, some games will flicker.
Sometimes, this is because the screen is being refreshed before
the system is done painting. For instance, the screen may be
refreshed after we have cleared the screen but not drawn all the
bitmaps. So for a fraction of a second, you may see a blank frame,
immediately followed by one filled with graphics. On some devices
this doesn't happen because the screen is automatically double
buffered.

Double buffering is a method used to make sure this flickering
effect doesn't happen. Essentially you have two buffers: a front
buffer and a back buffer. The front buffer is what is displayed, and
all of your drawing is done to the back buffer. When you finish all
of your drawing, you then either swap buffers or copy the back
buffer's bitmap to the front. This way, there is always a full screen

of graphics to be displayed regardless of when the handset refreshes the screen.

In order to determine if the handset you are running on is automatically double buffered, you can use the method isDoubleBuffered in the Canvas class:

```
public boolean isDoubleBuffered()
```

This method returns true if the device is double buffered, false if not. What do you do if the device isn't double buffered? Easy, you just roll your own system. The basic idea is to create an Image that is your off-screen buffer. All of your drawing is done to this Image instead of the graphics context of the display. After you do all of your drawing operations, you draw the off-screen Image to the graphics context of the Canvas. Don't worry if you're confused; you'll see this in action in our full game example.

Anyway, note that double buffering has some drawbacks. It uses up extra memory (a full screen-sized buffer's worth), there may be some performance penalty in drawing the entire image to the front buffer, and in some cases you may still get flickering displays as the refresh may catch you in the middle of copying the off-screen image over. Overall, I still consider it a win if you are dealing with hardware that isn't double buffered automatically.

Coordinate Systems

One thing we should probably get out of the way before we go any further into the graphics APIs is the coordinates that you are using when drawing a Graphics object. For instance, if I draw a bitmap at 0, 0, it appears in the upper left-hand corner of the screen. But what happens if we try to draw something at 600, 600 and the screen is only 120 by 130 pixels in size? The coordinate space used when plotting pixels, images, and other graphics operations is actually independent of the screen resolution.

So, if you start drawing Images at 600, 600, how do you see them? MIDP allows you to translate the origin of the screen view in the larger coordinate space so you can see these far off-screen locations. By default, the origin of the screen is at 0, 0 — which is why when you draw an Image at 0, 0 it appears in the upper left-hand corner. If you wish to make the upper left-hand corner of the screen 600, 600, use the translate method in the Graphics class:

```
public void translate(int x, int y)
```

This method will move the upper left-hand corner of the screen by the number of pixels in the x and y dimensions specified by the arguments. So, if we wanted to translate the coordinate space to be at 600, 600, we would do this:

```
g.translate(600, 600);
```

Now if we draw an Image at 600, 600, it will appear in the upper left-hand corner. What if we want to go back to 0, 0? Any future translations are added to the current x and y translation. So we need to translate back to 0, 0 by using negative numbers:

```
g.translate(-600, -600);
```

Now we are back at 0, 0. Sometimes you may not know the precise origin of the coordinate system. For this reason you can get the value of the current x and y translation by using these two accessor methods:

```
public int getTranslateX()
public int getTranslateY()
```

These two methods will return the x and y translation value respectively. So, if you want to go back to the origin you could do something like this instead:

```
g.translate(-g.getTranslateX(), -g.getTranslateY());
```

Translation also comes in handy when dealing with the varying screen resolutions of each device. You can translate the entire coordinate system to center all the graphics on the screen relative to the size. Thus you don't have to make a separate build for each handset; instead it will dynamically center the screen based on its size. We will go into this in a little more detail when we talk about hardware issues later in the book.

Figure 6-9: Our view into the larger coordinate system

Conclusion

In this chapter you have learned the basics of using bitmap Image
objects. Later on you will become versed in the techniques of
sprites and tiles, both of which MIDP 2.0 provides native support
for. But even with those niceties, the Image class is invaluable and
way more flexible. You will most likely be using this in conjunction
with sprites and tiles for most games.

Chapter 7

Text and Geometric Graphics

Introduction

Now that we have trudged through the muck and mire of bitmap graphics, it is time to turn our focus to text and geometry. MIDP contains various functions for drawing not only text but also various geometric shapes such as squares and lines. In some cases, using geometric shapes instead of bitmaps can not only save space, but boost performance of your MIDlet as well. In this chapter we will take a brief tour of drawing both shapes and text.

Drawing Text

Before we dive into shapes, we'll first cover text. MIDP provides some basic functionality for drawing strings of text, including drawing text in various colors and fonts. The actual text drawing method is found in our old friend, the Graphics class:

```
void drawString(String str, int x, int y, int anchor)
```

First, we pass a String object with the text we want to display. Next, we pass the x and y pixel location. Finally, we have an anchor. We saw how to use the anchor in Chapter 6, "Bitmap

Graphics"; however, with text there is a special anchor we can use — BASELINE.

The BASELINE anchor uses the bottom of the string as the anchor point — but not the absolute bottom. With most any font there are things called *descenders*, the part of letters such as "p" and "q" that drop below the bottom, or baseline, of the string, as seen in Figure 7-1. You can use the BOTTOM anchor to reference the absolute bottom of the text, or use BASELINE to use that line above the descenders.

forget your p and q

Figure 7-1: Portions of letters such as "g," "p, "and "q" drop below the baseline. Those insolent letters!

Changing Colors

There are a number of ways you can customize text. Perhaps the most common way is to alter the color of the text. The Graphics object includes the setColor method, which is used to determine the current drawing color for all graphics operations. The setColor method is defined like so:

```
public void setColor(int red, int green, int blue)
```

This method takes three arguments: red, green, and blue components. Each argument is a value from 0 to 255 that represents its respective color component. For instance, if we wanted to draw our text in red, we'd make this call before using drawString:

```
g.setColor(255, 0, 0);
```

With a red color component of 255, this sets the current color to pure red. Of course, even though using three bytes to specify a color gives you millions of color possibilities, usually your phone has a restricted palette. Most current phones have 12- or 16-bit screens, which have far fewer hues than full 32-bit color space. When you specify a color with this method, the device will find the closest color available that matches the one you specify. So if you pick a few colors that are all fairly close to each other, they may end up being the exact same color on the device.

There is also another, less commonly used method to specify the color. With this method, you can use a single integer instead of three individual arguments. The overloaded version of setColor looks like this:

```
public void setColor(int RGB)
```

Instead of passing each component individually, this lets you send one integer with the format (in hexadecimal) of 0x00RRGGBB. What this means is that the second byte contains the red color component, the third byte contains green, and the fourth is blue. The first byte does nothing. You may recognize this format from the previous chapter when dealing with creating Images from arrays of pixel data. This is the same format. So, if we wanted to set the color to red using this method, it would look like this:

```
g.setColor(0x00FF0000);
```

As you can see, the second byte is set to 0xFF, which in hexadecimal is 255. Using single integers for colors is a good way to simplify your data structures or pull colors out of raw binary data and files.

Using Fonts

The other major stylistic change you can make to text is through fonts. A *font* is a typeface used for the lettering of any text you draw — but I'm sure you already know that. Anyway, most MIDP devices support several different typeface styles you can use to create custom fonts. You really can't go crazy with lettering, as the type always looks like regular letters. Still, you can play around with size, italics, and other styles to get a unique look. It is not guaranteed that every device will have all of these font options, despite being prominently listed in the MIDP specification. Much like selecting colors, any fonts you create will be matched to the closest one supported by the device. So you really should test your drawing on different devices to make sure the text looks right on each one.

To set the current font, you need to use the setFont method inside the Graphics object:

```
void setFont(Font font)
```

Okay, that looks simple enough. Just pass it a Font object and you are in business. Any text you draw after this will use the font passed to this method. The big question is, how do you create a Font object? There are a few different ways to do this, all involving the system's Font object and the getFont method. The easiest one to use is defined like this:

```
public Font getFont(int fontSpecifier)
```

This version of getFont takes an integer that specifies a predefined font to get. There are only two font specifiers defined in the Font object: FONT_INPUT_TEXT and FONT_SYSTEM_TEXT. The FONT_INPUT_TEXT specifier is for the font that is used when entering text in text controls. FONT_SYSTEM_TEXT is the text you see in any GUI components such as static text controls and the like. The result of this method is a Font object representing the font you specified with the argument. So, if we wanted to get the font used for text input controls, we would do something like this:

```
Font textFont = Font.getFont(Font.FONT_INPUT_TEXT);
```

Okay, so now we have a font. But this only gives us two options. There has to be a better way to do this, right? Yes indeed. The second, overloaded version of getFont looks like this:

```
public Font getFont(int face, int style, int size)
```

The first argument is an integer for the face. The three faces are listed in Table 7-1. After the face, there is the style. There are also three styles, as listed in Table 7-2. Finally there is the size argument. There are also three sizes, as listed in Table 7-3. By using a combination of these three properties, you can create your own custom fonts. However, many handsets do not support all of these options, so you may get a font that the device considers "close" to the one you specified. In particular, many handsets don't seem to support italics.

Table 7-1: Font faces

Face	Description
FACE_MONOSPACE	A "monospace" font similar to Courier, which you might have on your word processor. Each letter takes a fixed amount of space.
FACE_PROPORTIONAL	A "proportional" font. This kind of font has letters that are of varying width. The font uses *kerning*, a technique that adjusts the spaces between letters.
FACE_SYSTEM	The "system" font face. This font is used for system screens such as the launcher interface that lets you select the MIDlet to run.

Table 7-2: Font styles

Style	Description
STYLE_BOLD	The "bold" style. This is usually represented by darker coloring or thicker letters.
STYLE_ITALIC	The "italic" style. As with any other italicized text in a word processor or web browser, italic text is slanted to the right for emphasis.
STYLE_PLAIN	The "plain" style is the basic, normal style used for most regular text.

Table 7-3: Font sizes

Size	Description
SIZE_LARGE	Large sized text.
SIZE_MEDIUM	Medium sized text.
SIZE_SMALL	Small sized text.

So, let's say we wanted to create a small, monospace, italic font. We would do something like this:

```
Font ourFont = Font.getFont(Font.FACE_MONOSPACE, Font.STYLE_ITALIC, Font.SIZE_SMALL);
```

The result should be ourFont, referencing a font that is at least similar (or what the handset considers similar) to the font we requested. As I said earlier, you can't depend on this being even remotely close to what you asked for. Also, in many cases you may get this font in the emulator but not the real device. So you really should test your code on a variety of handsets.

Note   Not only may some devices fail to support various fonts, others may even fail to return proper string screen sizes, which makes resolution-independent layouts a nightmare.

Drawing Geometry

Now that text is out of the way, it is time to venture into drawing geometric primitives. Geometric primitives are things such as squares, lines, and other simple shapes that can be combined to create more complicated scenes. Unlike a bitmap, which is an explicit pixel-level representation of an image, geometric primitives are just a description. For instance, to draw a box, I just need to tell MIDP the position and size of the rectangle to draw.

This is where the space savings of geometry come in. If I were to, say, have a 64 x 64 box in a bitmap at an 8-bit color depth, it would take up 4096 bytes, or 4 kilobytes of data. However, if I were to just draw the box as geometry, all I would really need is an x and y position along with a width and height. That's 4 integers, or 16 bytes — something like .004% of the size of the bitmap. In the interest of conserving precious JAR space and RAM, using geometry wherever appropriate is recommended.

Also, because geometry is a description of an image, this description can be modified in real time. This means you can change the size and shape of your primitive on a per-frame basis. For instance, you could have a square grow in height over a period of time, or spin a line around like the hands on a clock. These lend themselves to interesting algorithmic animation effects, but also can be used to scale your graphics to the size of the screen. This comes in handy when dealing with a MIDlet that needs to run on a wide variety of devices. Instead of having new bitmaps for each screen format, you simply alter the description of your shapes based on the width and height of the screen.

Although providing somewhat less geometry support compared to other mobile APIs, MIDP's geometric graphics are all accessed via the Graphics object. The following sections illustrate how to use each relevant method.

Strokes

Before we discuss each shape, we have to go over strokes. Aside from using setColor to change the color of your shapes (and text as well), you can also modify what is known as the *stroke style*. Each geometric shape is drawn with a "brush." The "stroke" used with this brush can be changed with the method setStrokeStyle:

```
public void setStrokeStyle(int style)
```

Okay, that's great, but what is a stroke? The *stroke* is how the object is drawn. There are only two types of strokes — solid or dotted — indicated by the appropriately named constants SOLID and DOTTED. So, if you wanted to draw a line as a dotted line instead of a solid one, you would use setStrokeStyle in a paint method like this:

```
g.setStrokeStyle(Graphics.DOTTED);
```

Then any subsequent geometric object will be drawn with dotted lines. To go back to solid, you would do this:

```
g.setStrokeStyle(Graphics.SOLID);
```

The stroke style does not affect drawing text, images, or filled geometric objects. So, now that we have covered strokes — let's go on to the actual shapes.

Lines

The Graphics object's line drawing method is defined like this:

```
public void drawLine(int x1, int y1, int x2, int y2)
```

Obviously, the first pair of integers references the x and y location of the starting point of the line, and the second pair is the end point of the line. So, if I were to draw a line from the upper left-hand corner of the screen to the lower right-hand corner, it would look something like this:

Figure 7-2: Drawing a line

```
g.drawLine(0, 0, getWidth(), getHeight());
```

You can see line drawing in action in Figure 7-2.

Rectangles

There are two ways to draw a rectangle. The first is to draw an outline using drawRect:

```
public void drawRect(int x, int y, int width, int height)
```

The first two arguments are the x and y location of the upper left-hand corner of the rectangle. The second pair is the width and height of the rectangle. The result of this operation is an outline of a rectangle drawn in the current color and stroke style, as shown in Figure 7-3.

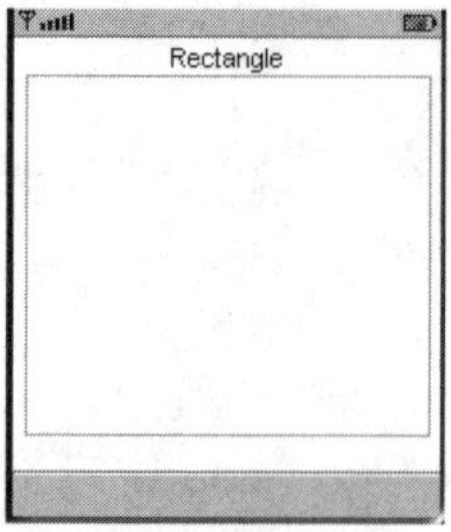

The second way to draw a rectangle is to fill one in with fillRect:

```
public void fillRect(int x, int y, int width, int height)
```

Figure 7-3: The barren and hollow shell of a line rectangle

This method has the same arguments as drawRect, except this time the result is a filled-in rectangle. The color of the fill is the current color set with setColor. The stroke style has no effect on this kind of shape.

Rounded Rectangles, Circles, and Ellipses

Sure, MIDP is lacking some basic common shapes, but yet we have the rounded rectangle. The rounded rectangle can be used to draw several different primitive types, actually. The rounded rectangle is basically a box with the sides rounded off. Make the sides round enough and you can even coax MIDP into drawing a circle or an ellipse. The method looks like this:

```
public void drawRoundRect(int x, int y, int width, int height, int arcWidth,
        int arcHeight)
```

Just like regular rectangles, the first four arguments are the x and y coordinates of the upper left-hand corner and the width and height of the rectangle. The two new ones on the end are for the width and height of the arc that will round off the sides of the shape. Each argument specifies the horizontal and vertical diameter of each rounded corner, respectively. If you want just the left and right sides to be rounded, then specify a small arcWidth and a large arcHeight. If you want it the other way around, then reverse the values. If you want a circle, you can draw a rectangle with the same width and height, and an arcWidth and arcHeight that are the same as the actual rectangle width and height. The call looks something like this:

```
g.drawRoundRect(0, 0, 25, 25, 25, 25);
```

This will draw a circle at coordinates 0, 0 25 pixels in diameter.

To draw an ellipse, use a different width and height, creating a rounded rectangle instead of a box — but keep the arc width and height the same as the rectangle's width and height. For example:

```
g.drawRoundRect(0, 0, 100, 25, 100, 25);
```

This draws an ellipse 100 pixels wide and 25 pixels high.

Note   For a handy Java applet that allows you to interactively play with rounded rectangle values, try this URL: cs.bluffton.edu/~jsorice/portfolio/roundrect/roundrect.html.

Naturally, you can also draw a filled-in rounded rectangle with this method:

```
public void fillRoundRect(int x, int y, int width,
        int height, int arcWidth, int arcHeight)
```

As with other fill operations, the fill color is the currently set color and the stroke style does not apply. See Figure 7-4 for an example of a rounded rectangle.

Figure 7-4: A rounded rectangle — you won't poke your eye out on this.

Arcs

You can also draw arcs in MIDP using the drawArc method in the Graphics class:

```
public void drawArc(int x, int y, int width, int height, int startAngle,
        int arcAngle)
```

Naturally, the first pair of arguments specifies the origin point of this arc. Next up is the width and height of this arc in pixels. Finally there are the startAngle and arcAngle arguments. The

startAngle is the beginning angle at which the arc starts, specified
in degrees. The arcAngle is the angle at which the arc ends, relative to the startAngle. This means that if the startAngle is 45
degrees and the arcAngle is 10 degrees, the ending angle of the
arc will be 55 degrees. It's hard to really visualize what I'm talking
about on paper. Instead, play around with the geometry source
code of the example MIDlet for this chapter to get a better feel for
the values. You can see drawArc in action in Figure 7-5, however.

As usual, there is a filled version of this method too:

```
public void fillArc(int x, int y, int width, int height, int startAngle,
    int arcAngle)
```

The end result of a filled arc is a pie slice
shape. Play around with the example MIDlet
source to get a feel for how this slice is
rendered.

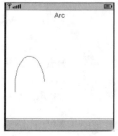

Triangles

New to MIDP 2.0 is the triangle primitive.
Strangely, there is no outline triangle, just a
filled triangle. The method looks like this:

Figure 7-5: An arc

```
public void fillTriangle(int x1, int y1, int x2, int y2, int x3, int y3)
```

This method takes three pairs of x and y positions, each one representing a corner of the
triangle. The result is a filled-in triangle using
the currently set color. A filled triangle can be
seen in Figure 7-6.

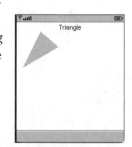

Figure 7-6: Brand new
for MIDP 2.0, the filled
triangle

Conclusion

In this chapter you have learned the basics of drawing text and primitive shapes. With this knowledge combined with the lessons learned in the previous chapter, you have the tools to create some impressive visuals. Although not analyzed line by line, the example program for this chapter shows how to draw each primitive discussed in this chapter.

Chapter 8

The Graphical User Interface

Introduction

One of the most important aspects of any game is the interface. Although quite simplified from its desktop big brother, J2ME and the MIDP API provide a lot of support for various GUI controls and features. This chapter will take you through the basics of MIDP's lcdui package, which is a replacement for J2SE's Abstract Windowing Toolkit. In addition to this, we will cover the basics of parsing key input as it is tangentially an interface issue.

Key Events

Before we begin the discussion of GUI objects and user interface issues, we might as well cover the basics of key input. Because MIDP is an event-based API, the primary way you capture input from the user is through key events. MIDP 2.0 has introduced more efficient ways of scanning input that will be discussed when we get to MIDP 2.0's Game API in Chapter 9.

Capturing Keys in the Canvas

If you noticed in our HelloWorld example, we used the Display object to set the current Displayable in the startApp method like this:

```
display_.setCurrent(canvas_);
```

This not only makes Canvas the currently displayed item on the screen, but also routes all keypress events to it as well. The Canvas object has three methods you can overload to capture all key events. The methods are:

```
protected void keyPressed(int keyCode)
protected void keyRepeated(int keyCode)
protected void keyReleased(int keyCode)
```

The first method, keyPressed, is called when a key is pressed, obviously. The second, keyRepeated, may or may not be called if a key is held down. Many handsets do not support keyRepeated messages and thus it is not wise to depend on this method for anything. If you are totally hell-bent on using it, use the hasRepeatEvents method to detect if the handset supports repeats. Finally, keyReleased is called when the user has taken his finger off a key. They all have the same argument, an integer called keyCode. The keyCode is one of several predefined fields inside the Canvas object. See Table 8-1 for their meanings.

Table 8-1: Key codes

Key Code	Description
KEY_NUM0	The 0 key
KEY_NUM1	The 1 key
KEY_NUM2	The 2 key
KEY_NUM3	The 3 key
KEY_NUM4	The 4 key
KEY_NUM5	The 5 key
KEY_NUM6	The 6 key
KEY_NUM7	The 7 key
KEY_NUM8	The 8 key
KEY_NUM9	The 9 key
KEY_STAR	The * key
KEY_POUND	The # key

So, let's say we want to detect if the user has pressed the 0 button in our HelloCanvas. We would define a method like this:

Listing 8-1: Detecting a specific keypress

```
protected void keyPressed(int keyCode)
{
    if (keyCode == Canvas.KEY_NUM0)
    {
        System.out.println("0 Pressed!");
    }
}
```

This is a simple case, where we send output to the console that the 0 key has been pressed. Not very useful, but you can see where we are going. The same technique applies to keyReleased and keyRepeated.

Game Actions

One problem with MIDP handsets (in America and Europe, at least) is the non-standard key layout of each device. You may find a control setup that works fine for the primary handset you use for development, but on other devices it may feel awkward because of that particular phone's key placement. Also, none of these key codes allow you to detect if the directional pad has been pressed. For this reason, the Canvas also includes the method getGameAction:

```
public int getGameAction(int keyCode)
```

With this method, you pass the keyCode received by the keyPressed, keyReleased, or keyRepeated method and it returns an integer that tells you which game action key we are dealing with. A game action is an alias for a button that is optimized for gameplay and/or a press of the directional pad. The game actions are listed in Table 8-2.

Table 8-2: Game actions

Action	Description
UP	The up action
DOWN	The down action
LEFT	The left action
RIGHT	The right action
FIRE	The fire button action

Action	Description
GAME_A	The "game a" action
GAME_B	The "game b" action
GAME_C	The "game c" action
GAME_D	The "game d" action

So, let's change our previous method to use game actions. Instead of detecting if we have hit the 0 key, we will try to see if we hit the UP button instead. Our code would look like this:

Listing 8-2: Using game actions

```
protected void keyPressed(int keyCode)
{
    int action = getGameAction(keyCode);

    if (action == Canvas.UP)
    {
        System.out.println("UP Pressed!");
    }
}
```

The cool thing about game actions is it allows you to avoid having to write separate event handlers for the keypad and the directional pad. You can't assume every handset has a directional pad; thus it is a good idea to have the keypad's 8, 4, 6, and 2 buttons also perform the same actions as pressing up, left, right, and down respectively. By using game actions, you just have to check for the UP, LEFT, RIGHT, and DOWN game actions. Devices that have no directional pads will most likely register the equivalent game action for each keypress.

The FIRE action is usually reserved for directional pads that can be pressed to select. However, some devices may have dedicated fire buttons or perhaps map the phone's SEND key to be FIRE. Also the GAME_A through GAME_D actions are undefined and up to the OEM to use if desired. They could be dedicated buttons, they could be just the unused keys on the keypad, or they could be nothing at all. I usually ignore them in my code because I can't depend on a handset manufacturer to use these actions logically.

Overall, key input is exceedingly easy to use; however, event-based input is pretty lousy for game development. In Chapter 9, "The Game API," you will learn new ways to parse key input in a more game-friendly manner.

Soft Buttons

One of the more novel innovations brought forth by J2ME is the concept of the soft button. Every MIDP device is mandated to have at least two soft buttons. Handsets often have two small physical buttons — one just below the screen to the left and another on the right. See Figure 8-1 as an example of where the soft buttons are on an average MIDP handset.

Figure 8-1: The buttons labeled "Exit" and "Back" are referred to as soft buttons. On most handsets, there will be actual physical buttons on the device below these labels that when pressed perform the action described on the button label.

The actual function of these two buttons is determined by the programmer. You can add labeled soft buttons to any object derived from the Screen class. When you add a soft button to a Canvas or GUI screen, you will usually see a small text label directly over one of the soft buttons beneath the screen. Processing the input from these buttons involves becoming familiar with MIDP's Command object.

The Command

A Command object is a description of a command. This description includes a label (that goes above the soft button), a priority, and type. The last two properties govern where the soft button is placed on the screen. Of course, each handset seems to treat these properties differently, so there is no guarantee that your button label will appear on the same soft button when running your code on different handsets.

The Command is only the description of the command. The actual code that performs the action once this Command is issued is found in the CommandListener associated with the Displayable object (such as a Canvas or Form).

Creating a Command

All you really need to know about the Command object itself is how to create one. The most commonly used constructor looks like this:

```
Command(String label, int commandType, int priority)
```

The first argument is the String for the label that is shown above the soft button. The second is a commandType integer that is one of the defined types in the Command class. See Table 8-3 for each type. Finally, there is the priority. This is a number that represents the importance of the command. The lower the number, the more important it is. The theory is that if you have more than one Command associated with the soft button, the one with the highest priority will show up on the screen. In some cases, I have seen handsets bring up a pop-up menu if there is more than one Command assigned to a soft button. You then have to scroll through the commands, with the highest priority being at the top of the list. Details like this are handset-specific and not really part of the MIDP specification. In the end, the priority and type are just "hints" to the device — whether your handset does anything with these hints is up to the OEM.

Table 8-3: Commands

Command Type	Description
BACK	A command that brings the user back to the previous screen.
CANCEL	A command that invalidates the current action.
EXIT	A command that exits the application.
HELP	A command that brings up help for the current action or on the usage of the application.
ITEM	A command that relates to the currently focused item in a list. Similar to selecting an item from a menu.
OK	A positive response to a request.
SCREEN	An application-defined command relating to the current screen. For example, we may have a screen that allows us to boost the statistics of our character in an RPG, or a command called "Dexterity" that when pressed will increase the DEX stat by 1.
STOP	A command that stops a currently running process, for example, the downloading of a file from a web server.

Command Actions

Now that you have a command, how do you glue it into your MIDlet so that it actually does something? This is where listeners come in. Back in the stone age of pre-Java 2 programming, handling events in Java was similar to Win32. You had a giant case statement in your code that received messages and you acted upon the desired messages. Now in this high-tech age of Java 2 and MIDP, we have event listeners instead.

Listeners

Events get sent to your MIDlet in the form of event objects. In this case, when a button is pressed, a Command object is sent to your MIDlet's commandAction method. This requires your MIDlet to implement the CommandListener interface. As an example, look at the definition of our old HelloWorld MIDlet:

```
public class HelloWorld extends MIDlet implements CommandListener
```

When we implement the CommandListener interface, we are required to provide a commandAction method in our MIDlet class. In HelloWorld, our commandAction did nothing. However, it is defined like so:

```
public void commandAction(Command c, Displayable s)
```

The first argument is the actual Command object that gets sent to our MIDlet in response to an event such as pressing a button. The second is the Displayable object. Displayable is the parent class for Screens, Forms, and Canvases. Thus, when you attach soft buttons to any of these objects, a reference to the currently active Displayable from which the Command came will be passed to the method. This helps you determine which screen the user was on when the button was pressed, and thus perform the correct action given the context of the MIDlet's execution.

To process individual events, you can switch on the Command argument and compare it against the Commands you have created in your MIDlet. For a basic MIDlet that has, say, a Command object for exiting the MIDlet, it might look like this:

Listing 8-3: Command actions in action

```
public void commandAction(Command c, Displayable s)
{
    if (c == exitCommand)
    {
        destroyApp(false);
        notifyDestroyed();
    }
}
```

Here you see a really simple example of Command processing. We check to see if the Command passed in is our exitCommand object. If so, we destroy the MIDlet by calling destroyApp and then use notifyDestroyed to tell the application manager to kill this MIDlet.

Adding Commands to a Displayable

Now that we know how to create Commands and process events, we need to know how to add Commands to Displayables as well as allow them to send events back to our MIDlet to be processed by our listener method.

Any object extended from Displayable has the method addCommand:

```
public void addCommand(Command cmd)
```

Here we simply pass the Command we previously created to the method and it will add it to the soft button commands that are already on the screen if there are any. Despite all the hints for priority and type, I find that most handsets seem to simply position the Commands in first-in last-out (FILO) order. That is, when you add a command, the previously added command gets pushed to the soft button on the left.

We can also remove commands in a similar fashion:

```
public void removeCommand(Command cmd)
```

This allows us to remove a specific Command object from the Displayable that we previously added. Annoyingly, there is no method for removing all currently added Commands from a Displayable. Instead, you have to track them yourself and explicitly remove each one with the removeCommand method.

Making MIDlets Listen

Now that we've added the Commands to the Displayable, we need to tell it to send the Commands to our MIDlet class. This is done with the Displayable's member method, setCommandListener:

```
public void setCommandListener(CommandListener l)
```

Here we pass an object that implements the CommandListener interface. In our case, this is our MIDlet class itself. Now, whenever a Command event happens, it will be sent to the commandAction method inside our MIDlet. You can switch the listener to another class by calling this again, and remove the existing listener by passing null as the argument.

Putting It All Together

So, to review, let's show a block of code that creates a Displayable object, adds some commands to it, and makes the MIDlet listen for events. This code would probably best fit in the startApp method of our old HelloWorld MIDlet from Chapter 4:

Listing 8-4: Our startApp method

```
public void startApp()
{
    canvas_ = new HelloCanvas();
    exitCommand_ = new Command("EXIT", Command.EXIT, 1);
    display_ = Display.getDisplay(this);
    canvas_.addCommand(exitCommand_);
    display_.setCurrent(canvas_);
    canvas_.setCommandListener(this);
}
```

Here we see the construction of our HelloCanvas object that is extended from Canvas. The Canvas class is derived from Displayable, and thus able to have Commands added to it. Then we create an exitCommand as we have seen earlier in this chapter. Next we get the display, add the command to the Canvas, and then set the current display to our newly created HelloCanvas. Finally, we set the HelloCanvas' listener to be the MIDlet itself by passing setCommandListener a this reference. This in combination with our commandAction method defined earlier is a fine example of a simple event processing MIDlet. Don't worry if these bits and pieces of code are confusing; you can see all of these concepts put together in the example source code for this chapter in the companion files.

Forms and Screens

The MIDP GUI works on the concept of Forms and Screens. These are both classes inside the javax.microedition.lcdui package. In fact, Forms are actually extended from Screens. A Screen represents a GUI element — and each GUI element takes up an entire screen. If you want to have a list control, for instance, this list will take up the entire display as a descendant of the Screen object. Although the Form is also derived from Screen, a Form is a kind of screen that acts as a container for multiple GUI controls. For instance, inside a Form you could have static text and a text input box on the same page. Each GUI element added to a Form is derived from the Item class, which we will discuss when detailing the inner workings of the Form class.

A Screen is a base class for four different types of GUI elements: Alerts, Lists, TextBoxes, and the aforementioned Form. Of course, both Screens and Forms are derived from Displayable, which allows them to have Commands added to them for user input. These controls will capture their own user input for things like scrolling text, moving a cursor, and such, but it is up to the programmer to write Command event handling code to process user interaction with the soft buttons. With this said, let's begin our tour of each individual GUI object.

Alert

An Alert is a full-screen display that alerts the user to an error or some other event. You might compare this to the simple MessageBox function in the Win32 API. The Alert can display a string and/or image that informs the user of the current situation. You can see an Alert in action in Figure 8-2.

Creating the Alert

This screen can be set to expire after a certain amount of time, after which the display will revert to the next Displayable object in the display manager's list of objects.

Alerts can also be modal, meaning they will stay on the screen until the user presses a button or otherwise performs some input that causes the Alert to be destroyed.

Before we do anything, we must create our Alert object. There are a few different constructors, but the easiest one to use is:

Figure 8-2: The Alert

```
Alert(String title)
```

This constructor takes a String as its only argument. This string passed to the constructor will be the Alert's title, which is usually text displayed along the top of the screen.

Setting the Alert Text and Image

After constructing the Alert, adding text to it is a simple matter of calling the setString method:

```
public void setString(String string)
```

Here you pass in a String with the text you want to display inside the Alert. If the text you place in an Alert is too large to fit on the screen, it will scroll and be forced into being modal. If you want to set an image to display inside the Alert, you use the setImage method:

```
public void setImage(Image image)
```

Here we pass a reference to a mutable or immutable image. In the case of a mutable image, it displays the image in the state it was as you passed it to the Alert. This means that if you modify the contents of that image later, it will not be reflected in the Alert unless you call setImage again with that reference, or make a call like this:

```
alert.setImage(alert.getImage());
```

This code will cause the Alert to take another snapshot of the mutable image and display it in its changed state. Now, when you display an Alert, your bitmap image will be shown in the center of the screen (or wherever the OEM felt like putting it).

Alert Gauges

New to MIDP 2.0 is the ability to add a Gauge in the Alert, as in a progress bar or some other progressive indicator of a task's completion status. To add a Gauge, you must pass a Gauge object to the method, setIndicator:

```
public void setIndicator(Gauge gauge)
```

This member method takes a reference to a Gauge as its only argument. You can then use the Gauge object to indicate the progress of a task such as loading all of your PNGs or some other processing that causes the MIDlet to block execution for a while.

There are restrictions to this functionality, however. The Gauge itself must be non-interactive, not owned by any other Alert or Form container, not have any Commands associated with it, not have an ItemCommandListener, not have a label, have no preferred width and height, and must have the layout value set to LAYOUT_DEFAULT. We will discuss Gauges in detail when we discuss the usage of Forms later in this chapter.

Alert Timeouts

So, let's say we want to create an Alert that informs the user of an invalid selection and displays on the screen for a few seconds. The code would look something like this:

```
Alert alert = new Alert("Warning!");
alert.setText("Invalid Selection!");
alert.setTimeout(2000);
display_.setCurrent(alert);
```

This assumes we are doing this inside a MIDlet similar to our HelloWorld architecture. We create the Alert object with the title string "Warning!" We then set its text and the delay, and use the MIDlet's Display object to make the Alert the currently shown screen. The method setTimeout specifies how many milliseconds we want the Alert to display. In this case, we use 2000 milliseconds, which is two full seconds. Alternatively, you can use the constant FOREVER to create a modal Alert like so:

```
alert_.setTimeout(Alert.FOREVER);
```

Now, the Alert will not be automatically dismissed after a period of time and thus must be manually dismissed by a Command or other event. As stated earlier, if the text of the Alert is too large to fit on the screen, the Alert will be forced into the modal state because it has to scroll the text.

AlertTypes

Alerts can also be associated with different AlertType classes. By setting the AlertType, you can cause the device to display the Alert with a certain look representative of these types. The AlertType class has five fields that are used to indicate the type of Alert we are displaying. They are listed in Table 8-4.

Table 8-4: AlertType Fields

Field	Description
ALARM	An Alert type that alerts the user to an event that the user has already been notified of.
CONFIRMATION	An Alert type that is used to confirm the user's selection or input.
ERROR	An alert that notifies the user of an error such as a failed network connection or invalid text in a text control.
INFO	An Alert that provides information about something.
WARNING	An alert that warns the user of a dangerous operation.

To set the current AlertType, you use the setType method in the Alert class:

```
public setType(AlertType type)
```

Here you simply pass an AlertType that you want to use. For instance, if we wanted to set this to be a warning, we would do something like this:

```
alert.setType(AlertType.WARNING);
```

Of course, this is just a "hint" to the system to treat this as a warning alert. The device may change the look (perhaps adding an exclamation point to the display), or do nothing at all. This is yet another per-device difference that you may have to test for when launching your MIDlet commercially.

Alert Sounds

The AlertType class also includes the method playSound:

```
boolean playSound(Display display)
```

This takes the current Display as an argument and plays the appropriate sound for the AlertType instantiated. Back in the MIDP 1.0 days, this is all we had for sound. Usually the sound played, if any at all, was an annoyingly loud beep. Keep in mind that this, as with the other AlertType properties, is only a "hint" to the device to play a beep. The device may not do anything at all. If the method returns true, then you know the user was alerted. Otherwise, nothing probably happened.

List

The List class is a simple menu control that lets you pick from a number of different choices. It is similar to a drop-down list on the web, except all of the options are given at once. Being another object extended from Screen, the List takes up the entire display, making it a rather inflexible and ugly GUI component.

Figure 8-3: A List in action

Creating the List

Among the few constructors for List, the easiest to use is this:

```
List(String title, int listType)
```

The first argument is the title String. Similar to the title in an Alert class, this is text that is drawn at the top of the screen when the List is being displayed. The second argument is the listType. There are four different list types, all represented by fields defined in the interface javax.microedition.lcdui.Choice. We will examine the ChoiceGroup and Choice interface when we discuss items for Forms. Until then, look at Table 8-5 for what each of these list types do. So let's say we want to make a main menu for our game that only allows one item to be selected at a time. The constructor call would look something like this:

```
List list = new List("Main Menu", Choice.EXCLUSIVE);
```

Table 8-5: List types

List Type	Description
EXCLUSIVE	A list in which only one element can be selected.
IMPLICIT	A list in which the currently highlighted item is selected upon a Command event.

List Type	Description
MULTIPLE	A list in which more than one item can be selected simultaneously.
POPUP	A list in which only one element is selected at a time. This selected element is visible, while the others are hidden. The user must scroll through the choices upon performing a keypress or other input. This is similar to the pop-up or drop-down list menus. This is a feature brand new for MIDP 2.0.

Adding Items

Now that we have created a List, we need to add selectable items. MIDP 2.0 allows you to insert strings as well as images in a List; however, it is required that you at least have a string for each item. One of the methods used to add items to the List is append:

```
public int append(String stringPart, Image imagePart)
```

This method will add an item to the bottom of the list. The first argument is the String containing the text for this selectable item; this is a required argument. The second is a reference to an Image that can be a small icon or other decoration to spruce up the look of the List display. This is optional; if you pass null to imagePart, no image will be shown for this item.

You can also insert an item at an arbitrary position in the List through the insert method:

```
public void insert(int elementNum, String stringPart, Image imagePart)
```

This is similar to append with one difference, the elementNum argument. This specifies where you want to insert the item. For instance, if you want to put this item at the top of the list, elementNum would be 0. If the index is greater than the number of elements in the list, this method will throw an IndexOutOf-BoundsException, so watch where you put stuff.

Removing Items

You can also delete individual items, or the entire list, with these two methods:

```
public void delete(int elementNum)
public void deleteAll()
```

The first method allows you to specify a particular element to delete. The range checking restrictions present in insert are also in effect here. The deleteAll method will remove every element in the list — effectively clearing it out.

List Commands and Events

Now that you have a bunch of items in the List, how do you select items and retrieve the selection? The first thing you need to do is make the MIDlet a listener for the List. Much like we did in the Command part of this chapter, we can set the MIDlet to be the List's listener much like a Canvas can. This should look familiar to you:

```
List list = new List("Main Menu", Choice.EXCLUSIVE);
list.setCommandListener(this);
```

Now the List object can notify the MIDlet of a Command action when a soft button is pressed or a select operation is performed. Some phones have a special select key. When this button is pressed, a special select command is sent. This command is defined inside the List class as SELECT_COMMAND. Thus, inside the MIDlet's commandAction method, you can check if the Command argument is equal to List.SELECT_COMMAND. If this is the case, then the phone's select button has been pressed. On phones that do not have select buttons, you have to use a soft button to select items on the list. You do this by adding your own select Command object to the List, and then putting the selection logic inside your MIDlet's commandAction method.

Dealing with Selections

Whether processing a SELECT_COMMAND or your own custom soft button event, you need to know what the current selection is on the List in order to perform the requested action. There are a number of methods inside the List class for dealing with selected items. The simplest method of the bunch is getSelectedIndex:

```
public int getSelectedIndex()
```

This method returns an integer that is the number of the element in the List that is currently selected. If nothing is selected, the return value will be set to –1. This method only deals with single selections for EXCLUSIVE type Lists. What if you have multiple items selected instead? That's where getSelectedFlags comes in:

```
public int getSelectedFlags(boolean[] selectedArray)
```

This method takes an array of Booleans as an argument. This array must be as large as the number of elements in the list. After this method executes, each element will be either true or false, based on whether or not it is selected. The return value is how many items are currently selected. If the array passed to this method is shorter than the size of the list, it will throw an IllegalArgumentException.

You can also set the currently selected item. This is done for EXCLUSIVE Lists through the setSelectedIndex member:

```
public void setSelectedIndex(int elementNum, Boolean selected)
```

Here you simply pass in the element you want to set the state of, and then a Boolean. If selected is set to true, then this element will be set to selected. Otherwise, it will be deselected. Obviously, this method will throw an exception if you pass an element-Number that is beyond the range of elements in the List.

If you have a List that can have multiple selections, you use setSelectedFlags:

```
public void setSelectedFlags(Boolean[] selectedArray)
```

This method takes an array of Booleans as the argument. For each element in the array, it will set the corresponding element in the List to selected or unselected depending on the value of the Boolean. If the array is shorter than the size of the list, it will throw an exception.

TextBox

A TextBox is another screen-based GUI control that allows the user to input text. It may seem ridiculous to have an entire screen dedicated to inputting text when all you might be typing in is a name for a high score, and it is, but such is the MIDP GUI. You can set the size of the control, but that will just make it a smaller text box on a largely blank screen.

Creating a TextBox

Anyway, enough ranting — to create a TextBox you use its one and only constructor:

```
TextBox(String title, String text, int maxSize,
        int constraints)
```

Figure 8-4: The text box as seen in the emulator

The first argument is a title String. This will be a line of text displayed at the top of the display, as is the standard with these Screen-based controls. Next you pass in the text that will be in the TextBox by default. If this is null, then the TextBox will start out empty. Next you pass in the maximum number of characters this TextBox will hold via the integer argument, maxSize. Finally, there is the constraints argument, which describes an input constraint for the text control.

TextBox Input Constraints

There are a number of different inputConstraints values available in the TextField class. Yes, I said TextField class. We'll discuss TextFields when we get to Forms later in this chapter, but for now just know that TextField and TextBox share many of the same properties. Hence the interchangeable constraints. What these do is limit the kind of data that can be entered into the text box. For instance, if you want only numbers to be typed into your text box, you use the constraint constant NUMERIC like this:

```
TextBox textBox = new TextBox("Number", null, 8, TextField.NUMERIC);
```

The constraint is actually a combination of two values that can be ORed together. First, there are the restrictive constraint settings, as shown in Table 8-6. Then one of those values can be ORed with any number of the modifier flags in Table 8-7.

Table 8-6: Restrictive constraints

Constraint	Description
ANY	No input restriction
EMAILADDR	Email addresses (periods, @ symbols, etc.)
NUMERIC	Numbers only
PHONENUMBER	Numbers, parentheses, and dashes
URL	For web addresses — includes periods, slashes, and such
DECIMAL	Decimal numbers (basically, a numeric that allows periods)

Table 8-7: Constraint flags

Flag	Description
PASSWORD	Hides input from user (replacing text with asterisks, for instance)
UNEDITABLE	Text control is not able to be modified by user
SENSITIVE	This is sensitive data and should not be cached (passwords, credit card numbers, etc.)
NON_PREDICTIVE	Doesn't use the device's built-in text-prediction system if any is available
INITIAL_CAPS_WORD	Automatically capitalizes the first letter of each word
INITIAL_CAPS_SENTENCE	Automatically capitalizes the first word of each sentence

Input Modes

While we are on the subject of input constraints, we might as well mention input modes. This new feature of MIDP 2.0 allows the programmer to "hint" to the device that a certain kind of information will be entered in a given TextBox. It is up to the device to facilitate the input of this text by perhaps changing the interface to suit that kind of input. For instance, you can hint to the device that Korean Hangul text will be input into a TextBox. Depending on the implementation of the device, it may bring up a different on-screen keyboard with Korean characters instead of defaulting to English when using this TextBox. However, since this is just a hint, it very well may not do anything. To set the input mode, you use the method setInitialInputMode:

```
public void setInitialInputMode(String characterSubset)
```

The sole argument to this function is the String characterSubset. There are a number of strings recognized by MIDP as input modes. For instance, if you want this TextBox to support the input of Greek characters, you would call the method like this:

```
textBox.setInitialInputMode("UCB_GREEK");
```

Now you are set to support the explosive Greek mobile gaming market. (Well, that is if the Greek government doesn't ban all cell phone games.) If you are interested in input modes, you can see all the available strings in the documentation.

TextBox Commands and Events

Much like the List control, you have to add soft button commands to the screen and make the MIDlet the listener for these events. It is done pretty much the same as with the List. Inside our MIDlet's startApp method, we might do something like this:

```
TextBox textBox = new List("Enter Name", null, 32, TextBox.ANY);
textBox.setCommandListener(this);
```

Seem familiar? Since Alert, List, TextBox, and Form are all derived from Displayable, they deal with command and event processing the same way. You can add Commands to the TextBox and process them in the MIDlet's commandAction method as described previously. For instance, you probably need a command to either cancel the text input or accept the text and proceed to the next screen. That functionality would be performed by the Commands.

Getting the Contents of the TextBox

Retrieving the actual text inside the TextBox is accomplished with the method getString:

```
public String getString()
```

That's it. This method returns a string containing the contents of the TextBox. Note that if you have used constraints such as PHONENUMBER, what is displayed in the TextBox is not necessarily the contents of the string. For instance, the phone number entered may include parentheses around the area code and a dash after the prefix, but the string returned by getString will simply be a bunch of numbers.

TextBox Tickers

A new feature for MIDP 2.0 is the ability to add a Ticker to the TextBox screen. This is done with the method setTicker:

```
public void setTicker(Ticker ticker)
```

Here you pass a Ticker object to the TextBox. The Ticker is an Item-based control and is discussed in the following section. However, what this does is provide a way to display a simple scrolling string of text on the same screen as the TextBox. Exactly how this is displayed is up to the implementation on the actual handset. In some cases it may modify the size and appearance of the TextBox itself.

Form

And now the final control, the Form. The Form isn't really a GUI control class. It is more of a container for a different kind of GUI object. In this case, GUI controls derived from the Item class can be added to a Form in much the same way Commands can be added to a Canvas. This sort of solves my major complaint about screen-based controls in that it lets you have multiple GUI objects on the same screen. Some of the Item controls are smaller versions of their screen-based big brothers, while others are unique altogether.

Creating a Form

The simplest Form constructor looks like this:

```
Form(String title)
```

As with most any screen-derived GUI object, the title is a string of text displayed at the top of the display. Now that we have created a Form, we need to add Items to it.

Items

Classes extended from the Item class are small GUI objects that can be added to the Form and automatically laid out on the screen. There are eight different Items in MIDP 2.0: ChoiceGroup, CustomItem, DateField, Gauge, ImageItem, Spacer, StringItem, and TextField. We will go through a brief overview of each one. For detailed usage information, check Sun's documentation and the sample MIDlet for this chapter.

ChoiceGroup

A choice group is a collection of selectable items. The ChoiceGroup can be used as either a single selection or multiple selection control — similar to the behavior of a List. As with all GUI elements, the look of the ChoiceGroup is not standardized and thus it may appear as radio buttons, check boxes, or whatever else the OEM felt like doing when they made their MIDP implementation. You can also associate an image with each selection to further customize the look. See Figure 8-5 for a ChoiceGroup in action.

Figure 8-5: The Choice-Group as seen in a Form. You can see other items in this view, but the ones we will be looking at are outlined with a black rectangle.

Creating a ChoiceGroup

Creating a ChoiceGroup is a simple matter of calling the constructor:

```
public ChoiceGroup(String label, int choiceType)
```

The first argument is the label text that will appear above the ChoiceGroup item. The second is an integer that determines the selection type. You may be familiar with this concept from the List class. These are the same predefined choice fields we used with the List:

EXCLUSIVE, MULTIPLE, IMPLICIT, and POPUP. Each one represents a behavior similar to that of the List.

Adding Choices

Now that you have created a ChoiceGroup, you need to add things to choose from. This is done via the append method:

```
public int append(String stringPart, Image imagePart)
```

This method takes a mandatory String argument that is the text that goes next to the choice's check box or radio button. Next is an optional Image argument that is used to display a small image that goes alongside the choice. If this is set to null, then no image will be displayed. This returns an integer that is the index of the element in the ChoiceGroup's internal array of choices. As with all other append operations, the appended choice is added to the bottom of the list. If you want to explicitly insert a choice in the list, use insert:

```
public void insert(int elementNum, String stringPart, Image imagePart)
```

This is pretty much the same thing as append, except the first argument specifies explicitly where in the list you want this choice to appear. Naturally, if you give an invalid index, an exception will be thrown.

Removing Choices

If you want to delete a choice, you simply use the delete method:

```
public void delete(int elementNum)
```

This removes the choice specified by the argument elementNum. This is an index — like what is returned from the append method. You can also delete all of the choices with the deleteAll method:

```
public void deleteAll();
```

That's all there is to it. Calling this will clear the ChoiceGroup of choices.

Detecting Selections

Finding out what is selected in a ChoiceGroup is basically the same as doing so in a List. You have two familiar methods:

```
public int getSelectedIndex()
public int getSelectedFlags(boolean[] selectedArray_return)
```

The first method returns the index of the selected choice for EXPLICIT ChoiceGroups. The second method takes an array of Booleans as an argument. These will be set to true or false depending on the corresponding choice's selected or unselected state. Naturally, you can manually select items as well:

```
public void setSelectedIndex(int elementNum, boolean selected)
public void setSelectedFlags(boolean[] selectedArray)
```

The first method takes the element you want to select as a first argument and a Boolean, selected. If the Boolean argument is set to true, then the index will be set to selected. Otherwise, it will be flagged as unselected. The second method is similar; however, it takes an array of Booleans and then uses the array to select or unselect each corresponding choice.

CustomItem

The CustomItem is a brand new class for MIDP 2.0. Basically, this is a class used to create your own custom GUI Item objects. It has all the parts necessary to create a wide variety of widgets, including the ability to write your own paint method for much-needed flexibility in the appearance of the control. The class includes methods for detecting input that is normally automatically handled by the existing Items. Instead of only getting a listener call when the control is modified, the CustomItem derived class has methods that are called for every keypress and pointer move (if the device has a stylus).

DateField

The DateField is a control that can be used to either display or enter the time and date. This is an exceedingly simple control with few member methods. It does the job, though. Depending on the handset's implementation of MIDP 2.0, trying to set the time may bring up another clock interface, and setting the date may bring up a full-screen calendar. See Figure 8-6 for a DateField in action.

Gauge

The Gauge is basically a progress bar. In most implementations it represents the value of an integer as a line or collection of bars. There are two kinds of Gauges: interactive and non-interactive. Interactive Gauges respond to keypresses by increasing or decreasing the fill level. Non-interactive Gauges are not influenced by the user, and thus are ideal for showing progress, such as loading a level or some other automatic task. See Figure 8-7 for a Gauge in action.

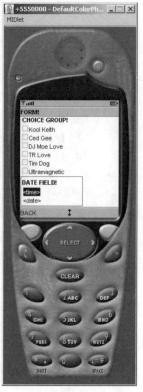

Figure 8-6: The DateField as seen in a Form

Creating a Gauge

To create a Gauge, we use the one and only constructor:

```
public Gauge(String label, boolean interactive, int maxValue, int initialValue)
```

The first argument is a String with the text that will be displayed above the Gauge as a label. The second is a Boolean that tells if this Gauge is interactive or not. Not only are both drawn differently, but if a Gauge is interactive, then keypresses from the user will automatically increase or decrease the Gauge's value. Finally there is the maxValue and initialValue. The initialValue argument represents the initial value of the Gauge. The maxValue represents the integer value that will completely fill the gauge. If you make this number too large, it will take too long to fill the gauge.

Setting and Getting the Value

To set the Gauge's value, use setValue:

```
public void setValue(int);
```

This method will return the current value the Gauge is set to.

To determine the current value, you use getValue:

```
public int getValue();
```

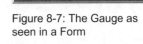

Figure 8-7: The Gauge as seen in a Form

This will return the current Gauge's value. So, let's say we want to set the Gauge to be 1 greater than it is currently. You can do it like this:

```
Gauge gauge = new Gauge("Progress", false, 10, 1);
gauge.setValue(gauge.getValue() + 1);
```

We created the Gauge with 1 as its starting value (one-tenth filled). The end result after our setValue method is a Gauge with a value of 2.

ImageItem

An ImageItem is used to place bitmap images in a Form. Mutable or immutable, the ImageItem lets you set the image to any exiting Image class and will appear in your Form alongside other GUI controls. See Figure 8-8 for an example of the ImageItem's usage.

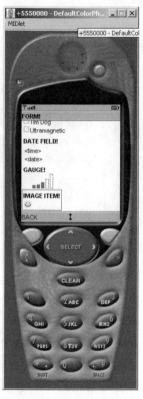

Creating an ImageItem

The ImageItem is pretty basic. To create one, use the constructor:

```
public void ImageItem(String label, Image img,
        int layout, String altText)
```

The first argument is a String that will be shown along with the Image as a label. The second is a reference to the Image we want to use with this ImageItem. The next is a layout directive. The ImageItem has a number of different layout directives as illustrated in Table 8-8. These directives are similar to those used when adding Items to a Form as discussed later

Figure 8-8: The ImageItem

in this chapter. The final argument is a string that will be displayed in lieu of the Image if for some reason the bitmap can't be shown.

Table 8-8: Valid ImageItem directives

Directive	Description
LAYOUT_CENTER	Item has horizontally centered layout.
LAYOUT_DEFAULT	Item follows the default layout policy of its container.
LAYOUT_LEFT	Item has left-aligned layout.
LAYOUT_NEWLINE_AFTER	Item becomes last item in its line or row, with the next item appearing at the beginning of a new line or row.
LAYOUT_NEWLINE_BEFORE	Item is placed at the beginning of a new line or row.
LAYOUT_RIGHT	Item has right-aligned layout.

Spacer

A new class for MIDP 2.0, the Spacer is a simple blank Item that allows you to place gaps between your GUI controls on a Form. You can determine the width and height of the spacer to give some added control over the layout of your Items.

Creating a Spacer

This constructor creates a spacer with the minimum width and height in pixels specified by the two arguments:

```
public Spacer(int minWidth, int minHeight)
```

StringItem

The StringItem is a non-interactive static display of text that can be inserted into your Form alongside other GUI components. See Figure 8-9 for an example of a StringItem's usage.

Creating a StringItem

Creating a StringItem is very simple:

```
public StringItem(String label, String text)
```

The first argument is a String containing a label that will appear alongside the text specified with the text argument. You can put newlines in your text to force the StringItem to appear on multiple lines instead of just one.

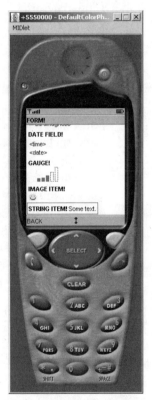

Figure 8-9: A StringItem as seen in a Form

TextField

Similar to a TextBox, the TextField is a small editable box into which the user can type text. The TextField Class shares some properties with the TextBox and works in a very similar manner. See Figure 8-10 for an example of a TextField in action.

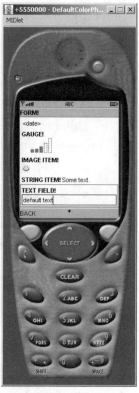

Creating a TextField

Create a TextField by using its only constructor:

```
public TextField(String label, String text,
      int maxSize, int constraints)
```

Much like the TextBox, this takes a label that will be displayed at the top of the Item as a first argument. It also takes a String, text, that is used as the default text that appears inside this control. It can be set to null if you want it blank. The next argument, maxSize, is the maximum number of characters this TextField can hold. The final argument, constraints, is the same argument we used in the TextBox. Using various predefined constraint values defined in the TextField class, you can restrict input to just numbers, web addresses, and other filters.

Figure 8-10: A TextField as seen in a Form

Getting the Contents of the TextField

Retrieving the text from a TextField should be familiar to you by now. You use the method getString:

```
public String getString()
```

This method returns a String with the contents of the TextField. Remember that depending on the constraints used, the String will not be exactly what is displayed on the screen. For instance, when using the PHONENUMBER constraint, the parentheses around the area code will not be present in the string but will be shown in the control itself.

Adding Items to a Form

Once you have created an Item, you need to add it to the Form. This is done with the append method:

```
int append(Item item)
```

Here we pass a reference to the Item we wish to add to the Form. Internally, the Form maintains an array of all Items contained in it. Therefore, you can explicitly insert an Item into the order you want. This is achieved with the insert method:

```
void insert(int itemNum, Item item)
```

The first argument is the position in the Form's internal array and the second is a reference to the Item you are inserting. Obviously if you specify an itemNum greater than the number of items in the Form, it will throw an exception.

You can also delete items with the delete method:

```
void delete(int itemNum)
```

Here you pass in the number of the Item you wish to delete. The same rules apply here. If you pass an invalid item number, it will throw an exception.

Item Layout

Sure, you can just add Items to the Form, but do you have any control over where they appear? In MIDP 1.0 you had very little control over the position of Items. However, MIDP 2.0 does support the concept of layouts. Your ability to control the placement of Items in a Form is very limited, but it's way better than it used to be.

Note   The screen shots of Items in Figures 8-4 through 8-10 show the default layout of each Item when added successively to a Form.

The Form is broken down into rows and columns. As you add Items to a Form, by default each successive Item is added in a row below the previous one. If the Form grows too much vertically, it will be necessary for the user to scroll down to view the rest of the Items.

It is possible to influence the positioning of the next Item in various ways by using the Item's layout attribute. To set the layout of an Item, you need to use the method setLayout:

```
public void setLayout(int layout)
```

This takes a single integer argument, layout. This argument must be set to one of the predefined layout fields in the Item class as shown in Table 8-9.

Let's say you want the next Item to be aligned along the left side of the Form. In this case, you would make this call before adding the Item to the Form:

```
StringItem stringItem = new StringItem("String Item", "Contents");
StringItem.setLayout(Item.LAYOUT_LEFT);
```

Now, this item will be drawn against the left side of the screen. The layout may be recomputed if you change the size or otherwise alter the appearance of an Item as well.

Table 8-9: Layout directives

Directive	Description
LAYOUT_DEFAULT	Item follows the default layout policy of its container.
LAYOUT_LEFT	Item has left-aligned layout.
LAYOUT_RIGHT	Item has right-aligned layout.
LAYOUT_CENTER	Item has horizontally centered layout.
LAYOUT_TOP	Item has top-aligned layout.
LAYOUT_BOTTOM	Item has bottom-aligned layout.
LAYOUT_VCENTER	Item has vertically centered layout.
LAYOUT_NEWLINE_BEFORE	Item is placed at the beginning of a new line or row.
LAYOUT_NEWLINE_AFTER	Item becomes last item in its line or row, with the next item appearing at the beginning of a new line or row.
LAYOUT_SHRINK	Item's width may be reduced to minimum width.

Directive	Description
LAYOUT_EXPAND	Item's width may be expanded to fill open space.
LAYOUT_VSHRINK	Item's height may be reduced to minimum height.
LAYOUT_VEXPAND	Item's height may be expanded to fill empty vertical space.
LAYOUT_2	Item uses MIDP 2.0 layout rules instead of MIDP 1.0 style.

An Exception will be thrown if an illegal combination of layout directives are used.

Form User Interaction

When multiple Items are contained in one Form, the user can switch the focus to any of the selectable controls by using the directional pad on the device. This action is handled automatically by the Form itself and requires no additional programming. However, when the state of an item changes, you can have the Form call a listener that can act upon this event. Changing the state may be something like selecting something in a ChoiceGroup or entering text in a TextField. To set up the listener for Item state changes, you use the method setItemStateListener:

```
public void setItemStateListener(ItemStateListener iListener)
```

ItemStateListener is an interface that your MIDlet must implement in order to be able to process the change events from Form Items. For instance, we would modify our HelloWorld MIDlet declaration like so:

```
public class HelloWorld extends MIDlet implements CommandListener, ItemStateListener
```

Now that our MIDlet class implements the ItemStateListener interface, we have to set the HelloWorld object as the Form's listener with setItemStateListener:

```
Form form = new Form("A Form!");
form.setItemStateListener(this);
```

The ItemStateListener interface requires us to write an itemStateChanged method in our MIDlet class. The definition looks like this:

```
public void itemStateChanged(Item item)
```

When an Item's state changes in a Form, the reference to the changed Item is passed to this method. We can then do any kind of processing we need to do inside this method. For instance, let's say we have a TextField in our MIDlet and we want to get the contents of it when the contents change. Our itemStateChanged method might look something like this:

Listing 8-5: The itemStateChanged method

```
public void itemStateChanged(Item item)
{
    if (item == textField_)
    {
        contentString_ = textField_.getString();
    }
}
```

Here we check if the changed Item is our TextField object. If so, we copy the contents of it to another private member variable, contentString_. This technique should be familiar to you if you followed our implementation of commandAction earlier in this chapter. Since the Form is derived from Screen, you can also add Commands to it as with any other GUI Screen object.

Managing the Display

All of these GUI screens are actually derived from Displayable, as is our Canvas (which is also included in the lcdui package). Thus, we manage the display of GUI objects much like we do with the Canvas. This means we have to use the Display object's setCurrent method to set the currently active GUI Screen class as the one that will be drawn on the screen.

One annoying thing about GUI screens is that you cannot explicitly call for a repaint. Theoretically, MIDP is supposed to handle it for you. But I have seen some "lazy" MIDP implementations that seem to forget to draw the screen when setting them to be current. If you need to force a screen to redraw, you can try things like adding and removing an Item, changing the size of a TextBox and then changing it back to the original value, etc. These methods will usually force a repaint on the handset if for some reason it does not do so automatically.

Third-Party GUI Packages

The basic MIDP GUI is rather primitive and ugly. For this reason there have been several GUI packages for MIDP released over the past few years. Some of these are free, while others require a license fee. These GUI controls can be much more flexible and visually impressive than MIDP's rather garish set of classes.

Note   Yes, the MIDP GUI is horrifically ugly and inflexible. The philosophy behind this bare-bones GUI is that the entire phone interface should be "skinnable" with downloadable themes much like you might have on your Windows desktop. Therefore, you have no control over lcdui's color or general appearance because this will be set at the OS level by the user.

kAWT

The kAWT package is an attempt to provide a slimmed-down version of AWT for KVM (and thus MIDP). This is not a free package and requires a license fee when used for commercial products. For educational and non-commercial use, it is completely free. Controls supported by the package include tabs, scrolling text windows, radio buttons, and other GUI components common to desktop systems. An upcoming color version promises to be a bit more attractive on modern devices. More information is available at www.kawt.de.

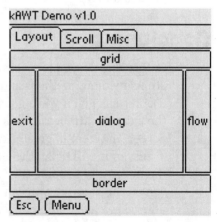

Figure 8-11: kAWT has a series of useful widgets and controls for MIDlets.

Nextel Open Windowing Toolkit

Being one of the first carriers in the U.S. to support J2ME, Nextel has long provided some open source toolkits for the MIDP development community. Nextel's OWT is a GUI package designed to be used on their exclusive Motorola iDEN handsets. Although you may have some success using OWT on other devices, it is not recommended. This package (and other Nextel projects) can be found at nextel.sourceforge.net.

Motorola Lightweight Windowing Toolkit (LWT)

Motorola has also provided a GUI package for J2ME. The LWT is designed to be used with just about any MIDP 1.0 device, unlike Nextel's offering. The LWT contains your standard array of alternate GUI controls and widgets such as text fields, buttons, and images. Although embedded on certain Motorola handsets (such as the T720i), LWT can be used on other devices. Being free and cross-platform, this may be the one for you. Check developers.motorola.com for the latest LWT and other Motorola APIs and tools.

Conclusion

In this chapter you have seen the basics of the MIDP GUI. There are many more methods and features of each class. However, this chapter has given you a good overview of the major features. Also, the example MIDlet for this chapter shows how to use each Screen and Item in greater detail.

Even in MIDP 2.0 the GUI is rather ugly and restrictive. In the interest of keeping the GUI consistent for every application run on the handset, you can't change the color of the controls or otherwise change their appearance much. This might be okay for address book and calculator programs, but for games it's horrible. Because of this and other limitations, I wrote custom GUI classes for my own projects. You may consider doing this too, or try using one of the various third-party MIDP GUI packages available on the net.

Chapter 9

The Game API

Introduction

Up until this point, most of our graphics discussion has focused largely on techniques that have been around since the MIDP 1.0 days. Sun has listened to the complaints and demands of the game development community and added a new Game API to MIDP 2.0 designed to address the needs of game developers. This chapter will discuss the major features of the Game API — most notably the Sprite and TiledLayer classes as well as the new GameCanvas.

The Game API

Early on, the most popular use for mobile Java was gaming. Even before MIDP was ratified, Japanese carriers had been using various flavors of mobile Java to provide enormously popular gaming services such as iAppli and J-Sky. Despite the pre-MIDP prevalence of gaming, MIDP 1.0 provided little if any support useful to game developers.

The basics were there, such as bitmap images and limited geometric drawing; however, developers were clamoring for more. Popular 2D gaming techniques such as sprite and tile graphics have been implemented in wireless Java since the stone age of the late '90s, but the main issue has been performance. The Game API attempts to provide a way for handset manufacturers to offer some optimized functionality for game programming — largely in the area of sprites and tiles — by providing dedicated classes for these common graphics techniques.

What exactly is the Game API? The Game API is located in the package javax.microedition.lcdui.game. This package contains classes covering many aspects of game development including sprites, tiles, and the efficient polling of input. We begin our discussion of each major class with the bedrock of the Game API, the GameCanvas.

GameCanvas

From reading the previous chapters, you have probably noticed that the Canvas object, while functional for displaying bitmaps and geometry, isn't exactly the greatest when it comes to processing input. MIDP 1.0's key message architecture is fine for address books and even turn-based strategy or puzzle games, but it really starts to show its limitations when trying to do anything fast-paced or arcade-like in nature.

Creating the Canvas

To create a GameCanvas, we have a slightly different constructor:

```
protected GameCanvas(boolean suppressKeyEvents)
```

This method must be implemented in any GameCanvas subclass for your code to properly compile. The single Boolean argument, suppressKeyEvents, determines whether the GameCanvas will receive events for game keys (UP, DOWN, etc.). If you are using GameCanvas' new input polling method, you don't need these messages sent to the class. On some devices, performance may improve as the overhead of receiving these events may speed things up a bit. The GameCanvas will continue to receive messages for normal keypresses if true is passed to the constructor; however, game actions will be disabled. As you saw in our example, any class derived from GameCanvas must make a call to the super and pass this argument along.

Polling Input

Among other enhancements, GameCanvas' biggest new feature is the ability to poll input. Instead of waiting for the application manager to feed your MIDlet key events, you can query the state of the gamepad at any time. This not only lets you sync game action input with your main loop, but also allows you to detect if more than one button is held simultaneously (given the hardware supports this feature).

Multiple keypress is the holy grail for mobile games developers. They've had it in Japan for years, but only now is the rest of the planet able to run and shoot at the same time. Most likely you will have to plan for input with both multiple keypress and single key input for quite some time.

In order to poll input, you use the getKeyStates method:

```
int getKeyStates()
```

This simple method returns an integer as a result. This integer is a bit pattern representing the state of all game action buttons. The bit patterns are defined in the GameCanvas class as a series of fields. These fields are detailed in Table 9-1.

Table 9-1: Fields

Field	Description
DOWN_PRESSED	Bit for the DOWN game action key.
FIRE_PRESSED	Bit for the FIRE game action key.
GAME_A_PRESSED	Bit for the GAME A game action key.
GAME_B_PRESSED	Bit for the GAME B game action key.
GAME_C_PRESSED	Bit for the GAME C game action key.
GAME_D_PRESSED	Bit for the GAME D game action key.
LEFT_PRESSED	Bit for the LEFT game action key.
RIGHT_PRESSED	Bit for the RIGHT game action key.
UP_PRESSED	Bit for the UP game action key.

So to see if the FIRE button is being pressed, we would do something like what is shown in Listing 9-1.

Listing 9-1: Key polling in MIDP 2.0, finally!

```
int pattern = getKeyState();
if ((pattern & GameCanvas.FIRE_PRESSED) != 0)
{
    System.out.println("Fire!");
}
```

We simply perform an AND operation with the bit we want to check. The respective bit will be set to 1 if it's pressed and 0 if not. This lets you check for multiple keys being held by making several different checks in a row. For instance, after this we could check to see if any other direction is being pressed to perform a special move in a fighting game or a combination of actions. As mentioned previously, some handsets simply cannot detect multiple keypresses, so only one bit may be on at any given time. Some handsets also can only support certain simultaneous button combinations. Check the OEM's developer documentation on your handset to get more information on its input capabilities.

Accessing the Frame Buffer

Another great new feature of the GameCanvas is the ability to get a graphics context for the screen itself. The method involved is getGraphics:

```
protected Graphics getGraphics();
```

This method returns a Graphics class associated with the screen itself. The screen is double buffered. Therefore, the graphics context is for the off-screen buffer, not the currently displayed image. Because this method creates a new Graphics object as its return reference, you need to call this at the start of the game and reuse the reference throughout the life cycle of the MIDlet whenever you want to perform drawing operations directly on the screen.

Now that you have the reference, you can draw to this Graphics object all you want, but you will not see the results until you call the flushGraphics method:

```
public void flushGraphics()
```

This method "flips" the second buffer and displays it to the screen. It is also possible to flush a subsection of the off-screen buffer to the display with the overloaded version:

```
public void flushGraphics(int x, int y, int width, int height)
```

By using the x, y, width, and height arguments, we specify a subsection of the off-screen buffer to flush to the display. Only flush the display when you have completed all of your drawing operations for the frame. Calling flushGraphics after every drawing operation is not only unnecessary, but may slow your MIDlet to a crawl. Don't worry if you don't get the concept of double buffering just yet; this will be discussed in detail when we create a complete game as an example.

The Layer

The next major object is the Layer. We won't spend too much time on this as the real meat of the Game API is in the Sprite and TiledLayer classes derived from this object. However, because Layer is the parent of these two major new classes, we should discuss the basics here.

What Is a Layer?

The Layer class is the graphical building block of the Game API. All displayable images are based on Layers. Layers are essentially bitmaps that can be drawn, hidden, and moved, as well as depth sorted. Depth sorting the drawing order of the Layers causes different layers to draw on top of others. The abstract Layer class contains a few basic methods, some of which are listed here:

```
public void setPosition(int x, int y)
public void Move(int dx, int dy)
public void setVisible(Boolean visible)
```

The first method, setPosition, sets the position of the layer relative to its upper left-hand corner in absolute coordinates. If you wanted to place the layer in the upper left-hand corner of the screen, you would do something like this:

```
derivedLayerObject.setPosition(0, 0);
```

Obviously, you would never access the method inside a Layer object directly, as this is an abstract class. But assuming derivedLayerObject is a class we created that extends Layer, this would place it at 0, 0 in absolute coordinates.

Alternatively, the Move method describes a displacement from the current position. If we wanted to move the Layer object down vertically by five pixels, we would call the method like so:

```
derivedLayerObject.Move(5, 0);
```

Now the Layer is at the coordinate 5, 0. We have essentially added five pixels to the y coordinate with the Move method. If we wanted to move it up by two pixels, we would make this call:

```
derivedLayerObject.Move(-2, 0);
```

Now the Layer is positioned at 3, 0. We have displaced the Layer up by two pixels.

The Layer also can be hidden using the method setVisible. By passing true as an argument, it is visible. By passing false, the Layer is now invisible. When the method's paint method is invoked, nothing will happen.

Speaking of paint, the Layer includes an abstract paint method that must be defined in any subclass you define. You can create your own graphical primitive subclassed by Layer, but must write your own paint method to handle the drawing of this object.

Sprite

The first Layer subclass we will discuss is the Sprite. A *sprite* is another term for a moving object in a game. For instance, a ghost monster in Pac-Man and a bullet in Asteroids are both considered a sprite. Back in the day, a Sprite used to be a hardware feature built into the graphics subsystem of a machine, but today a Sprite is more of an API feature. How the API and hardware actually accomplish Sprite graphics is no longer an issue — the Sprite officially now exists as bits and bytes in an API, not actual circuitry in a chipset. On some handsets, there may actually be accelerated sprite hardware — on others it may be just as slow as using an Image. Therefore, the mere presence of the Game API does not guarantee fast game performance on a MIDP 2.0 device.

The Sprite contains functionality not only for drawing and moving an image, but also performing animation and collision detection, as well as rotating and flipping the bitmap in various ways. First we will examine the basics of the non-animated Sprite, and then proceed into animation.

Creating a Sprite

To create a simple, non-animated Sprite, you use the basic constructor:

```
public Sprite(Image image)
```

This takes an Image as a single argument. You now have a single-frame Sprite positioned at 0, 0. Since this Sprite is a Layer, you can position, move, and hide it just as we discussed previously. Sprites also have a paint method. You can call this directly from inside your Canvas' paint method, or use the LayerManager to manage the drawing ordering of your Sprites. We will discuss the LayerManager later in this chapter.

Reference Pixel

By default, all positions reference the Sprite at its upper left-hand corner. In lieu of anchor points, the Sprite has what is termed a *reference pixel*. Known in game programming circles as a "handle," "hotspot," or even "registration point," the reference pixel determines what the coordinates are relative to. Instead of simply being able to select from a combination of top, left, right, and bottom as with anchor points, the reference pixel lets you reference any point in the device's coordinate system. In fact, this point can even be outside of the sprite dimensions.

The reference pixel is set with the method setRefPixel-Position:

```
public void setRefPixelPosition(int x, int y)
```

Obviously, the x and y arguments refer to the pixel position you wish to reference. In the case of animated Sprites, this position is relative to the frame itself, not the entire image.

See Figure 9-1 for an illustration of how reference pixels work in relation to coordinate locations.

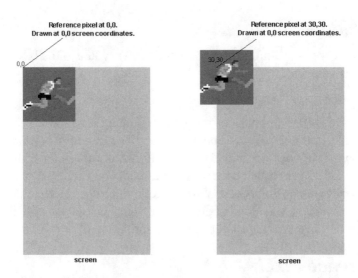

Figure 9-1: The reference pixel is the "origin" of the sprite — about which its x and y coordinate will be centered. The image on the left has the reference pixel at 0, 0. So, when we draw the bitmap at 0, 0, its upper left-hand corner is in the upper left-hand corner of the screen. The image on the right has its reference pixel at 30, 30. So when we place the image at 0, 0 on the screen, the upper left-hand corner is actually 30 pixels above and to the left of the screen — thus it is cut off.

Transforms

A great new feature of the Sprite is the ability to perform transforms on the image. This means you can flip and rotate the image before you draw it. This is exactly the same functionality as discussed in Chapter 6 when we talked about the drawRegion method.

You can set the transform for the Sprite via the setTransform method:

```
public void setTransform(int transform)
```

This method takes a single argument, transform, to select which transform to perform on this Sprite when painted. The argument must be one of the predefined fields seen in Table 9-2. Keep in mind that the rotation transforms are all performed in 90-degree increments. Smooth rotation is still not possible; however, it is useful for flipping objects to face different directions such as left or right and up and down. This can dramatically cut down on the number of frames you need to represent an object, depending on how your artwork is designed.

All transforms are done relative to the reference pixel. For instance, if you want an object to rotate about its center, set the reference pixel to be in the middle of the frame. If, perhaps, you want the object to orbit around a character's hand, you could set the reference pixel to be on the hand of the character before performing the transform. See Figure 9-2 for the relationship between reference pixels and transforms.

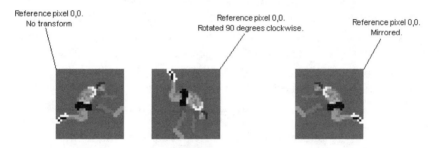

Reference pixel 0,0.
No transform

Reference pixel 0,0.
Rotated 90 degrees clockwise.

Reference pixel 0,0.
Mirrored.

Figure 9-2: You can use the transforms to rotate a Sprite about its reference pixel. The first image is the Sprite with no transform and a reference pixel at 0, 0. The second is that same Sprite rotated about its reference pixel 90 degrees. The third is the image mirrored about its reference pixel.

Table 9-2: Transforms

Transform Field	Description
TRANS_NONE	The image is copied unchanged.
TRANS_ROT90	The image is rotated clockwise by 90 degrees.
TRANS_ROT180	The image is rotated clockwise by 180 degrees.
TRANS_ROT270	The image is rotated clockwise by 270 degrees.
TRANS_MIRROR	The image is reflected about its vertical axis (flipped horizontally).
TRANS_MIRROR_ROT90	The image is reflected about its vertical axis and then rotated 90 degrees clockwise.
TRANS_MIRROR_ROT180	The image is reflected about its vertical axis and then rotated 180 degrees clockwise (flipped vertically).
TRANS_MIRROR_ROT270	The image is reflected about its vertical axis and then rotated 270 degrees clockwise.

Animation

Now that we have covered the basics of the Sprite, it's time to talk about animation. We saw in Chapter 8 that we can provide a strip of images and display a single frame out of this group through the use of clip rectangles or regions. The Sprite operates in a similar fashion.

Creating Animated Sprites

With the Sprite, it is possible to create a Sprite strip of various dimensions and have the Sprite automatically display the frame you specify upon drawing itself. In Chapter 8, we used a simple horizontal strip. However, the Sprite class can use horizontal, vertical, and even rectangular Sprite pages. The only stipulation is that every frame in the bitmap must be the same size. When you create an animated Sprite, you use the following constructor:

```
public Sprite(Image image, int frameWidth, int frameHeight)
```

The first argument, as with the original constructor, is the Image you are using as a basis for this Sprite. However, with an animated Sprite, this Image must be a Sprite strip as previously described. See Figure 9-3 for an example of a horizontal Sprite layout. The remaining arguments specify the width and height of each frame. Note that you do not have to specify whether the strip is vertical, horizontal, or square. Using the dimensions of the Image and the frame size specified, it will automatically pull the frames out in the correct sequence.

Figure 9-3: Look familiar? This is the same sprite layout we used in Chapter 6, "Bitmap Graphics." We can use a vertical strip or a square layout as well.

Frame Sequences

Now that you have a Sprite with a bunch of frames, how do you display each one? The key is the frame sequence. Each Sprite has what is called a *frame sequence*, that is, a list of frames to display. By default, a Sprite is created with a frame list as long as the number of frames. Each entry in this list is set to the next frame. So, if you have a four-frame Sprite, by default the frame sequence is set to 0, 1, 2, 3. How do you select which entry in the frame sequence to display? Use the method setFrame:

```
public void setFrame(int sequenceIndex)
```

The lone argument, sequenceIndex, is the entry in the frame sequence we want to display. So, if we have just constructed a Sprite and we want to display the third frame, we would do it like this:

```
Sprite sprite = new Sprite(animImage, 32, 32);
sprite.setFrame(2);
```

The first thing you have to remember is that the frame list is an array, and thus it is zero-relative. Hence the use of 2 to reference the third frame. Secondly, I cannot stress enough the concept that this is a list of frames to display, not a setting for the frame itself. It just so happens that by default the frame in the frame sequence is the same as its position in the array. But we can set our own frame sequence with the setFrameSequence method:

```
public void setFrameSequence(int [] sequence)
```

This takes an array of any length and makes it the frame sequence for the Sprite. If you pass null as an argument, the frame sequence will be set back to the default. That is, having an entry for each frame that is in order of the frames in the Image. Anyway, let's say we want the frame sequence to go backward and then forward: 3, 2, 1, 0, 1, 2, 3. We could do it like this:

```
int[] frameSequence = {3, 2, 1, 0, 1, 2, 3};
sprite.setFrameSequence(frameSequence)
```

Now, if we set the frame to be 0 like this:

```
sprite.setFrame(0)
```

the frame that will actually be displayed when we paint the Sprite is frame 3. Get it? I agree that the method setFrame is rather confusing. But once you separate in your mind the frames in the Image from the actual frame in the list, it becomes much easier.

You can also navigate the frame sequence backward and forward with the following two methods:

```
public void nextFrame()
public void prevFrame()
```

The nextFrame method sets the current frame to be the next one in the frame sequence; prevFrame travels backward in the sequence. These calls wrap — that is, if you go past the beginning of the sequence with prevFrame, it will go back to the last and vice versa.

Collision

The final major feature of the Sprite class is collision. MIDP 2.0's collision system is actually quite robust. You have two basic options: pixel-level and rectangle collision. The former is more accurate, actually checking if the individual pixels intersect the pixels of another Sprite, Tile, or Image. The latter is a more general algorithm that uses collision rectangles to determine collisions. See Figure 9-4 for an example of how these two collision systems work.

Rectangle Collision

Rectangle collision is the simpler of the two methods to understand. Each object has a *collision rectangle* — a rectangle representing the boundaries of the Sprite or frame. By default, MIDP 2.0 assumes the collision rectangle is the boundaries of the frame. If you want to change it, you can use the method defineCollisionRectangle. There are three different collision methods in the Sprite class:

```
public boolean collidesWith(Image image, int x, int y, Boolean pixelLevel)
public boolean collidesWith(Sprite s, Boolean pixelLevel)
public boolean collidesWith(TiledLayer t, Boolean pixelLevel)
```

The first of the three methods detects if there is a collision between the Sprite and an Image. Unlike Layers, Images have no coordinates or reference pixels. Thus, you must specify the x and y location of the Image, and it is assumed that we are using positions relative to the upper left-hand corner of the Image. The last argument of this method, pixelLevel, is a Boolean that determines if we are going to do a pixel detection or not. By setting this to false, it will simply check if the boundaries of the Sprite intersect those of the Image. If so, it returns true. Otherwise, it returns false.

The second method detects if the Sprite has collided with another Sprite passed in via the first argument. This method takes the reference pixel and transforms of both Sprites into account when performing the test. As with the previous implementation, this method takes a Boolean, which determines if we are doing a pixel-level check or not.

Finally, we have a method that detects if the Sprite has collided with anything in a TiledLayer. TiledLayers will be discussed later in the chapter. This method essentially uses the Sprite's position, reference pixel, and transform, and checks it against the TiledLayer to see if we have collided with anything in the map. As with the rest of these methods, a Boolean is used for the last argument to determine if we are doing a pixel-level test or not.

By default, all of the rectangle checks use the frame boundaries as the collision rectangles for both the source and destination. This makes it somewhat useless for many games as usually you want a collision rectangle slightly smaller than the frame to give the player a little bit of a break. For instance, you might shrink the collision rectangle of your player character by one quarter so that anything that brushes against your character's arms or legs will not register. There is nothing more frustrating in a game than an unfair collision system. MIDP 2.0 gives you the ability to define the collision rectangle using the method defineCollisionRectangle:

```
public void defineCollisionRectangle(int x, int y, int width, int height)
```

Here we pass the x and y coordinate of the upper left-hand corner of the rectangle, and then two more integers for the width and height. You might want to set this per-frame if your sprite changes shape as it animates. If you need even more accurate collision, pixel-level detection solves this problem, potentially at the expensive of speed.

Pixel Collision

As previously described, a pixel-level collision occurs when the pixels of one bitmap intersect those of another. This is necessary for images that have transparent pixels, because those pixels that are opaque are considered part of the object. Transparent pixels are blank, and thus should not trigger collisions. This is the main advantage over rectangle collisions, as a single rectangle cannot accurately represent the boundaries of an irregularly shaped bitmap with transparent pixels. However, the trade-off is that pixel checks are considerably more computationally expensive than a simple rectangle check.

Depending on the handset, there may be hardware acceleration for pixel checks. One would hope that the OEMs perform a rectangle check to see if the two sprites intersect at all before checking the individual pixels. However, if there is anything I have learned over the past few years of developing wireless games, it is to never underestimate the carelessness of handset manufacturers and OS providers. To perform a pixel check, simply pass true as the final argument to any of the collidesWith methods of the Sprite class.

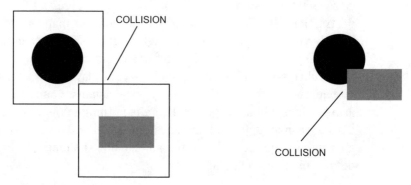

Figure 9-4: Bounding boxes versus per-pixel collision detection. In both of these pictures there is a collision. On the left, the bounding boxes of the sprites collide, but there is no contact between the solid portions of each image. On the right, you can see that per-pixel is more accurate.

Tile Graphics Explained

The next major class of the Game API is the TiledLayer. Much like Sprite, this is derived from Layer and thus inherits some of its behaviors. The TiledLayer is used to display background graphics in the form of tile maps. These tile maps can be parallaxed, scrolled, and even animated for various effects. Before we get into the minutiae, we should probably give a brief overview of tile graphics in general.

What Are Tile Graphics?

Game graphics are typically categorized as either sprite or background graphics. Sprite graphics are usually the moving characters in the game, as seen in our discussion of the Sprite class. Backgrounds are typically defined as the graphics behind the sprite characters that they travel over and interact with. For instance, the maze in Pac-Man and the dungeon in Legend of Zelda would be considered backgrounds.

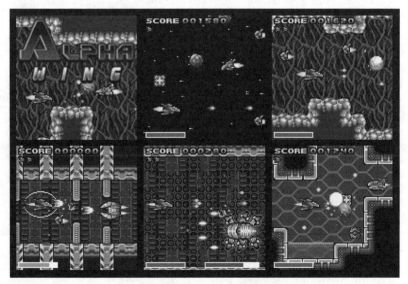

Figure 9-5: Macrospace's Alpha Wing is a prime example of sprites and backgrounds. Image copyright Macrospace Ltd., 2003-2004.

If you look at most any background in one of these games, you will notice that parts of the background seem to repeat. For instance, you may see the same door graphic on each wall or the same floor pattern repeated over the screen. This is because instead of storing backgrounds as one large image, the backgrounds are broken up into repeating elements, or tiles, that can be pieced together in various ways to create a variety of backgrounds in much less space.

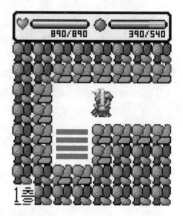

Figure 9-6: GameVIL's Last Warrior uses tile graphics for its backgrounds. Note the repeating patterns used for the dungeon walls.

Instead of using up a lot of memory to store a bunch of background images, a small set of tiles and some instructions to tell the code where to place them on the screen is used to represent background graphics. This storage mechanism not only saves vast amounts of memory, but has other advantages when referring to the background for collision, artificial intelligence, and other game-specific tasks.

So, what exactly is a tile? A *tile* is basically a square bitmap. Tiles are then arranged in "tile maps" to make an entire picture or background image. For example, say you have the two tiles shown in Figure 9-7.

Figure 9-7: The two tiles we are using to draw a background

These two tiles will be known as 0 and 1. A tile map using these two images may be a simple two-dimensional array like so:

```
char map[][] = {{0, 0, 0, 0},
                {1, 1, 1, 1},
                {0, 0, 0, 0},
                {1, 1, 1, 1}};
```

If we were to draw this tile map on the screen, we would get an image like Figure 9-8.

This does not look like much, but I am sure you can start to see the possibilities. For instance, we could make an empty room that looks like Figure 9-9.

It is possible to save this background as a single large bitmap. For the sake of our calculations, let's assume we're dealing with uncompressed PNGs — straight bitmaps, if you will. This would involve an allocation of about 16 kilobytes to store this 128 x 128 8-bit image. However, the image is really composed of two tiles: the maze wall and the floor. If we use tiles instead and save the maze as a tile map, we have a huge memory savings. The two tiles will end up being 16 x 16 8-bit PNGs. Both images together consume approximately 2K. Of course, these sizes would be much smaller in practice as PNGs are compressed — and can even be shrunk further with the use of tools like Pngcrush.

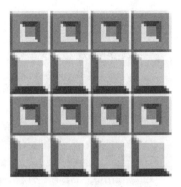

Figure 9-8: The tile background represented by our array

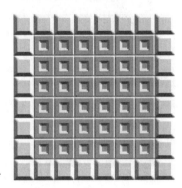

Figure 9-9: An empty room scene made of tiles

In order to make a 128 x 128-pixel scene out of 16 x 16 tiles, we need an 8 x 8 tile map. This is because 8 multiplied by 16 pixels is 128. Therefore, with an 8 x 8 tile map we would reproduce our original 128 x 128 image. If our tile map is an 8 x 8 array of single-byte entries, the map itself would consume 64 bytes. To reproduce the scene, our tile map has to look like this:

```
char map[][] = { {1, 1, 1, 1, 1, 1, 1, 1},
                 {1, 0, 0, 0, 0, 0, 0, 1},
                 {1, 0, 0, 0, 0, 0, 0, 1},
                 {1, 0, 0, 0, 0, 0, 0, 1},
                 {1, 0, 0, 0, 0, 0, 0, 1},
                 {1, 0, 0, 0, 0, 0, 0, 1},
                 {1, 0, 0, 0, 0, 0, 0, 1},
                 {1, 1, 1, 1, 1, 1, 1, 1}};
```

With the two tiles and map data together we have to use slightly over 2K to reproduce an image that originally was 16K. With memory at such a premium on mobile devices, tile maps are invaluable for most games.

Another great feature of tile maps is that they are an internal representation of the scene that is easily used in code to read and store information about the game world. For instance, in this case we know a tile entry of 1 is a wall. Therefore, we can perform collision detection against the walls of the maze by detecting if our game character is attempting to enter a tile that has an index of 1.

If you want to get more complicated, you can create a small tile class and make the tile map an array of these structures instead of simple bytes. For instance, you might need a Boolean member variable in your tile class to determine if there is a gold piece on a given tile. If this Boolean is set to true, when the tile is drawn, you also draw a piece of gold on top. If the character picks up the gold, you then clear out the Boolean. Then, the next time you draw the screen, the gold will be missing from that tile.

Note   As mentioned earlier, you can check pixel-level collision with a Tile and a Sprite. The collision occurs when non-transparent Sprite pixels collide with non-transparent Tile pixels. For this reason, you may have to keep a simplified collision tile set that you use only for checking collisions — not for display. This collision tile set would be made of simple black-and-white pixels, with white set to transparent. This way you can still have non-collideable areas in your Tiles that aren't transparent when drawn.

Larger Worlds

Another advantage of tile maps is the ability to create a large world and make the display a smaller viewport into it. Let's say a hypothetical handset has a 128 x 144 screen resolution. If we use small 8 x 8 tiles, we can display about 16 x 18 tiles on the screen at once. However, we can create a tile map much larger than this — as large as heap memory will afford. Therefore we can make mazes and worlds that span multiple screens.

The relationship of the viewport to the larger map is like laying a sheet of paper with a hole in it over a photo. As you move the paper around, you see different portions of the photo. As you move the viewport around the map, you see different sections of the background tile map. This concept is similar to the coordinate space discussion in Chapter 6, "Bitmap Graphics." Using the maze example again, we can have it so that if your character walks off the side of the screen, we move the viewport over one screen width to show the next section of the map. Or, you can slide the viewport around to create a smooth scrolling effect.

Modifying Worlds

Making your environment interactive is another way to make a game deeper and more interesting. For instance, you could have a bridge that needs to be blown up in order to prevent the enemies from advancing or a secret wall that is revealed with the flick of a switch.

Because we are storing our worlds in the form of tile maps, it is easy to do this. All we need to do is modify the indices of the tiles we want to change and redraw the screen. For instance, if you want a secret door to appear in a wall after a certain event, you just modify the tile indices in the wall to those of the secret door and redraw. The possibilities are endless.

Creating Tile Maps

If you have very small maps, then perhaps creating arrays by hand will work. But with complicated and graphically rich games, you most likely want to import tile maps from an external editing tool used by designers and artists. In the old days, everyone used to write their own tile editor for their games. In many cases people still do; however, there are a number of commercial and freely available tile editors that are quite powerful. Some of them also allow you to configure the output so that you can include any special game-specific data in your maps that the editor normally does not keep track of.

Mappy

The tile editor I use most often is Robin Burrows' Mappy, available at www.tilemap.co.uk. Mappy can output a large file format known as FMP with many data fields and multiple tile map layers. However, it also has a simple binary file with a tile index array like we used at the beginning of this chapter. Mappy also has a few different playback utilities that allow you to view your maps outside of the editor with various environments and graphics libraries, such as Allegro, OpenGL, Java, or DirectX. Also, if you really need some extra features added, the C source code is provided, which allows you to create your own custom versions of Mappy suited for your game.

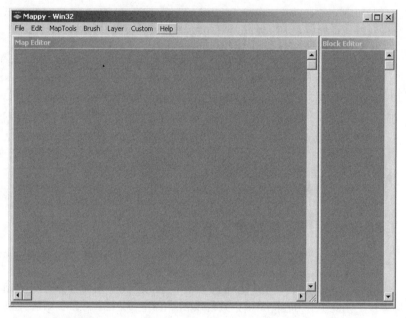

Figure 9-10: Mappy's main screen

When you first load Mappy, you will see the Map Editor window on the left and the Block Editor window on the right. The Block Editor window is really a tile window with some extra benefits. The first thing you need to do is create a new map by clicking on **File ▸ New Map.**

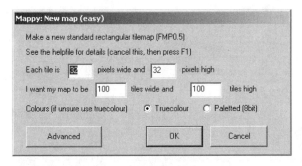

Mappy: New map (easy)

Make a new standard rectangular tilemap (FMP0.5)

See the helpfile for details (cancel this, then press F1)

Each tile is `32` pixels wide and `32` pixels high

I want my map to be `100` tiles wide and `100` tiles high

Colours (if unsure use truecolour) ⊙ Truecolour ○ Paletted (8bit)

| Advanced | OK | Cancel |

Figure 9-11: Mappy's New Map dialog

Figure 9-11 shows the New Map dialog. In it, you see your block settings. Here you determine the pixel width and height of the tiles you will be using, as well as the bit depth.

Below these settings are the map attributes. These include the width and height of the map in tiles. You can resize the map later, so you are not locked into the settings you make in this dialog.

At the bottom of the dialog is a button for advanced settings. If you click the Advanced button you get more options, including settings for isometric tiles. *Isometric tiles* are tiles that are shown from a slightly skewed overhead perspective. Instead of square-shaped tiles, they look like little diamonds. This provides a much more detailed perspective and gives you the ability to represent height in a 2D environment. In this book we are only using basic 2D tiles, so you can ignore these settings. For the maps in this chapter, we use the settings as shown in Figure 9-11 and leave the advanced settings at their defaults.

You also can determine the type of FMP file you wish to output when saving the map. This is to maintain backward compatibility with game engines that use Mappy's older FMP 0.5 format. In this case, it does not matter since we are just going to use the raw bitmap output for our example code in this chapter.

Once we have a blank map with the appropriate settings, we need to import our tiles. The tiles are stored as a long PNG with each tile juxtaposed so that Mappy can cut them up into individual blocks. Our tile PNG file, tilegfx.png, can be found in the chap09\loadtilemap\res folder in the companion files. It is the same graphic shown in Figure 9-7.

To import the tiles, we click **File ▸ Import**.

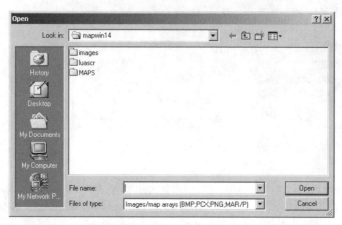

Figure 9-12: The import dialog

Now, we simply pick the image we wish to use for our tiles. In this case, we use tilegfx.png, found in the companion files. If, for example, we already had tiles loaded, Mappy would then ask if we wanted to import them as new graphics. Since we are starting from scratch, Mappy will just import the BMP automatically.

Now, you should see your tiles in the Block Editor window with the map consisting entirely of the blank entry. If you want to import different tiles and overwrite the existing ones, you can import another BMP and you'll have the opportunity to overwrite the current set of tile graphics with the ones in the BMP you are loading. Or, you can add to the end of the list of tiles, essentially appending your tile collection with new graphics.

Now that you have tiles, you can simply click on one in the Block Editor window and paint with it in the Map Editor window. However, if you want to see the FMP file we used to create the map for the example code, simply load the mazemap.fmp file from the chap09 folder in the companion files.

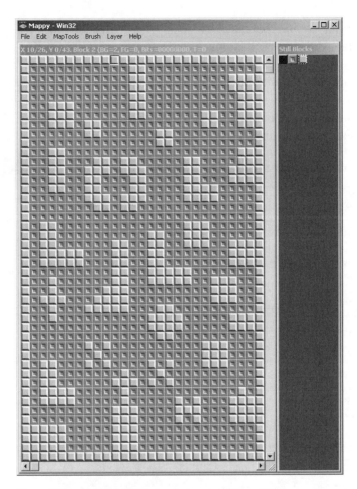

Figure 9-13: The entire map loaded and visible in Mappy

Looking at the Mappy interface, you can see a window into our larger map on the left and the tile palette on the right. If you want to edit the map, simply click on a tile block on the right, and then paint with it in the Map Editor window. You can then save your modified map and use that instead.

Our sample code will not read FMP files directly. These are too large and have lots of things included that we are not concerned with now. However, for more advanced games, converting the FMP files into a more compact binary format with a custom command line tool may be a possibility. Instead, we will use Mappy's raw MAP file format.

The MAP format is a simple binary file that begins with the width and height of the map in tiles followed by a raw array of bytes representing the tile indices. Luckily, Mappy allows you to customize the output format of the MAP file in its own INI file. My custom Mappy.ini file looks like this:

Listing 9-2: An example Mappy INI file

```
; Be sure you know what you are doing editing this file,
; comments start with a ';' at the beginning of the line,
; all other lines must have an equals sign for values
width = 640
height = 480
grid = 1
zoom = 1
picklayer = 1
transred = 255
transgreen = 0
transblue = 255
trans8bit = 0
apmode = "640*480 8bpp ?hz"
importskip = 1
csvadjust = -1
maptype = "LW4H4A1-1"
mapdefw = 100
mapdefh = 100
mapdefbw = 32
mapdefbh = 32
mapdefBMP = "nodefault.bmp"
mapstaggerx = 0
mapstaggery = 0
mapclickmask = 0
```

As you can see, there are a variety of settings you can configure in this file. The one we are interested in is *maptype*. The string LW4H4A1-1 determines how Mappy will format the raw binary MAP file.

The first character, "L," indicates the endian format of the data. The only thing you need to be concerned about is that L means we are using the little endian format that all PCs use.

The next character, "W," indicates the first group of bytes in the file will represent the width of the map in tiles. The number 4 following the letter says that the width will be stored as 4 bytes (an integer). You can probably guess the character pair "H4" means the next 4 bytes will store the height in tiles of the map.

The "A" character means the next chunk of data will be the map array. The "1" following the "A" tells Mappy that the tile indices will be stored in 1 byte. That means a tile entry in the map array can have any value from 0 to 255. If you need more tiles you can choose to expand the byte size of the map array elements to any size you would like. For most mobile games, 255 different values is sufficient.

The final part of the string, "-1," tells Mappy to subtract 1 from each tile index. If you look in the block array on the right in Figure 9-13, you will see a "blank" tile at the start of the tile array. Mappy creates a default "blank" tile when importing tile BMPs. Therefore, there are actually three tiles when we really only imported two. To fix this offset, you must subtract 1 from each tile value so that the first tile really is referenced as 0 and not 1. As a result, we ignore the blank tile completely. So, the string "LW4H4A1-1" means the binary MAP file is stored in little endian format, beginning with 4 bytes representing the width, 4 bytes representing the height, and then an array of zero-relative single-byte entries containing the tile map data.

To export a MAP file, you simply need to select the MAP file format when saving the file. Mappy will warn you that you are discarding important map information by doing so. Just as long as you save a corresponding FMP file for each MAP you export, you will easily be able to recreate this data. You can also load MAP files in directly, just as long as you remember the BMP file that you used for the tile graphics

What extra information is stored in an FMP? Mappy allows you to save attribute bits on tiles, have multiple parallax layers of tile maps, and all sorts of advanced features. These features may be useful for more complicated games, which is why you might look into reading FMP files directly or converting them to a slightly more complicated binary format for your games.

Now that we have seen the basics of Mappy usage, you need to know how to load one in your game. First, we'll explain how to use the tiling system in MIDP 2.0, then we'll show you how to load an actual MAP file.

TiledLayer

You could manually create your own tile scroller by drawing sub-sections of the tile set Image according to a 2D array of indices. In fact, this is how it was done in the MIDP 1.0 days. Now, the Game API has introduced the TiledLayer, which does all this heavy lifting for us. The class is fairly simple: You give it an Image for your tile set and set the viewport position through the move and setPosition methods in the Layer parent class. First, we will discuss the constructor.

Creating a TiledLayer

The TiledLayer class has a single constructor:

```
public TiledLayer(int columns, int rows, Image image, int tileWidth, int tileHeight)
```

The first argument is the number of columns in the tile map. This is essentially the width of the array. The second argument, rows, is an integer that determines how many rows, or how high, the tile map array is. Next up is a reference to an Image — this will be the bitmap data with your actual tiles in it. This Image is otherwise known as a static tile set. Tiles can be delivered in the same exact way as sprites — a vertical, horizontal, or square bitmap collection of tiles. Next up we have the tileWidth and tileHeight arguments. These tell the system how wide and high the individual tiles in the bitmap are. All tiles have to be the same size. The width and height must be a multiple of the image width and height; otherwise, an IllegalArgumentException will be thrown.

You can change this static tile set with the method setStaticTileSet:

```
public void setStaticTileSet(Image image, int tileWidth, int tileHeight)
```

This takes largely the same arguments as the constructor and works much in the same way. If there are fewer tiles than the previous set, all contents (animated tiles and the actual cells) will be deleted. Otherwise, they will be preserved.

Setting the Tile Map

Now that you have the tile set bitmap loaded and the TiledLayer object initialized, how do you actually create the tile map itself? The TiledLayer object refers to the tile map as cells. Each cell is simply a tile index into your static tile set. Think of the cells as the two-dimensional array of tile indices we covered when talking about Mappy. Unfortunately, you have to set each cell individually. The fumbly method used to do this is setCell:

```
public void setCell(int col, int row, int tileIndex)
```

This method takes the column and row (zero relative) you wish to modify the index of, and then the actual tile index value you are going to set this cell equal to. The actual tileIndex is one relative. If you set the cell to 0, it will be a blank cell that is totally transparent. A tileIndex of 1 will get you the first tile in your static tile set. You can also fill a range of cells with a single tile index using the method fillCells:

```
public void fillCells(int col, int row, int numCols, int numRows, int tileIndex)
```

Here you specify the starting column and row, and then the number of columns and rows you wish to fill with the value specified in the final argument, tileIndex. I suppose this is good for clearing out large areas of your map, but otherwise it is ultimately useless.

You can also query the value of the cell with the accessor method, getCell:

```
public int getCell(int col, int row)
```

Obviously, this returns the tile index at the specified column and row.

Tile Animation

Until now, we have only discussed static tiles. The TiledLayer also includes the ability to animate background tiles for creating interesting effects and adding detail to the scene. A simple way to animate tiles is to set the cells you wish to change every frame. Once you redraw the TiledLayer after modifying the cells, you will see the next frame of the animated tiles. While this method will work, you still have to manually modify a large number of tile indices if large portions of your map are animating. This messy process can impede the performance of your application if much processing per-cell is necessary.

The TiledLayer class avoids this issue by creating new tile indices for animated tiles. These indices can then be associated with a tileIndex. The tileIndex can be changed every frame, and thus every animated tile associated with that index will be drawn with a different frame upon repainting.

These special animated tiles use negative numbers as their tileIndex. The negative value tells the TiledLayer that this is not a direct index into your static tile set, but instead a reference to an animated tile association. To associate a negative tileIndex with a static tile index, you must use the method createAnimatedTile:

```
public int createAnimatedTile(int staticTileIndex)
```

You pass this method the static tile you wish to be associated with the animated tile index. It returns a negative number, which is an available animated tile index. So, if we have not created any animated tiles previously, it will return –1, and so on. Now, when you set a cell to be –1, the tile will be drawn with the tile index specified in the staticTileIndex argument.

So, to perform animation, you need to change the staticTileIndex associated with the animated tile index, –1, every frame. You do this with the method setAnimatedTile:

```
public void setAnimatedTile(int animatedTileIndex, int staticTileIndex)
```

This method takes the animated tileIndex you wish to modify (in our case –1) and a static tile index you wish to associate with this animated tile. If you pass an animated tile index that hasn't been created yet, an IndexOutOfBounds exception will be thrown. So, let's say we create an animated tile like so:

```
int animTileIndex = tileLayer_.createAnimatedTile(1);
```

The integer variable animTileIndex should be set to –1. All cells with –1 as an index will be drawn as tile 1. Next frame, we want to advance to tile 2 in our tile animation sequence. We could do something like this in a timer task or thread:

```
tileLayer_.setAnimatedTile(animTileIndex, 2);
```

Now, when we repaint, every tile with the –1 index will be drawn as tile 2. The reason for this indirection is that you can now have a whole block of tiles set to –1, but you only have to call setAnimatedTile once for that index in order to make all those draw as a different static tile. Manually, you would have to go into the cells and modify each one to be the next tile in the frame sequence.

Drawing the Tile Map

Now that we have the cells set up and our static tile set ready to go, you can manually draw the TiledLayer by using the paint method. You can move around the tile map by using the move method in the Layer parent class. When used with a TiledLayer, this will move the position of the upper left-hand corner of the map — essentially moving the viewport around. So, if we want to move across the TiledLayer to the right a few pixels every frame, we would do something like this every frame:

```
tileLayer_.move(-5, 0);
```

You can also use clip regions to make a smaller viewport into the TiledLayer. However, as we will discuss in the next section, using the LayerManager makes the drawing and managing of all types of Layers much easier.

LayerManager

As we have said with all of the aforementioned classes, you can manually draw each one by using the paint method. However, you need to manually keep track of the draw order, as well as the references to each window. Sure, it's not too much work — but the LayerManager simplifies this process by giving us a single class that handles the sorting, drawing, and reference tracking of Layers.

Creating the LayerManager and Adding Layers

There's not much to be done here; just call the constructor:

```
public LayerManager()
```

Now that we have a LayerManager, we can append Layers like we would Items to a Form. In fact, LayerManager has its own append method:

```
public void append(Layer l)
```

We simply pass in a reference to a Layer that we want to add to the LayerManager's internal list of Layers. This could be a sprite, tile, or our own custom class extended from Layer.

Drawing Layers

To draw the Layers contained inside the LayerManager, simply call the paint method:

```
public void paint(Graphics g, int x, int y)
```

This method takes a Graphics object and an x and y location in the Graphics object's coordinate space at which to draw the Layers. The handset may actually skip drawing layers altogether that are not visible or are completely outside of the Graphics object's clip rectangle. If this is the case, the paint method will not be called. So don't put any processing in your Layer subclass' paint method that you absolutely need to execute every time the screen is drawn.

Draw Order

When you add a Layer to the LayerManager, it is put at the back of the list. When the LayerManager draws all of its Layers, it draws them in descending order. Starting with the last Layer added to the LayerManager, it draws each subsequent Layer beneath the previous one. The order of the Layers is commonly referred to as the z-order. You can manipulate the z-order by using the insert method instead of append when adding Layers:

```
public void insert(Layer 1, int index)
```

Much like append, this takes a reference to the Layer you are inserting. However, it also takes an explicit index as an argument. This is the position in the list where you want this layer. If the Layer already exists in the LayerManager, the old reference will be removed and a new one will be placed at this index. So, if we wanted to move a Layer to the top of the list, and thus drawn in front of everything else, we would do something like this:

```
layerManager_.insert(tileLayer_, 0);
```

Now the tileLayer is at the beginning of the list and thus will be drawn in front of everything else.

You can also remove Layers with the method remove:

```
public void remove(Layer 1)
```

Here we pass a reference to the Layer we wish to remove from the TiledLayer.

You can also get a reference to a Layer at an explicit index with the getLayerAt method:

```
public Layer getLayerAt(int index)
```

This method returns a reference to the Layer located at this location in the TiledLayer's internal list of Layers.

A Simple Example

For this chapter I have created a functional, but ultimately useless example program. This will illustrate the basics of creating and displaying sprites, tiles, and animation. Later on we will create something that looks more like a game with these techniques, but this code serves to illustrate the basics of the concepts described in this chapter.

The Interfaces

Before we get into the code, the first few things you may notice are the interfaces: ImageNumbers and Constants. ImageNumbers only has a few members:

Listing 9-3: The ImageNumbers interface

```
interface ImageNumbers
{
    public static final int IMG_TILE = 0;
    public static final int IMG_SPRITE = 1;
}
```

This is a handy way to give your images unique indentifiers. Granted, we only have two assets to keep track of, but when you create real games you are going to need a way to manage all of your bitmaps and other resources. In the code these are used for indices into our array of Image objects. The code is much more readable if you use IMG_SPRITE as an index into our Image array rather than the literal 1.

The second interface, Constants, is where we keep a few handy constants that we may reuse in the code several times:

Listing 9-4: Constants stored in a handy interface

```
interface Constants
{
    public static final int MAX_IMAGES = 10;
    public static final int TILE_HEIGHT = 16;
    public static final int TILE_WIDTH = 16;
    public static final int ANIM_PERIOD = 30;
    public static final int SPRITE_SPEED = 5;
}
```

The reason we put these in an interface is because we might want to use them over and over again in several different classes. Having to find every location of tile size 16 in the code if we ever change the tile size is much harder than simply changing the appropriate value in the Constants interface.

The TimerTask

Next up is our TimerTask derived object, HeartbeatTask. This is the TimerTask that will be continuously executing at fixed intervals to update the game logic and draw the screen.

Listing 9-5: The HeartbeatTask

```
class HeartbeatTask extends TimerTask implements Constants
{
    private SpriteTileTest app;

    public HeartbeatTask(SpriteTileTest spriteTileTest)
    {
        app = spriteTileTest;
    }

    public void run()
    {
        app.update();
    }
}
```

TimerTask classes are used with the Timer object that is scheduled to execute after a certain delay. Each TimerTask must have a run method that is called when the Timer executes the task. In our case, we have a simple constructor that takes a reference to our MIDlet as an argument. In the run method, we call the update method inside our MIDlet class, which will update the logic and draw the screen.

The GameCanvas

The next class is our extension of GameCanvas, SpriteTile-TestCanvas. This is used to load our Images as well as process input and paint the screen.

Listing 9-6: Our SpriteTileTestCanvas

```
class SpriteTileTestCanvas extends GameCanvas implements ImageNumbers, Constants
{
    public Image[] imageArray;
    public int  viewX;
    public int  viewY;

    public SpriteTileTest app;

    public SpriteTileTestCanvas(boolean supressKeyEvents)
    {
        //this must be called
        super(supressKeyEvents);

        try
        {
            //create and fill our image array
            imageArray = new Image[MAX_IMAGES]
            imageArray[IMG_TILE] = Image.createImage("/tilegfx.png");
            imageArray[IMG_SPRITE] = Image.createImage("/face.png");
        }
        catch (IOException e)
        {
            System.err.println("Failed loading images!!! " + e);
        }
    }

    public void paint(Graphics g)
    {
        //use the layer manager to paint all the layers
        app.layerMgr.paint(g, viewX, viewY);
    }

    public void update()
    {
        //poll the key state
        int keyState = getKeyStates();

        if ((keyState & LEFT_PRESSED) != 0)
        {
            app.sprite.move(-SPRITE_SPEED, 0);
        }

        if ((keyState & RIGHT_PRESSED) != 0)
        {
            app.sprite.move(SPRITE_SPEED, 0);
        }
```

```
if ((keyState & UP_PRESSED) != 0)
{
    app.sprite.move(0, -SPRITE_SPEED);
}

if ((keyState & DOWN_PRESSED) != 0)
{
    app.sprite.move(0, SPRITE_SPEED);
}

//update our sprite animation
app.sprite.nextFrame();

//update tile animation
if (app.tiledLayer.getAnimatedTile(app.animIndex) == 1)
    app.tiledLayer.setAnimatedTile(app.animIndex, 2);
else
    app.tiledLayer.setAnimatedTile(app.animIndex, 1);
    }
}
```

The first thing we do is declare an array of Images, imageArray. This will be used to hold the two Images we will create for the Sprite and static tile set. Next are the integer members viewX and viewY. These are used to keep track of the origin of our TiledLayer. Finally, we have the reference to our MIDlet class with the member variable, app.

If you look at SpriteTileTestCanvas' constructor, it's fairly standard. Inside a try/catch block, we create an imageArray large enough to hold our two Images, and then create them from PNGs stored in the JAR. Check the res folder in the project folder to see what they look like. Note that we call the super's constructor as well. This is absolutely necessary. In this case, we pass it the argument supressKeyEvents.

The paint method simply calls the MIDlet class LayerManager object's paint method. This will handle all the drawing for us. Although we never really use them, we pass the viewX and viewY methods as the origin. You can play with these values if you want to experiment with moving the scene around.

The final method in this class is the update method. This will be called from the MIDlet when the MIDlet's own update method is called upon TimerTask execution. This method takes the keyState and moves the sprite depending on the state of the keys.

Note that we check for all directions simultaneously, so it is possible to move diagonally by pressing two buttons. Finally, we advance to the next frame of the sprite, as well as alternate the animated tile's static tile index with the setAnimatedTile call, as shown below.

```
//update tile animation
if (app.tiledLayer.getAnimatedTile(app.animIndex) == 1)
    app.tiledLayer.setAnimatedTile(app.animIndex, 2);
else
    app.tiledLayer.setAnimatedTile(app.animIndex, 1);
```

What we do is if the static tile associated with our animated tile index is 1, we set it to 2. Otherwise, we set it to 1. This allows the animated tiles to alternate between the two every frame.

The MIDlet Class

Last but not least is our MIDlet class, SpriteTileTest.

Listing 9-7: The SpriteTileTest MIDlet class

```
public class SpriteTileTest extends MIDlet implements CommandListener,
        Constants, ImageNumbers
{
    boolean firstTime;
    public int appFlags;
    public Sprite sprite;
    public TiledLayer tiledLayer;
    public int animIndex;
    public LayerManager layerMgr;

    private Timer timer_;
    private SpriteTileTestCanvas canvas_;
    private Display display_;
    private HeartbeatTask heartTask_;

    private int[] frameSequence_ = {0, 1, 2, 1, 0};

    public SpriteTileTest()
    {
        firstTime = true;
    }

    public void startApp() throws MIDletStateChangeException
    {
        if (firstTime)
```

```
    {
        display_ = Display.getDisplay(this);
        canvas_ = new SpriteTileTestCanvas(true);
        canvas_.app = this;

        //add tile map
        tiledLayer = new TiledLayer(16, 16, canvas_.imageArray[IMG_TILE], 16, 16);

        for (int i = 0; i < 16; i++)
            for (int j = 0; j < 16; j++)
                tiledLayer.setCell(i, j, 1);

        //create an animated tile
        animIndex = tiledLayer.createAnimatedTile(0);

        //make a line down the middle that's animated
        for (int y = 0; y < 16; y++)
        {
            tiledLayer.setCell(5, y, animIndex);
        }

        //create sprite
        sprite = new Sprite(canvas_.imageArray[IMG_SPRITE], 16, 16);
        sprite.setPosition(0, 0);

        //create a ping-pong style animation sequence
        sprite.setFrameSequence(frameSequence_);

        //create the layer manager
        layerMgr = new LayerManager();

        //add to the layer manager
        layerMgr.append((Layer)sprite);
        layerMgr.append((Layer)tiledLayer);

        timer_ = new Timer();
        heartTask_ = new HeartbeatTask(this);
        timer_.schedule(heartTask_, 0, ANIM_PERIOD);

        firstTime = false;
    }

    display_.setCurrent(canvas_);
    canvas_.repaint();
}

public void pauseApp()
{
}
```

```
public void destroyApp(boolean unconditional)
{
}

public void commandAction(Command c, Displayable s)
{
}

public void update()
{
    canvas_.update();
    canvas_.repaint();
}
```

```
} //class
```

The first method is the constructor. Note that the only thing we do is set our member Boolean, firstTime, to true. We do our startup processing in the startApp method because this is when the MIDlet environment is guaranteed to be initialized properly. On a real device, doing things such as retrieving the Display object may have undefined behaviors in the MIDlet's constructor.

The startApp method is where the real meat of this MIDlet is.

```
public void startApp() throws MIDletStateChangeException
    {
        if (firstTime)
        {
            display_ = Display.getDisplay(this);
            canvas_ = new SpriteTileTestCanvas(true);
            canvas_.app = this;

            //add tile map
            tiledLayer = new TiledLayer(16, 16, canvas_.imageArray[IMG_TILE], 16, 16);

            for (int i = 0; i < 16; i++)
                for (int j = 0; j < 16; j++)
                    tiledLayer.setCell(i, j, 1);

            //create an animated tile
            animIndex = tiledLayer.createAnimatedTile(0);

            //make a line down the middle that's animated
            for (int y = 0; y < 16; y++)
            {
                tiledLayer.setCell(5, y, animIndex);
            }
```

```
//create sprite
sprite = new Sprite(canvas_.imageArray[IMG_SPRITE], 16, 16);
sprite.setPosition(0, 0);

//create a ping-pong style animation sequence
sprite.setFrameSequence(frameSequence_);

//create the layer manager
layerMgr = new LayerManager();

//add to the layer manager
layerMgr.append((Layer)sprite);
layerMgr.append((Layer)tiledLayer);

timer_ = new Timer();
heartTask_ = new HeartbeatTask(this);
timer_.schedule(heartTask_, 0, ANIM_PERIOD);

firstTime = false;
        }

    display_.setCurrent(canvas_);
    canvas_.repaint();
    }
```

Note that most of the processing occurs only if firstTime is true. This way we don't re-initialize the MIDlet if it is coming back from being paused by the Application Manager. With that out of the way, the first two things we do is get our display and create our SpriteTileTestCanvas. Note that we pass true to the constructor so we suppress the directional key events. Since we are not using key messages in the GameCanvas, they don't need to be sent.

Now we create our TiledLayer. We call the TiledLayer constructor to create a map 16 cells wide and 16 cells high, using the Image referenced by IMG_TILE in our GameCanvas' Image array. This Image contains two 16 x 16 tiles.

Now we get into creating the map. Here we do it manually by looping through and setting each cell to the first tile, 1. Remember that tile indices are 1-relative. If we set it to 0, the cell will be totally transparent. After this, we create an animated tile index and save it off in our animIndex member variable. Now notice that we go through the cells once again, setting every tile in the fifth column to be our new animated tile index.

Now that we have taken care of the tiled background, we need to create our sprite. We simply call the constructor using the image referenced by our IMG_SPRITE index. This sprite contains 16 x 16 frames, hence the passing of the size as the final two arguments in the constructor call. Look at Figure 9-14 to see the frames of our Sprite.

Figure 9-14: Our three-frame smiley face Sprite animation strip

After initializing the Sprite's position to the upper left-hand corner of the screen, we then create a frame sequence. By default, the frame sequence is 0, 1, 2 because it is a three-frame Sprite. We want the animation to ping-pong. That is, we want it to advance all the way to the last frame and then once there, go backward. This will make our little face smile then frown then smile again ad infinitum. To do this, we create a six-frame sequence: 0, 1, 2, 3, 2, 1. Now when we advance the frame in the GameCanvas' update method, it will appear to ping-pong back and forth between smiling and frowning.

Finally, we create our LayerManager and add the Sprite and TiledLayer to it. Note that we add the TiledLayer last, ensuring that the Sprite will be drawn in front of the background. Otherwise, you wouldn't be able to see the Sprite as the TiledLayer would be drawn in front of everything.

Finally we create a Timer and our HeartbeatTask object. We then use the Timer's schedule method with the ANIM_PERIOD constant to make the HeartbeatTask execute every 30 milliseconds.

At the end of this function, we set the current display to be our GameCanvas and repaint the whole screen. Since the HeartbeatTask is scheduled, the MIDlet will execute until you quit out of the emulator or hit the red phone button. You can move your smiley face around the tiled background as it animates and a column of tiles in the middle will blink between the two different tile images.

Yeah, I told you it was useless, but this code gives you a basic example of the major features discussed here. With this knowledge, you have the building blocks necessary to start creating a real game.

Figure 9-15: Mission complete! Our smiley face tile maze in action.

Another Example

Now that we've shown the functionality of the tile system, we need to know how to load up our tile maps from a file generated from a tile editor such as Mappy. If you look at the code for loadtilemap, you'll see something that looks very similar to the previous example with one major change. In our startApplet method, we load the file map.MAP from our JAR using getResourceAsStream. You can view the code in its entirety in the project itself, but for the sake of our illustration, let's just look at this method in Listing 9-8.

Listing 9-8: Loading our map file

```
public void startApp() throws MIDletStateChangeException
    {
        if (firstTime)
        {
            display_ = Display.getDisplay(this);
            canvas_ = new LoadTileMapCanvas(true);
            canvas_.app = this;

            //add tile map
            tiledLayer = new TiledLayer(32, 32, canvas_.imageArray[IMG_TILE], 16, 16);

            InputStream is;
            is = getClass().getResourceAsStream("/map.MAP");

            try
            {
                if (is != null)
                {
                    byte data[] = new byte[1];

                    is.read(data, 0, 1);

                    mapWidth = (int)data[0];

                    is.read(data, 0, 1);

                    mapHeight = (int)data[0];

                    mapArray = new byte[mapWidth * mapHeight];
                    is.read(mapArray, 0, (mapWidth * mapHeight));

                    is.close();

                    int tileX, tileY;

                    for (int i = 0; i < (mapWidth * mapHeight); i++)
                    {
                        tileY = i / mapWidth;
                        tileX = i - (tileY * mapWidth);

                        tiledLayer.setCell(tileX, tileY, mapArray[i]);
                    }
                }
            }
            catch (IOException e)
            {
                System.err.println("Failed loading MAP!!! " + e);
```

```
        }

        //create the layer manager
        layerMgr = new LayerManager();

        //add to the layer manager
        layerMgr.append((Layer)tiledLayer);

        firstTime = false;
    }

    display_.setCurrent(canvas_);
    canvas_.repaint();
}
```

The difference here begins with the declaration of our Input-
Stream, is. After this, we open the file map.MAP, which you will
find in our project's res folder. If the stream has been acquired
(and is non-null), we start the process of parsing the file. We're
using Mappy's MAP file that is as close to raw data as you can get.
The maptype setting used in the mappy.ini file is this:

```
maptype="LW1H1A10"
```

You can see here that the width and height values are 1 byte wide,
as is each individual map cell. Finally, we do not subtract anything
from the indices so that our tiles begin at 1. Otherwise, any tile
cell set to 0 will be transparent. So, the first thing we do is read a
byte, set our mapWidth integer to its value, and then read the second byte and set the mapHeight integer to that. Now the stream
should be at the start of the map data. Here's where we do the
heavy lifting (which really isn't that heavy).

   First, we read in all the remaining bytes in the file into a large
byte array that we allocate to fit this data (i.e., mapWidth *
mapHeight bytes in size). We then have a simple loop that iterates
through every byte (i.e., mapWidth * mapHeight amount of bytes)
and sets the appropriate cell in our TiledLayer to the value of this
byte. To compute the x and y location we do a little simple math to
convert a 1D array index to 2D coordinates. The end result is a
map that looks very similar to our sample map (with no animation). This should be a decent example to build any loading routine
you may use to support custom map formats and such.

Conclusion

This chapter has been a whirlwind tour of the Game API. The example code located in the chap09 folder gives a basic example of most of the techniques described here. Using these building blocks you can pretty much write an entire game. However, there are a few other odds and ends we should go over before delving into a completely functional game MIDlet.

Chapter 10

Sound and Music

Introduction

Back in the MIDP 1.0 days, there was no sound. The only standardized sound method was the use of Alert's beep notifications. Soon after the release of MIDP 1.0, many handset manufacturers had begun to include custom APIs to access the MIDI playback functionality they already used in the firmware for advanced ringtones and such. Of course, well before MIDP was ratified, Japanese flavors of mobile Java had quite advanced sound using Compact MIDI among other formats. MIDP 2.0 has introduced the Media API. Along with other media types, including streaming video, the Media API finally standardizes the playback of MIDI and other sound formats. This chapter will detail the basics of getting a sound engine up and running.

What Is MIDI?

Although the Media API can theoretically be used to play different media types including digital sounds in WAV format, we will be mostly discussing MIDI here. MIDI stands for Musical Instrument Digital Interface. MIDI was developed in 1983 as a protocol for digital musical hardware to talk to each other. For instance, by plugging a MIDI keyboard and drum machine into a computer with a MIDI interface, you could control both from your PC — issuing commands from a single interface to play sounds on all connected devices instead of needing a second pair of arms to control both machines simultaneously. In the end, a MIDI file essentially consists of a list of instructions that tell the device to play certain notes and sounds at various durations and times. Music is constructed by the receiving device by taking this MIDI data and playing sound according to the instructions inside. Because a MIDI file is a simple series of instructions instead of raw music data, it can be very small and thus is well suited for mobile devices where memory is at a premium.

Note   Even though MIDI is a standard, your MIDI tune will most likely sound different on every device you try it on. The instrument sounds used by each handset are not totally standardized, even though they are in the same general category. (For example, a drum on one device will sound tinnier than on another.)

The Media API

The MIDP 2.0 Media API is actually a subset of a previous API, the Mobile Media API (JSR 135). The Mobile Media API was designed to accommodate a range of devices considered much more powerful than the average handset, and thus there is support for rich media such as motion video in the standard. Because of the constraints of the average handset, the functionality of the Mobile Media API has been thinned out to a small set of requirements in MIDP 2.0. MIDP 2.0's Media API has removed video playback and other features to bring a subset that focuses on basic sound, including MIDI and tone generation.

The Media API is set up into three major classes and interfaces: Manager, Player, and Control. The Manager is a simple class used to request Player objects to play back audio data. The Player is responsible for the control of the audio playback. This includes starting, stopping, looping, and other navigation features. Controls are special interfaces that are used to alter the playback in ways such as altering the tone or volume of the currently playing audio.

The Manager

The first object we'll look at is the Manager. This is a static system object that we can use at any time.

Creating a Player

As previously described, the Manager is largely used to construct Players, which are used to play back the audio itself. To create a Player, we use the createPlayer method. The first version looks like this:

```
public static Player createPlayer(String locator)
```

This method takes a string containing a Uniform Resource Identifier (URI) pointing to the media clip we wish to play. It returns a Player object we can then use to play back the data. This method must be placed in a try/catch block where you catch MediaException.

Finding Out What You Can Play

Not every device is capable of playing the same sorts of media. In some cases you may only be able to play MIDI tunes, while in other cases you may be able to also use digital sound files such as WAV or MP3 data. Regardless of the type of data played, the Player class interface handles the playback of everything. However, you may want to know at run time which media formats are supported. To do this, you use the method getSupportedContentTypes:

```
public static String() getSupportedContentTypes(String protocol)
```

This method takes a protocol (such as "http") and returns an array of strings that contains the MIME types of every format supported under that protocol. If null is passed as an argument, it will return an array of all MIME types supported under all available protocols. MIME types will be discussed later in this chapter; however, there are universal MIME types for many common formats such as MIDI, MP3, and WAV. By checking the array for the presence of these MIME type strings, you can determine which types of media the device is capable of playing.

Locating Resources

A URI is a standardized string used to identify a resource. For instance, the web address http://www.flarb.com is a URI. The URI has gone beyond the normal web page resources and can be used to reference all sorts of resources. The format is <scheme>:<scheme-specific part>. So, if you look at http://www.flarb.com, the scheme is http — meaning it uses the Hypertext Transfer Protocol. The //www.flarb.com portion is the so-called scheme-specific part, or rather the location of the resource itself. So, if we had a MIDI file sitting on a web server somewhere, we might do something like this:

```
Player player = Manager.createPlayer("http://www.wordware.com/song.midi");
```

Now, if the resource exists and can be loaded properly off the server, the resultant Player object can be used to play this resource. Most likely, you will be using MIDI tunes that are located in the JAR itself, however. This is done through the use of streams.

Using Streams

MIDP 2.0 has no real file system to speak of. However, it is possible to get files inside your MIDlet's JAR using the method getResourceAsStream. This method is found in the primitive abstract class called Class. The method is defined like so:

```
public InputStream getResourceAsStream(String name)
```

The String argument is basically the path to the resource. If we have a MIDI file in our root directory (in the case of KToolbar, in the res folder), then we would make a call like so:

```
InputStream is = getClass().getResourceAsStream("/theme.midi");
```

You need that beginning slash for the path to work (although some development environments may differ). Also, in order to call this method, you need to get a reference to the Class object itself; thus the call to getClass. Now the InputStream can be used in the second version of createPlayer:

```
public static Player createPlayer(InputStream stream, String type)
```

This version takes our InputStream as the first argument, and then a second stream that specifies the MIME type of the stream's contents. When you use this method, you must place it in a try/catch block where you catch IOException.

MIME Types

MIME types deserve some discussion. MIME stands for Multipurpose Internet Mail Extensions. You might be able to glean from the name that originally MIME types were used to identify the contents of attachments in emails. Today, MIME types are used to identify resource types in all sorts of applications.

Essentially a MIME type is a simple string that has two parts separated by a slash. The first part is the type and the second part is the subtype. For instance, a common MIME type is text; however, there are numerous subtypes for the different formats in which the text can be represented. For instance, there is "text/plain" for normal, plain-vanilla text files. Or, "text/html" for text stored in the HTML format. For the purposes of this chapter, we are interested in MIDI. So, when calling createPlayer using our newly created InputStream, we would do it like this:

```
Player player = Manager..createPlayer(is, "audio/midi");
```

Now we have a Player that can be used to play the MIDI data available in the InputStream. The elegance to this method is that when new media formats are introduced to MIDP, we should only need to pass a new MIME type to createPlayer instead of having to deal with a completely different creation call.

Playing Tones

Somewhat unrelated to the creation and management of Players, the Manager can also be used to play Tones. A Tone is a simple algorithmically generated musical note. A series of Tones can be combined to create ringtones. Many of you may have experience with the built-in ringtone composers of various popular handsets. In order to play a Tone with the Manager, we use the playTone method:

```
public static void playTone(int note, int duration, int volume)
```

The first argument is the note we wish to play. This number ranges from 0 to 127. The MIDP 2.0 documentation gives the formula used to compute the precise MIDI note specified by each of these 128 values. It is listed like so:

```
SEMITONE_CONST = 17.31234049066755 = 1/(ln(2^(1/12)))
note = ln(freq/8.176)*SEMITONE_CONST
The musical note A = MIDI note 69 (0x45) = 440 Hz.
```

Okay, well that may look like Greek to you, and it sure does to me. But if you are really concerned about using tones to create sound, that is what you can reference to make sure your notes are accurate. The duration is the amount of time in milliseconds that this note will play. The volume argument is a number from 0 to 100 that represents the loudness of the note. 100 is the loudest, 0 is usually inaudible. Of course, this is also relative to the volume setting on the handset. If the global setting of the handset has the volume set to 0, a tone playing at 100 still won't be heard. So, an example of playing a brief tone would look like this:

```
Media.playTone(10, 1500, 100);
```

This plays note 10 for a second and a half at the maximum volume. You can painstakingly craft an array of notes and durations to construct a series of tones that sound like music — or you can opt to use MIDI files like the rest of us.

The Player

Now that we know how to create a Player based off a media clip either on the web or from a file internal to the JAR, we will focus on using it to play back MIDI files. The Player has quite an extensive array of methods for controlling the playback of media, as well as generating events for listeners to trigger actions at different points in the stream. Note that many of the Player methods force you to catch MediaException.

Playback

First, we will look at an exceedingly simple example of playback. To start playing our music, we simply use the start method:

```
public void start()
```

This method will begin playing the stream, although this may not occur immediately. The Player itself can be in several different intermediate states and unable to start. For instance, if we have created the Player based off of a URI, the Player may need time to cache the data from the Internet.

Player States

What are the various states of the Player, and how do you know which one it is in? This is done through the use of getState:

```
public int getState()
```

The getState method returns an integer that is set to one of five different states: UNREALIZED, REALIZED, PREFETCHED, STARTED, and CLOSED. Let's examine each state in detail:

- UNREALIZED: This is the state of the Player when it is first created. This usually means that the player is in the process of being initialized by the system itself, including fetching data off of a server specified by the URI. When the player is in the UNREALIZED state, the methods getContentType, getMedia-Time, getControls, and getControl must not be called. Otherwise, an IllegalStateException will be thrown. To force the Player to go into REALIZED mode, the realize method can be called.

- REALIZED: In REALIZED state, the Player is ready to begin playing music. Notice I said "begin." Once in the REALIZED state, the Player may still have to acquire the hardware's audio device, among other setup duties. For instance, if there is another sound currently playing and the device has no mixing capabilities, the Player may wait around in REALIZED state until the sound stops playing and it can acquire the sound device itself.

- PREFETCHED: In PREFETCHED state, the Player is in the process of acquiring the device, setting up buffers, and performing other housekeeping duties. To invoke PREFETCHED state, the prefetch method must be used. Now that the Player is in PREFETCHED state it can be started — and thus the music can play.

■ STARTED: As we saw with the illustration of the start method, the STARTED state is where the Player is when it is playing a media clip. Once the music has stopped playing, it returns to PREFETCHED. Note that the UNREALIZED and REALIZED states are never encountered again. This means that the latency of playback is minimized after the first play-back, or after forcing a Player into the PREFETCHED state with a call to the prefetch method.

■ CLOSED: This is the state the Player is in when it has released its resources. It can never be used again once it is in the CLOSED state.

A simple example of playing the MIDI file we grabbed in the previous section would look something like this:

```
Player player = createPlayer(is, "audio/midi");
Player.start();
```

Okay, so what happens here? When you call start, the player must first go through the UNREALIZED, REALIZED, and PREFETCHED states. Then it will enter the STARTED state and play the MIDI file back. This may introduce a considerable delay between when you call start and when you actually hear something. Therefore, what you could do is create a bunch of Players for each MIDI tune you wish to play — and call prefetch on each one like this:

```
Player player = createPlayer(is, "audio/midi");
player.prefetch();
```

Now, later on you might start the playback as usual:

```
Player.start();
```

But this time the delay between calling start and hearing the sound may be much shorter, if not nonexistent. This is because the data is loaded, the audio device has been acquired, and it's ready to go.

Looping

The Player interface also has an easy way to loop. Looping is for when you want the tune to start at the beginning once it finishes — usually for ambient background music and things like that. To do this, simply call setLoopCount:

```
public void setLoopCount(int count)
```

The count argument specifies how many times the Player will loop the content. This can be –1 or any nonzero number. If count is set to –1, it will loop indefinitely until you manually stop the Player or alter the loop count again. The catch is that the Player cannot be in STARTED or CLOSED states. So set the loop before you play the tune, not after.

Player Events

Players generate different events that can be processed by listeners much like Command events. These events will tell you when the tune has stopped, started, changed volumes, and other incidents of note. To assign a listener to a Player, we use the addPlayerListener method:

```
public void addPlayerListener(PlayerListener playerListener)
```

This method takes a PlayerListener object as the sole argument. Much like CommandListener, PlayerListener is an interface. If we implement PlayerListener in a class, we need to provide a playerUpdate method. This behaves in much the same way as commandAction for CommandListener. The method looks like this:

```
public void playerUpdate(Player player, String event, Object eventData)
```

The first argument is the Player that generated the event. This argument is followed by a string that identifies the event being sent, and finally, an Object reference that is used to pass along data associated with the event. Different events may send different types of objects through this argument, and thus it must be cast to the right one.

So, let's say we want to detect if our previously created player has finished. If we want to include playerUpdate in our MIDlet class, we need to implement the interface like this:

```
public class HelloWorld extends MIDlet implements PlayerListener
```

When we create the Player, we now have to set the MIDlet class to be the listener like this:

```
Player themeSongPlayer = createPlayer(is, "audio/midi");
themeSongPlayer.prefetch();
themeSongPlayer.addPlayerListener(this);
```

As we have seen with other listener operations, we pass a reference to the MIDlet class and set it as the listener. Note that if we want to remove the MIDlet class as a listener, we can use the removePlayerListener method as well. Now, inside the MIDlet, we would have a playerUpdate method like this:

```
Public void playerUpdate(Player player, String event, Object eventData)
{
    if (player = themeSongPlayer)
    {
        if (event == PlayerListener.END_OF_MEDIA)
        {
            System.out.println("Finished!");
        }
    }
}
```

This method sees if we are processing the right player, and if so checks if we are acting upon the END_OF_MEDIA event. END_OF_MEDIA is one of the String fields defined in the PlayerListener interface. See Table 10-1 for a brief explanation of each field.

Table 10-1: Player listener fields

Field	Description
CLOSED	Player is closed.
DEVICE_AVAILABLE	The exclusive sound device is free to be used.
DEVICE_UNAVAILABLE	The exclusive sound device is being used by something else.
DURATION_UPDATED	The duration of the media has changed. This might occur for media types that can algorithmically speed up or slow down at different key frames, for example.
END_OF_MEDIA	The Player has reached the end of the media data.
ERROR	An error has occurred.
STARTED	The Player has started.

Field	Description
STOPPED	The Player has been forcibly stopped with the stop method.
VOLUME_CHANGED	The volume of the audio device has been modified.

Controls

The last topic we need to discuss is Controls. The Control interface allows us to alter the playback in a few different ways. Well, actually only two for now in the current version of MIDP 2.0. Before we do anything, we need to actually get a Control object. We do this via the Player class' getControl method:

```
public Control getControl(String controlType)
```

This method returns a Control object, of the type we specify with the String controlType. This method cannot be used when the Player is in the UNREALIZED or CLOSED state. There are only two strings you can pass to getControl: VolumeControl and ToneControl.

VolumeControl

The VolumeControl is obviously used to control the volume of the Player's sound output. So, if we want a VolumeControl from our Player, we do it like this:

```
VolumeControl volumeControl = themeSongPlayer.getControl("VolumeControl");
```

The end result is a VolumeControl that we can now use to modify the volume. This is done through the method setLevel:

```
public int setLevel(int level)
```

This takes an integer from 0 to 100, with 0 being the quietest and 100 being the highest level of volume for the sound. As with Tone volumes, this is also governed by the global settings of the device itself.

If you want to squelch audio altogether, use the setMute method:

```
public void setMute(boolean mute)
```

Pass the value true, and you will mute the Player. Pass false and it will be unmuted if it was muted in the first place. Note that setting the level or altering the mute status will trigger a VOLUME_ CHANGED event to the listener.

ToneControl

The ToneControl is a control of a different sort. This control allows you to use a Player to play a list of Tones. Previously, we described a process of manually making an array of Tones and playing each note using the Media class. Although you can do this, a better method is to use the ToneControl. The ToneControl is created by passing the string ToneControl to getControl:

```
ToneControl toneControl = themeSongPlayer.getControl("ToneControl");
```

Now that we have a ToneControl, we can use its interface to load an array of Tone data and use the normal Player methods to play it back. The array itself is an array of bytes, which is in a format defined in the documentation. Once you have initialized your array of data, you can assign it to the Player using ToneControl's setSequence method:

```
public void setSequence(byte[] sequence)
```

Obviously, this takes our hand-crafted array of Tone data and uses it as the Player's media source. Now you can use the normal Player methods to start, stop, and otherwise manipulate the playback of the Tone sequence.

A Simple Example

The example program for this chapter is an exceedingly simple exercise in playing a MIDI tune. All enclosed in one MIDlet class, the code looks like this:

Listing 10-1: The SoundTest MIDlet

```
public class SoundTest extends MIDlet
{
    private boolean firstTime_;
    private Display display_;
    private Player player_;

    public SoundTest()
    {
        firstTime_ = true;
    }

    public void startApp() throws MIDletStateChangeException
    {
        if (firstTime_)
        {
            InputStream is;

            display_ = Display.getDisplay(this);
            firstTime_ = false;

            is = getClass().getResourceAsStream("/tune.midi");

            try
            {
                if (is != null)
                {
                    player_ = Manager.createPlayer(is, "audio/midi");
                    player_.setLoopCount(-1);
                    player_.start();
                }
            }
            catch (IOException e)
            {
                System.err.println("Failed loading MIDI!!! " + e);
            }
            catch (MediaException e)
            {
                System.err.println("Failed playing MIDI!!! " + e);
            }
        }
```

```
    }

    public void pauseApp()
    {
    }

    public void destroyApp(boolean unconditional)
    {
    }

} //class
```

The only method of note here is startApp. Here we declare our InputStream and get the Display. Then we use getResource-AsStream to retrieve the MIDI stored in the JAR. Inside our try/catch block, we create a player if the stream isn't null. We then set our loop count to –1, which will make the song loop indefinitely. Then we start the tune. Note that you must set the loop count before starting the Player. Otherwise you'll get an exception.

Conclusion

In this chapter you have seen how it is possible to play MIDI tunes and tone sequences for sound effects through the Media API. Once again, how the device supports this is handset-specific. Some handsets may allow you to play and dynamically mix multiple MIDIs simultaneously, while others will require each Player to obtain exclusive access to the audio device. I have seen some impressive upcoming handsets with 256 wavetable synthesis and all sorts of mixing options. When these handsets will be the mainstream is anybody's guess.

Chapter 11

Odds and Ends

Introduction

This chapter contains a bunch of odds and ends that do not fall under any one cohesive category. Many of the techniques discussed here may be familiar to seasoned Java programmers. However, it is worth illustrating a few useful techniques here as both an introduction and a refresher.

Persistent Storage

J2ME's sandbox security model does not allow for writing to the file system. In fact, reading from the file system is somewhat restricted as well; the only way you can read data from files inside your JAR is via getResourceAsStream. We detailed this method in Chapter 9, "The Game API." That's all well and good if you want to read in a file, but what about writing persistent data, such as saving your position in a game or recording high scores? For this reason, MIDP has introduced the RecordStore.

RecordStore

Located in the javax.microedition.rms package, RecordStores are simple databases that can have arrays of bytes read from and written to. In MIDP 1.0, only RecordStores created inside the context of the MIDlet's JAR could be accessed — as the sandbox security model prevents MIDlets from accessing files outside of their JAR. However, MIDP 2.0 has some APIs to get around this problem. RecordStores are actually files that are kept in a hardware-specific location in the device's file system. Thus, each RecordStore that you create within the context of a MIDlet suite must have a unique name, as they are all present in the same directory. However, two different MIDlet suites can create RecordStores with the same name, as the MIDlet suite's name is appended to the file name on the device. When the MIDlet suite associated with the RecordStore is uninstalled, all of its RecordStores are removed as well.

Creating a RecordStore

To create or otherwise open a RecordStore, you use the openRecordStore method inside the static RecordStore system class. The method looks like this:

```
public static RecordStore openRecordStore(String recordStoreName,
    boolean createIfNecessary)
```

This method takes a string containing the name of the Record-Store and a Boolean that tells MIDP to create a RecordStore with this name if it doesn't already exist. The return value is a reference to the opened or newly created RecordStore object. Aside from making sure RecordStore names are unique within the context of the MIDlet suite, you must also restrict your names to 32 characters or less. This method throws exceptions for various reasons, including not being able to find the RecordStore, passing an invalid name as an argument, or if the RecordStore is full and cannot be opened. In addition to these exceptions, the RecordStore exception must be caught, and thus RecordStore operations need to be put inside try blocks. Note that this method creates a RecordStore that cannot be shared between MIDlet suites. We will show a new MIDP 2.0 method of sharing RecordStores later in this chapter.

Adding a Record

Now that you have a RecordStore opened or created, we can get on with the process of reading and writing data. To add a record, we use the addRecord method:

```
public int addRecord(byte[] data, int offset, int numBytes)
```

This method takes an array of bytes we will write into the RecordStore, an offset into this array that we want to begin writing from, and the number of bytes out of this array we wish to store. The return value is the recordID of this new record. This number can then be used to access this record and read or further modify it. So, let's say I wanted to create a RecordStore and save my name as the first record. The code would look something like this:

Listing 11-1: Using RecordStores

```
try
{
    String nameString = "Ralph";
    RecordStore nameRecord = RecordStore.openRecordStore("names", true);
    nameId = nameRecord.addRecord(nameString.getBytes(), 0, nameString.length());
    nameRecord.closeRecordStore();
}
catch (RecordStoreException e)
{
    e.printStackTrace();
}
```

So, what we do is first create a string with my name in it. Then we open or otherwise create a RecordStore called "names." Then we write the name to the RecordStore by converting the string to a byte array and using addRecord to put it in the RecordStore. We save the resultant recordId in our nameId member variable. Note that we close the RecordStore once we are done with it. Although the RecordStore access operations are automatic and will not become corrupted when multiple threads are writing to them simultaneously, it is still good practice to close them when you aren't accessing them. Many phones have strict limits on how many RecordStores can be open simultaneously. For instance, the Motorola T720i can only have four simultaneously open RecordStores. So keep your open RecordStores to an absolute minimum.

Note   Not only are there limitations on how many open connections you can have, but many devices have strict limitations on how much data can be saved in a RecordStore. Some of these file space restrictions are quite small.

Retrieving a Record

Now that we have stored a record, how to we get it back? We use the method getRecord:

```
public byte[] getRecord(int recordId);
```

This method uses the recordId integer returned by addRecord as the key to finding the byte array associated with that record. The return value is the byte array of the data stored under that recordId. If the RecordStore is not open, or you pass in a recordId that does not exist, the method will throw an exception. So, since we stored the recordId of our nameString entry in the nameId variable, we could do something like this:

Listing 11-2: Retrieving data from a RecordStore

```
byte[] recordData;
try
{
    RecordStore nameRecord = RecordStore.openRecordStore("names", true);
    RecordData = nameRecord.getRecord(nameId);
    nameRecord.closeRecordStore();
}
catch (RecordStoreException e)
{
    e.printStackTrace();
}
```

Now that we have the byte array stored under the recordId saved in nameId, we can convert this back to a String or do anything else we want with it. But what if we don't know the recordId in advance? What if we have a bunch of names in the RecordStore and we want to search for "Ralph"?

Finding a Record

There is no search functionality in the RecordStore class; however, there are methods that can be used to access successive entries and thus search manually for the data we seek. Before we start, one thing we might need to do is find out how many records are in the RecordStore. To do this, we use getNumRecords:

```
public int getNumRecords()
```

This method returns the total number of records in the Record-Store. Now that we know how many records are in the RecordStore, we can manually retrieve each one and check the contents of its byte array to see if it's the data we are looking for.

Let's say that we have 10 records in the RecordStore. We can't simply loop through 10 times and increment the index for each call to getNumRecords. The recordIds are not necessarily sequential. For instance, if we had added three records with the recordIDs 1, 2, and 3, and then removed the second one, we would have a gap. Now there are two recordIds: 1 and 3. Stepping through sequentially would cause us to try to retrieve record 2, which does not exist, and thus would return a null array. Instead, we need to use the RecordEnumerator.

Record Enumerations

A RecordEnumerator is an interface that allows you to step through the records in a RecordStore without having to explicitly specify a recordId. So, we can iterate through all the records, even skipping over gaps in the recordId number sequence. In order to get access to the RecordEnumerator for our opened RecordStore, we use the enumerateRecords method:

```
public RecordEnumeration enumerateRecords(RecordFilter filter, RecordComparator
    comparator, boolean keepUpdated)
```

The first argument is a RecordFilter object. This is used to match the byte array of each record with a filter. Basically, this will prune the records stepped through by filtering out the ones that do not match what was set in the RecordFilter — kind of like a regular expression or wild card. We can pass null to the filter argument to ignore this, and thus step through every record in the Record-Store. The comparator argument is a RecordComparator object that is used to sort the records in any order you like. Essentially, if you implement the RecordComparator interface in an object, you have to write a compare method that takes the byte arrays of two records as arguments. This is the method that determines which record is greater than the other. A reference to this object can then be passed as the RecordComparator. Again, we'll ignore this for now and just pass null as the argument — this will iterate through each record in a sequential but undefined order. The final

argument, keepUpdated, is a Boolean that determines if this enumeration will be updated if the RecordStore is modified while we
are iterating through it. For instance, we may have another thread
that is adding or removing records as we are going through it. If
this argument is set to true, then the enumeration will be kept up
to date with any changes.

If all goes well, the RecordEnumeration object returned by the
method can then be used to traverse the records looking for the
one we want. We travel through the records with the nextRecord
and previousRecord methods of the RecordEnumeration class:

```
public byte[] nextRecord()
public byte[] previousRecord()
```

The nextRecord method returns the next record in the Record-
Enumerator's sequence. Both methods return an InvalidRecord-
IDException if we have traveled beyond the range of records in
the RecordStore. The return value is a byte array that contains a
copy of the contents of the current recordId. Remember, this is a
copy — any changes to this returned byte array will not be
reflected in the actual record. You'll have to find out what the
recordId is and manually change that record through the Record-
Store class itself. You can do this by using the nextRecordId and
previousRecordId methods:

```
public int nextRecordId()
public int previousRecordId()
```

Both methods return a recordId that can be used to retrieve the
actual record from the RecordStore class itself. These behave in
much the same way as the previously discussed methods.

Modifying a Record

So now we know how to add and retrieve records from a
RecordStore. How do we modify the data associated with a
recordId? This is accomplished with the setRecord method:

```
public void setRecord(int recordId, byte[] newData, int offset, int numBytes)
```

This method takes the desired recordId of the record we wish to
modify, a byte array of the data we want to write into this record,
an offset into the record, and the number of bytes we're writing

into the record itself. Obviously, an exception will be thrown if you specify an invalid recordId, the RecordStore is full, or it isn't open.

Sharing RecordStores

New to MIDP 2.0 is the ability to share RecordStores between MIDlet suites. This involves creating a special kind of RecordStore that allows any MIDlet to access it. This is done through an overloaded version of openRecordStore:

```
public static RecordStore openRecordStore(String recordStoreName,
      boolean createIfNecessary, int authmode, boolean writable)
```

This works in a similar fashion to the original version of open-RecordStore, except it takes two new arguments. The authmode integer can be one of two values defined as fields in RecordStore: AUTHMODE_PRIVATE or AUTHMODE_ANY. If AUTHMODE_PRIVATE is passed, then this RecordStore is only accessible from this MIDlet suite — basic MIDP 1.0 style. If AUTHMODE_ANY is passed as the authmode, then this will be a shared RecordStore and thus can be accessed by other MIDlet suites. The final Boolean argument, writable, determines if this will have read/write or read-only access when being used by outside MIDlet suites. If true is passed to this argument, it will be able to be written to by other MIDlet suites. This argument is ignored if the RecordStore already exists; therefore it is impossible to change the writable attribute once the RecordStore has been initially created.

Now, to open a shared RecordStore, you need to use an overloaded version of openRecordStore:

```
public static RecordStore openRecordStore(String recordStoreName, String vendorName,
      String suiteName)
```

This method works in a similar fashion to the original MIDP 1.0 version; however, there are a few new arguments. The vendor-Name string is the name of the MIDlet suite that originally created the RecordStore. This will be related to the vendor string in the JAD. The suiteName string is the MIDlet suite name of the creator. This is also related to the MIDlet suite's name in the JAD. Naturally, if you are not the creator of this RecordStore and the record was created with AUTHMODE_PRIVATE, then a SecurityException will be thrown.

The implications for game programmers could be dramatic. For instance, you could create an RPG that imports characters from other games. Or, you could create a series of games that unlock content in each other through the use of shared Record-Stores. For instance, you could store whether or not you have beaten a game in a shared RecordStore. Another related game could read this and then unlock a new level or character based on the player's progress in the other game MIDlet.

Note that in Sun's emulator, the RecordStore database files are sorted in the appdb folder under KToolbar. There should be a folder for each emulator profile that there are RecordStores saved for. If you want to clear out the RecordStore for your MIDlet, check the appropriate folder and delete it.

Random Numbers

Another invaluable technique for game programmers is the generation of random numbers. Through the use of Java's Random class, this process is easy and painless. First, you need to create a random number generator with the Random class's constructors:

```
Random()
Random(long seed)
```

The constructor we are most interested in is the second one. It takes a long as an argument. This is the *seed* — the original number used to generate the random number sequence. For debugging purposes, you can use the same seed twice and get the exact same number sequence. However, in the final product you want to use a number that is dynamic as the seed to more or less ensure you get a different number sequence every time you start the game. Usually the current time is used as a seed like this:

```
Random rand = new Random(System.currentTimeMillis());
```

For extra randomness, you can reseed the Random object at any time through the setSeed method:

```
public void setSeed(long seed)
```

This works in the same way as the constructor.

Now that you have a random object, you can pull values out of it with the nextInt and nextLong methods:

```
public int nextInt()
public long nextLong()
```

If we want to get a random number with our newly created Random object, it's as simple as this:

```
int value = rand.nextInt();
```

If you are really interested, the MIDP documentation gives more information about the algorithm used to generate and retrieve values from its random number sequences. But for me, it works — no need to question it.

Collection Classes

One nice feature of J2ME is the inclusion of Java's basic collection classes. A collection class is an object used to store multiple items. For instance, a linked list may be considered a collection class. In the case of MIDP, both the Vector and Hashtable classes are available. While some texts warn against using these for games, I have found no real performance problems with the Vector class in particular. We will only briefly discuss these classes as they have been included in Java since the dawn of time. But a brief overview may be in order.

Vector

The Vector class can be thought of as a simple linked list of objects. You can access elements in a Vector like an array or traverse it like a list. To lessen the impact of dynamic memory allocation, you may want to create a Vector using a predefined size with this constructor:

```
public Vector(int initialCapacity)
```

Otherwise, if you use the basic constructor, Vector(), memory will be allocated every time you add an element to the Vector. Using this version will create a fixed-size Vector. If you end up needing to add elements beyond the capacity you initially declared, you will have to increase the capacity using the method ensureCapacity:

```
public void ensureCapacity(int minCapacity)
```

This method will increase the capacity of the Vector to the amount specified by the minCapacity argument if it is currently smaller. You can avoid this altogether by using another form of the constructor:

```
public Vector(int initialCapacity, int capacityIncrement)
```

The second argument is the amount the capacity will be increased by if you attempt to add an element to a full Vector.

To add an element, use the method addElement:

```
public void addElement(Object obj)
```

Obviously, we pass a reference to the Object we wish to add to the Vector. This adds the element to the end of the Vector. Similarly, you can remove an element from the Vector like so:

```
public void removeElement(Object obj)
```

You simply pass the reference to the Object you wish to remove to this method. You can also clear out the entire Vector with the method removeAllElements:

```
public void removeAllElements()
```

To retrieve an element from the Vector, you can treat it like an array or use the elementAt method:

```
public Object elementAt(int index)
```

Pass the index of the item in the Vector you want to access and it will return the item. So, if I wanted to get the second element of a Vector, I could do it in two ways:

```
Object obj = ourVector[2];
```

or

```
Object obj = ourVector.elementAt(2);
```

These are both effectively the same thing. There is plenty more you can do with the Vector, including enumerating it like a RecordStore to sort the entries and such. Check the API documentation for details.

Hashtable

The next collection class is the Hashtable. In general, a Hashtable is a structure optimized for the quick access of data. The basic idea is that each item you add into a Hashtable is associated with an algorithmically generated key. The key can then be used to retrieve the data immediately, without having to search through the structure. A Hashtable can take up considerable amounts of memory as it has to pre-allocate a lot of space in anticipation of the insertion of data, as well as to aid in the generation of unique keys. You can create a Hashtable with one of two constructors:

```
public Hashtable()
public Hashtable(int initialCapacity)
```

The first method will create a Hashtable with a default size. The second version allows you to specify the capacity of the Hashtable.

Now that you have a Hashtable created, you can add elements to it with the put method:

```
public Object put(Object key, Object value)
```

The first argument is a reference to the key. The key is an object you create, which has to implement the hashCode method and equals operator. The hashCode method is a part of the Object abstract base class. This is the method responsible for generating the key associated with Hashtable entries. Refer to the object documentation for more information on hashcodes. The second argument is the object you are actually adding to the Hashtable for later retrieval. To retrieve this object, you then use the get method:

```
public Object get(Object key)
```

This method takes the key you used when putting the object in the Hashtable. The result is a reference to the Object that is associated with this key. Again, this is a basic fundamental object in Java — not necessarily MIDP-specific. Check the Java documentation for more detail on how to use Hashtables and Vectors.

TimerTasks and Threads

Although you have already seen an example of the TimerTask in our Game API example code, it's worth going over the basics of TimerTasks and Threads. These are the two basic ways you can keep continuous tasks running — such as the execution of your game loop and drawing of frames. They both are Threads at heart, but operate in different ways.

TimerTask

The TimerTask is an object that can be scheduled by the Timer to execute at regular intervals. This is what we used in the Game API example MIDlet to run the main loop for every frame.

Creating a TimerTask

The TimerTask object is a simple one, and the only method you must implement is run. A basic class might look something like this:

```
class OurTask extends TimerTask
{
    public void run()
    {
        System.out.println("Running!");
    }
}
```

Every time it is executed, this simple class will print the text "Running!"

Scheduling the TimerTask

Now, in our MIDlet, we need to schedule this TimerTask to run. We do it like this:

```
timer_ = new Timer();
task_ = new OurTask();
timer_.schedule(task_, 0, 100);
```

Now, our TimerTask object is scheduled to execute every 100 milliseconds. This is done through the Timer's schedule method. The one we use looks like this:

```
public void schedule(TimerTask task, long delay, long period)
```

This method will schedule the task to execute indefinitely at fixed millisecond delays specified by the final argument, period. The delay argument is an initial delay before scheduling the task. This is unnecessary for our purposes, so we set it to 0.

If you want to create a one-time event, you would use this method:

```
public void schedule(TimerTask, long delay);
```

Similar to our previous version, this simply takes a delay after which the TimerTask will be executed.

Thread

Now that we've talked about TimerTasks, we should briefly discuss Threads. Unlike some other mobile applications platforms, J2ME is *multithreaded*, which means you can have various tasks running simultaneously. For instance, you might have a Thread that is downloading a new game map from your web server executing in the background at the same time a Gauge indicating the percentage of progress in this download animates and is displayed to the user. A broad discussion of Threads is beyond the scope of this book; however, we will cover the basics here. If you want more information on exactly what Threads are and how they work, I suggest looking at Sun's official documentation.

Creating a Thread from a Class

There are two ways to create a thread. One way is to make a thread its own class that extends Thread; the other is to implement the Thread's runnable interface in your MIDlet class and essentially have a method in your class act as the Thread. For the former, the class must override the run method. This is the method that gets executed when the Thread is started — essentially a main loop that runs indefinitely. To start the Thread, we need to create the object and call its start method like this:

```
OurThread t = new OurThread()
t.start();
```

Now the Thread is away and executing the run method. Until the execution falls out of the run method's loop, it will continue to execute. There is no way to explicitly stop a Thread; rather the Thread must stop itself. For instance, you might have a method in your Thread class that sets a Boolean — if that Boolean is set to true, the run method will break its loop and thus the Thread will stop executing.

Creating a Thread from Runnable

To start a Thread based off of a class, such as our MIDlet, that implements the Runnable interface, we would do it like this (assuming our MIDlet class implements Runnable):

```
new Thread(this).start();
```

Now a Thread object has been created, which is executing the loop in our MIDlet class's run method. A reference to any class that implements the Runnable interface can be passed to Thread's constructor. The same rules of stopping Thread execution apply to Runnable implementing objects.

Telling Time

Most every kind of game needs to perform some kind of time-critical tasks. In many cases you need to measure how long it took for different events to occur. For this reason, we often need to find out what the current time is in milliseconds. MIDP supports this through the System class's currentTimeMillis method:

```
public static long currentTimeMillis()
```

This method returns a long that is the difference, in milliseconds, between the current moment in time and 12:00 midnight, January 1, 1970 UTC. You should be familiar with this method from normal Java programming — but it's worth noting that it is available in J2ME as well.

Conclusion

In this chapter you have learned about a few somewhat unrelated concepts. Check the code for this chapter for a fairly extensive RecordStore example. Now that we have these odds and ends covered, we are ready to start creating simple games.

Chapter 12

Putting It All Together

Introduction

If you have followed this book through the previous chapters, you have learned about most of the MIDP 2.0 components necessary for developing a game. In this chapter we will develop a very simple game to illustrate how everything works together. This is not a great game by any means. However, by studying the development of a complete and finished title, you can build upon this code or use the ideas presented to create your own masterpiece.

The Mobile Game Development Process

I have seen many different authors write books about how games should be designed or developed. The truth is, if you ask a dozen different developers you will most likely get a dozen different answers. There seems to be no one simple solution to developing a game. Depending on the type of game you are making, the people on the team, and many other factors, the process necessary to take your project from concept to completion varies wildly.

Because the games for mobile devices are often very simple, the development process is much like that of the early days of gaming. This means that often only one programmer and artist are necessary to put together a commercial-quality title.

The average major console or PC title can have a development time of 18 to 36 months. With a mobile game, it is often reduced to 1 to 3 months. Sometimes it is a matter of mere weeks. Games become more complicated once you enter the multiplayer realm, with server and network protocol development. However, for simple single-player games, you can bang out a great title in an astoundingly short period of time.

As I said before, there is no one way to develop a game. The process I describe in this chapter is not necessarily the one you should follow. It is just a method cobbled together from my own personal experience and industry observations. With mobile game development being so quick and informal, it is really up for debate whether you actually need a totally organized process in the first place. Regardless, I will detail a few major phases of the development process.

Design

Ideas come from anywhere. Although there are many "industry visionaries" running around doing interviews and giving lectures at development conferences, the truth is just about anyone can come up with a good game concept. The real value in a design is the implementation. If you can't figure out a way to develop your game concept and finish it, the idea is worthless. Whether your game is fun or not is up for the players to decide. By the time you finish a game, it is nearly impossible to have an objective opinion on the quality of the gameplay. Oftentimes the soldiers in the trenches developing the game may have a completely different opinion of the quality of their product than that of the general gaming public. Occasionally, I have assumed the game I was working on was headed for disaster when in reality the public loved it once the title was released. The fickle tastes of the public are hard to define. Also, when you are too close to a game's development, it is almost impossible to be objective about its quality or lack thereof. Luckily, the brief development time of the average mobile product greatly reduces the significance of this issue.

Catering to the Platform

With that said, creating a design for a mobile game is totally unique from that of the average multimillion-dollar console title. As a programmer, you are in the unique position to take the technical challenges and limitations into account when designing your game. Probably one of the greatest dangers in game development is for the design to be overly ambitious and just downright impossible given the technical limitations of the target platform and resources available to the developers. In this case, you must be very cautious of the tiny amount of available memory, limited graphics display capabilities, lack of storage space, and restrictive input schemes of most handsets. These limitations are becoming less of an issue as the relentless pace of progress creates more impressive phone hardware, but you still have to keep in mind the existing user base of older phones. You may have to target the low-end hardware with your design if you are interested in appealing to the widest possible audience.

Note   One of my basic design principles is to make sure the game can be easily controlled with one hand (usually a thumb on the directional pad).

With technical issues out of the way, what about actual game concepts? What kinds of ideas are suitable for mobile games? There are several key issues to take into account when developing for this venue. The first is length of play. If you want to play a game for long periods of time, most likely you would rather be in the comfort of your own home, sitting in front of your console or PC rather than hunched over your wireless phone fumbling around with the keypad and squinting at a tiny LCD screen. Because of the nature of the device, chances are the idle time a player has with her phone is brief. Therefore, games must be designed to be played in short bursts — while waiting for the bus or in line at a movie theater, for instance

This is not to say the game cannot be designed for long-term play. You can have a game with long-term goals that may require many hours of play to achieve. However, the game must still be able to be successfully played in short bursts and be interrupted at any time. It is highly annoying to lose your game because you got a phone call while in the middle of a climactic battle. Allow the user to pause and resume the game at any time with little or no effect on the game's progress.

Catering to Your Audience

If you are looking at this from a purely commercial perspective, you have to also take into account your audience's tastes. The audience for mobile games is not necessarily the same as that of console or PC games. People do not buy phones to play games, although this is slowly changing. As mobile phone handsets become closer in quality to the hardware present on Nintendo's GameBoy Advance and other more modern consoles, the desire for traditional games of normal lengths and play styles may over-ride the so-called "mobile" audience considerations. However, you have to keep in mind the small amounts of revenue generated from many of these titles. Just how much game are you going to give for $3?

Therefore, duplicating what is successful on consoles and PCs that appeal to a totally different market does not necessarily equate to a successful mobile game. Right now, we are still relatively early in the history of mobile gaming. Experimentation with all sorts of crazy and wild ideas not viable for PC titles with millions of dollars at risk may yield equally bizarre success stories.

Once this market matures, we will be able to see a pattern in mobile gaming tastes. Yet, even existing patterns can be wrong. Just look at how the entire PC gaming industry was turned on its head by the massive success of a "niche" market title such as Deer Hunter. In an era where every game seemed to be appealing to the bloodlust of your average teenage male, Sunstorm Interactive's low-budget hunting simulator went on to rack up sales higher than many high-profile so-called "A" titles. Who am I to say how you should design and develop a game? In the end, it is entirely up to you. You can only observe industry facts and the wisdom of others and determine if it makes sense in what you are trying to accomplish. Ultimately, the players will determine if they like it or not.

Development

The term "game development" encompasses a lot more than just programming. Design and programming are just two of the overall elements involved in creating a completed game. Granted, with mobile gaming that is about 99% of it. But in traditional game development there are management concerns, work flow, tool creation, and a host of other issues that are encompassed in the general term "game development."

Asset Creation

In the game industry, an *asset* is defined as any element of the game that is plugged into the engine for the creation of content. Usually you will hear people refer to "sound assets" or "art assets." What they usually are talking about is the sound (music, dialog, and sound effects) or artwork (sprites, 3D models, and textures). The creation of these assets involves many different tools like 3D modeling packages such as 3D Studio Max or Maya; bitmap drawing programs including Photoshop or Paint Shop Pro; sound editors like SoundForge or CoolEdit; and a host of other tools used by artists, musicians, and others to create graphics, models, music, animations, and just about any other content used to make a game.

Most of the graphics in mobile games are bitmaps and geometric 2D shapes. In the case of bitmaps, a large variety of programs are available for creating images. It is irrelevant to the programmer, as most of them output standard PNGs that can be used with MIDP. In the case of 2D geometric graphics, there currently are no tools for creating such content for use with MIDP. Perhaps a way to import data from structured drawing programs like Macromedia Flash will appear in the future. Also, we are beginning to see several J2ME devices such as the Sony Ericsson K700 make 3D APIs available. As hardware becomes more powerful and fast 3D is feasible, the use of high-end 3D modeling packages will become commonplace in the development of mobile games.

Source Control

Another important factor in game development is source control. A source control system, such as the open-source CVS, manages changes coming from different developers to the same code. Often this means only one programmer can modify a section of code at a time, and the source control application makes sure this is so. Although primarily a tool used when multiple software engineers are working on a project, source control can also serve some use for single developers as well. This is because most source control applications keep a log of all changes in each source file over the course of the entire project. You can then easily track changes and see exactly when problematic lines of code were added into any file. Checking the differences between different versions of the source code is invaluable when fixing hard-to-find bugs. Oftentimes, if you can look at the differences between the last working version of the source and the current one, it is quite easy to tell what the problem is.

The very same source control software can also be used to manage asset creation. If you have a project where multiple artists are modifying the same graphics assets, a source control tool can manage this potential logistical nightmare quite easily. Because artwork is usually stored in binary files, a source control program can usually not detect the differences in two versions of the same art asset. However, it can at least keep a log and backup of any changes in a given piece of artwork over the course of the project.

Testing

Once you have your game up and running, you have to make sure it is bug-free. Well, bug-free is perhaps a little extreme. It seems that most programs these days ship with many bugs. Some bugs are worse than others. In these cases, it must be decided which bugs are "showstoppers" (ones that the game cannot ship without fixing) and which bugs do not significantly impact the player's experience. Under the pressure of time and limited resources, oftentimes a publisher has to make the decision as to which bugs the game can ship with and which are worth spending more time to fix.

In the PC realm, this decision is much easier as patching the game after release is commonplace. In fact, many game developers announce the creation of a patch before the first version of the game even hits the shelves! On a console such as the PlayStation 2 or Xbox, standards are far more stringent. It is not possible to update the game later, despite the emergence of hard drives on some modern consoles. The game has to be totally stable before shipping as you cannot go back and correct your mistakes with a patch. Mobile games are more like consoles in that patching is really not an option. Also, carriers will demand that your product be stable before offering it to their customers to purchase.

Although you as the programmer can test the game yourself, there is a need for external testing to bang on the game for a bit and see if it breaks. These third-party testers can be anyone from a software quality assurance firm to your little brother. An impartial third party playing your game may try to use it in ways you never thought of. This process may reveal bugs that would otherwise have gone unnoticed and even give you a window into how much fun the game actually is.

With most carriers, your applet must go through a stringent testing process before being accepted for sale. This testing process may cost money. Therefore it makes economic sense to make sure you catch as many of your own bugs as possible before sending it off for carrier or OEM certification.

Attack of the **FLARB**

Now that I have gone through an overview of how a game is developed, we will create a simple game in this chapter: Attack of the FLARB. This is a mobile version of a really bad arcade action game I created as a Java applet back in 1996. I am even using the same graphics I created for that fine classic of web gaming. This is not going to turn any heads at the next Electronic Entertainment Exposition, but at least it is a simple enough game to provide as an example of a completely functional MIDlet that brings together some of the lessons learned in previous chapters. The source for this project is found in the chap12 folder in the companion files.

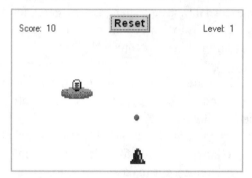

Figure 12-1: The original "classic," Attack of the FLARB, as a Java applet in 1996

In Attack of the FLARB you move the ship at the bottom of the screen (known as the GULLET-1) and fire projectiles up at the invading Flarb ship. The Flarb spacecraft travels across the screen from the left to the right, descending down a level when it reaches the edge and beginning back on the left side of the screen. When a bullet collides with the ship, the Flarb starts again at the top and descends at a faster pace. If the Flarb reaches the bottom of the screen, the game is over. Their death grip on planet Earth is complete! Eventually, the relentless pace of the advancing Flarb will make success impossible and humanity will die. But such is our lot in life. Hey, maybe Attack of the FLARB is actually some kind of existential metaphor for life. Well, perhaps not. Either way, it is an undeniably cheesy attempt at some late-'70s gameplay on a mobile phone.

Note   No, Flarb isn't my name spelled backward.

As I have said, this game is not a prime example of quality; however, it exhibits a few of the design principles illustrated previously. All gameplay is controlled by the directional pad, therefore all you really need is your thumb. The actual game is an exceedingly simple arcade challenge that lends itself to short bursts of play. However, the saving of the high score gives the player a long-term goal in trying to beat her personal best.

The Elements of the Code

This game uses various concepts discussed previously, including Sprite graphics, MIDI music, GUI classes, user input, and Record-Store usage. Here we do a little Sprite collision, as well as deal with the prospect of having the MIDlet suspended by a phone call and properly resumed. Although the code was developed using the DefaultColorPhone profile, it takes the dimensions of the screen into account, so it should work on just about any profile. Without further ado, let's start looking at the source file.

The Constants

Like some of the other examples in this book, we use a few interfaces to hold constants used throughout the code. This is so we can easily modify these attributes to tweak gameplay, layout, and other aspects.

Listing 12-1: Our interfaces

```
interface ImageNumbers
{
    public static final int IMG_SHIP = 0;
    public static final int IMG_FLARB = 1;
    public static final int IMG_BULLET = 2;
    public static final int NUM_IMAGES = 3;
}

interface Constants
{
    public static final int ANIM_PERIOD = 50;
```

```
public static final int START_SPEED = 5;
public static final int PLAYER_SPEED = 10;
public static final int BULLET_SPEED = 4;
public static final int FLARB_POINTS = 10;

public static final int START_Y = 20;

public static final int MENU_START = 0;
public static final int MENU_SCORES = 1;
public static final int MENU_EXIT = 2;

public static final int START_LIVES = 3;

public static final int GAME_MODE_NONE = 0;
public static final int GAME_MODE_PLAY = 1;
public static final int GAME_MODE_MAINMENU = 2;
public static final int GAME_MODE_SCORES = 3;
public static final int GAME_MODE_OVER = 4;
}
```

The first interface, ImageNumbers, is used to index into our array of PNGs when loading up and creating Sprites. We also use the NUM_IMAGES member to determine how large we want to make our Image array. The Constants interface has a lot of useful values for tweaking the gameplay as well as the layout of the screen. We also have some constants used for the List control as well as game mode definitions.

The RecordComparator

Next up is our extension of RecordComparator, ScoreCompare. This is used to enumerate the records in the high score RecordStore to display in descending order. If you look closely, you'll see the comparison is the opposite of the one we used in our previous RecordStore example.

Listing 12-2: The RecordComparator

```
class ScoreCompare implements RecordComparator
{
    public int compare(byte[] rec1, byte[] rec2)
    {
        //get the score out of the record
        String rec1String = new String(rec1);
        String rec2String = new String(rec2);
```

```
int score1 = Integer.parseInt(rec1String);
int score2 = Integer.parseInt(rec2String);

if (score1 > score2)
    return(PRECEDES);
else if (score1 < score2)
    return(FOLLOWS);
else
    return(EQUIVALENT);
    }
}
```

Here we simply convert the data in the record entries to integers and see which one is bigger. It's that easy.

The TimerTask

Next, we have our HeartbeatTask, an extension of TimerTask, which should also look familiar to you:

Listing 12-3: The HeartbeatTask

```
class HeartbeatTask extends TimerTask implements Constants
{
    private AttackOfTheFlarb app;

    public HeartbeatTask(AttackOfTheFlarb attackOfTheFlarb)
    {
        app = attackOfTheFlarb;
    }

    public void run()
    {
        if (app.gameMode == GAME_MODE_PLAY)
            app.update();
    }
}
```

Here we have a constructor that takes a reference to our MIDlet class itself so that it can call the update function inside the MIDlet every time the task is scheduled. If you look in our run method, you'll see that we only call the MIDlet's update member if the game is in the GAME_MODE_PLAY state. This is the only state of the game that requires a continuously executing method. The update method in the MIDlet is what does all the heavy lifting. This class merely serves to trigger it off.

The GameCanvas Extension

Our GameCanvas extended class, AttackOfTheFlarbCanvas, is also fairly simple. Because of MIDP's weird architecture, the Canvas is responsible for catching the key events. So we have some convoluted plumbing here that processes the keys inside the Canvas and then calls methods inside the MIDlet to do additional game processing. This method is called before the MIDlet actually goes through the rest of its game logic — effectively moving the ship according to the player's input before doing any AI, collision, or other tasks. Also, although totally unnecessary for the emulator and most modern MIDP devices, we have double buffered this Canvas to illustrate the concept. After the Image array and reference to the MIDlet class, you have the following members:

```
//image and graphics context for double buffering
private Image backBuffer_ = Image.createImage(getWidth(), getHeight());
private Graphics backGraphics_ = backBuffer_.getGraphics();
```

The first member, backBuffer_, is our Image that we will draw to. This Image will then be copied to the Canvas' Graphics context. This is the essence of double buffering — we don't update the screen until we are done drawing everything. This will do much to eliminate flicker on devices that don't have double buffering built in. However, in the case of the emulator, you won't notice anything. We'll show this process in detail when we look at the paint method.

The Constructor

The constructor for the GameCanvas is pretty straightforward. It loads up the PNGs, and that's about it.

Listing 12-4: The Canvas

```
public AttackOfTheFlarbCanvas(boolean supressKeyEvents)
    {
        //this must be called
        super(supressKeyEvents);

        try
        {
            //create and fill our image array
            imageArray = new Image[NUM_IMAGES];
```

```
        imageArray[IMG_SHIP]    = Image.createImage("/ship.png");
        imageArray[IMG_FLARB]   = Image.createImage("/flarb.png");
        imageArray[IMG_BULLET]  = Image.createImage("/shot.png");
    }
    catch (IOException e)
    {
        System.err.println("Failed loading images!!! " + e);
    }
}
```

Note that we have to call the constructor for the parent class via a call to super. If you don't do this, the code won't compile properly. Next up, in the try/catch block, we create our array of Images and then load up each one.

The Paint Method

The paint method is where we see double buffering in action. Notice that the Graphics object gets passed in as the g argument, but we do all of our drawing operations on backGraphics_, which is our off-screen buffer's Graphics object. First, we clear the screen with a call to fillRect, then draw the score at the top of the screen. Next, we call the LayerManager's paint method from inside the MIDlet class to draw all the Sprites. If we are in the game over state, we also draw the "Game Over" message in the center of the screen. Finally, you see where we use drawImage to draw the off-screen image, backBuffer_, to the Graphics object passed to this method. This performs the final act of double buffering, copying the back buffer to the front. It's easy to convert this back to single buffering; just replace all references of backGraphics_ with g, and get rid of the final drawImage call.

Listing 12-5: The paint method

```
public void paint(Graphics g)
    {
        //clear screen
        backGraphics_.setColor(255, 255, 255);
        backGraphics_.fillRect(0, 0, getWidth(), getHeight());

        //draw the score
        backGraphics_.setColor(0, 0, 0);
        backGraphics_.drawString("Score: " + app.score, 0, 0, Graphics.TOP |
            Graphics.LEFT);
```

```
//use the layer manager to paint all the layers
app.layerMgr.paint(backGraphics_, 0, 0);

//if we are in the game over state...say so!
if (app.gameMode == GAME_MODE_OVER)
{
    backGraphics_.setColor(0, 0, 0);
    backGraphics_.drawString("GAME OVER", getHeight() / 2, getWidth()
            / 2, Graphics.HCENTER | Graphics.TOP);
}

//paint the back buffer to the screen
g.drawImage(backBuffer_, 0, 0, Graphics.TOP | Graphics.LEFT);
}
```

As noted earlier in this book, double buffering isn't necessary on a lot of hardware. You can detect whether the device has automatic double buffering via the Canvas method, isDoubleBuffered. Also, double buffering may incur a performance penalty as you have to do a full-screen bitmap copy at the end of the process.

The Update Method

Here's where we act upon user input from inside the Game-Canvas. This method gets called in the MIDlet's update method that is called from our TimerTask at regular intervals.

Listing 12-6: Updating the game

```
public void update()
{
    //poll the key state
    int keyState = getKeyStates();

    if ((keyState & LEFT_PRESSED) != 0)
    {
        app.playerSprite.move(-PLAYER_SPEED, 0);

        if (app.playerSprite.getX() < 0)
            app.playerSprite.setPosition(0, app.playerSprite.getY());
    }

    if ((keyState & RIGHT_PRESSED) != 0)
    {
        app.playerSprite.move(PLAYER_SPEED, 0);

        if ((app.playerSprite.getX() + app.playerSprite.getWidth()) > getWidth())
```

```
            app.playerSprite.setPosition(getWidth() - app.playerSprite.getWidth(),
                app.playerSprite.getY());
    }

    if ((keyState & FIRE_PRESSED) != 0)
    {
        app.fireBullet();
    }
}
```

This method first gets the keyState to see which buttons are being held. We then use the predefined bit-flag fields to see which keys are being pressed. For the left and right buttons we move the player Sprite and perform checks against the sides of the screen to make sure it doesn't move off. If fire is pressed, we call the fireBullet method inside the MIDlet class to launch a missile if one isn't already in play.

The MIDlet Class

Now to the real meat of the game. The class begins with a bunch of public and private member declarations, most of which are self-explanatory.

Listing 12-7: The MIDlet class' declarations

```
boolean firstTime;

public Sprite playerSprite;
public Sprite flarbSprite;
public Sprite bulletSprite;

public LayerManager layerMgr;

public int score;
public int gameMode;
public int oldGameMode;

private Timer timer_;
private AttackOfTheFlarbCanvas canvas_;
private Display display_;
private HeartbeatTask heartTask_;

private List list_;
private Form form_;
```

```
private Command exitCommand_;
private Command backCommand_;
private Command selectCommand_;
private Command pauseCommand_;
private Command resumeCommand_;
private Command quitCommand_;
private Command continueCommand_;

private int lives_;
private int moveSpeed_;
private int level_;

private boolean suspended_;
private boolean paused_;
private boolean bulletInPlay_;

private Player player_;
```

First, we have all of our Sprites. These will be used to display the objects on the screen as well as perform collision tests. Next up we have the LayerManager that will be used to draw our Sprites. We then have the integer to store our current score, as well as two integers that store the current and previous game mode. Following this are our Timer, GameCanvas, Display, and TimerTask classes, which should all be familiar to you. We also have a List and a Form, which will be used to display the main menu and high score table respectively. Next up is a bunch of Command objects used for the soft button interface, as well as integers that track the number of lives left, the movement speed of the enemy ship, and the current play level. We also have three Booleans that track whether the game is suspended, paused, or a bullet is on the screen. We need to track the bullet status because the game only allows a single bullet on the screen at one time. Finally, we have a Player object that will be used to play the background tune.

The Constructor

Because the MIDlet environment isn't necessarily properly initialized when the constructor is called, we try to include only the creation of objects that don't deal with external system resources such as the Display.

Listing 12-8: The constructor

```
public AttackOfTheFlarb()
{
    firstTime = true;

    gameMode = GAME_MODE_NONE;
    oldGameMode = GAME_MODE_NONE;

    //construct commands
    exitCommand_    = new Command("EXIT", Command.EXIT, 1);
    backCommand_    = new Command("BACK", Command.EXIT, 1);
    selectCommand_  = new Command("SELECT", Command.OK, 1);
    pauseCommand_   = new Command("PAUSE", Command.OK, 1);
    resumeCommand_  = new Command("RESUME", Command.OK, 1);
    quitCommand_    = new Command("QUIT", Command.EXIT, 1);
    continueCommand_ = new Command("CONTINUE", Command.OK, 1);

    //initialize the record store
    try
    {
        RecordStore recordStore = RecordStore.openRecordStore("scores", true);

        if (recordStore.getNumRecords() == 0)
        {
            //initialize scores to 0
            String zero = "0";

            for (int i = 0; i < 3; i++)
            {
                recordStore.addRecord(zero.getBytes(), 0, zero.length());
            }
        }

        recordStore.closeRecordStore();
    }
    catch (RecordStoreException e)
    {
        e.printStackTrace();
    }

    timer_ = new Timer();
    heartTask_ = new HeartbeatTask(this);
    timer_.schedule(heartTask_, 0, ANIM_PERIOD);
}
```

The first thing we do in the constructor is set our firstTime_ Boolean to true. This way when we get into startApp we can do the initial processing required there and set it to false for subsequent calls. Next, we initialize the game mode members as well as construct all of our Command objects. We also create the RecordStore if it doesn't exist and fill it with blank entries. Finally, we create our TimerTask and get it going. The TimerTask won't do any real processing until we are actually playing the game, so don't worry about it running continuously in the background.

Starting the MIDlet

The startApp method can be called both after MIDlet creation and if the MIDlet is resumed after being suspended by an incoming phone call, SMS message, etc. For this reason we use the firstTime_ Boolean to distinguish between these two instances in the method.

Listing 12-9: The startApp method

```
public void startApp() throws MIDletStateChangeException
{
    if (firstTime)
    {
        display_ = Display.getDisplay(this);
        canvas_ = new AttackOfTheFlarbCanvas(true);
        canvas_.app = this;

        //create the layer manager
        layerMgr = new LayerManager();

        //create sprites
        playerSprite = new Sprite(canvas_.imageArray[IMG_SHIP]);
        flarbSprite = new Sprite(canvas_.imageArray[IMG_FLARB]);
        bulletSprite = new Sprite(canvas_.imageArray[IMG_BULLET]);

        firstTime = false;

        //set up our player object
        InputStream is;

        is = getClass().getResourceAsStream("/tune.midi");

        try
        {
            if (is != null)
            {
                player_ = Manager.createPlayer(is, "audio/midi");
                player_.setLoopCount(-1);
```

```
        }
    }
    catch (IOException e)
    {
        System.err.println("Failed loading MIDI!!! " + e);
    }
    catch (MediaException e)
    {
        System.err.println("Failed playing MIDI!!! " + e);
    }

    setGameMode(GAME_MODE_MAINMENU);
    }

    suspended_ = false;
}
```

Here we finally get the Display since it should be properly initialized by now. If we got it inside the constructor, the result would be unreliable. On some phones it may be a valid Display object, while on others it wouldn't, so we might as well play it safe. The rest of this method is fairly mundane as we create all of our objects including the game's Sprites. Before putting the game into the Main Menu mode, we also load a MIDI file and create a Player for it. This will be used for our background gameplay music loop.

Pause and Destruction

Our mandatory pauseApp method is very simple.

Listing 12-10: The pauseApp method

```
public void pauseApp()
{
    suspended_ = true;
}
```

We set the suspended_ member so the thread doesn't do any execution while the game is suspended by an incoming call or other non-game event.

Almost not worth mentioning is our destroyApp method, which does pretty much nothing.

Listing 12-11: The destroyApp method

```
public void destroyApp(boolean unconditional)
{
}
```

Here we just trust that Java's garbage collector will clean everything up for us.

Command Listening

Our obligatory commandAction method has the standard Soft Button and List selection processing.

Listing 12-12: The commandAction method

```
public void commandAction(Command c, Displayable s)
{
    if (c == pauseCommand_)
    {
        paused_ = true;
        pauseCanvas();

    }
    else if (c == resumeCommand_)
    {
        paused_ = false;
        unPauseCanvas();
    }
    else if (c == exitCommand_)
    {
        destroyApp(false);
        notifyDestroyed();
    }
    else if (c == backCommand_)
    {
        setGameMode(GAME_MODE_MAINMENU);
    }
    else if (c == quitCommand_)
    {
        cleanUpGame();
        setGameMode(GAME_MODE_MAINMENU);
    }
    else if (c == continueCommand_)
    {
        setGameMode(GAME_MODE_MAINMENU);
    }
    else if ( (c == List.SELECT_COMMAND) ||
            (c == selectCommand_) )
```

```
        {
            switch(list_.getSelectedIndex())
            {
                case MENU_START:
                setGameMode(GAME_MODE_PLAY);
                break;

                case MENU_SCORES:
                setGameMode(GAME_MODE_SCORES);
                break;

                case MENU_EXIT:
                destroyApp(false);
                notifyDestroyed();
                break;

            }
        }
}
```

Here we exit the MIDlet itself on some events, pause and resume the game on others, and set the current game mode to different states depending upon list selections.

It's worth looking into the pauseCanvas and unPauseCanvas methods before we go on.

Listing 12-13: Managing our Command objects

```
public void pauseCanvas()
{
    canvas_.removeCommand(quitCommand_);
    canvas_.removeCommand(pauseCommand_);
    canvas_.removeCommand(resumeCommand_);

    canvas_.addCommand(quitCommand_);
    canvas_.addCommand(resumeCommand_);
}

public void unPauseCanvas()
{
    canvas_.removeCommand(quitCommand_);
    canvas_.removeCommand(pauseCommand_);
    canvas_.removeCommand(resumeCommand_);

    canvas_.addCommand(quitCommand_);
    canvas_.addCommand(pauseCommand_);
}
```

Why are we doing all of this command juggling? Because we want to change the "Pause" soft button to be "Resume" once the game is paused. The problem is, we can't pick individual commands and swap them out. Instead, we need to remove all of the Commands on the Canvas and replace them with new ones. Although the priority and command types can govern where it appears on the Canvas, we are really relying on addCommand to push the buttons to the left every time one is added. Therefore, if we want Resume to appear on the right soft button, we need to add it last.

Game Modes

Another method called often in commandAction is setGameMode. This is used to switch the MIDlet between different states, such as gameplay and displaying the main menu.

Listing 12-14: Game mode management

```
public void setGameMode(int newGameMode)
{
    oldGameMode = gameMode;
    gameMode = newGameMode;

    if (oldGameMode == GAME_MODE_NONE)
        oldGameMode = gameMode;

    switch (gameMode)
    {
        case GAME_MODE_PLAY:
        initializeGame();

        try
        {
            player_.start();
        }
        catch (MediaException e)
        {
            System.err.println("Failed playing MIDI!!! " + e);
        }
        break;

        case GAME_MODE_MAINMENU:
        cleanUpGame();
        buildMainMenu();

        try
```

```
    {
        player_.stop();
    }
    catch (MediaException e)
    {
        System.err.println("Failed stopping MIDI!!! " + e);
    }
    break;

    case GAME_MODE_SCORES:
    buildForm();
    break;

    case GAME_MODE_OVER:
    checkHighScore(score);
    modifyGameOverCanvas();
    break;
    }
}
```

First, we assign the gameMode to be a new value and store off the old one. Then we get into the switch statement that performs different actions depending on what mode is currently being set. For instance, if we are setting the mode to GAME_MODE_PLAY, we are starting a new game. Thus we call initializeGame, which sets up the initial gameplay situation.

Listing 12-15: Initializing the game

```
public void initializeGame()
{
    score = 0;
    lives_ = START_LIVES;
    bulletInPlay_ = false;
    moveSpeed_ = START_SPEED;
    level_ = 0;
    paused_ = false;

    list_ = null;

    //initialize sprite positions
    playerSprite.setPosition((canvas_.getWidth() / 2) - (playerSprite.getWidth() / 2) ,
            canvas_.getHeight() - playerSprite.getHeight());
    flarbSprite.setPosition(-flarbSprite.getWidth() , START_Y);

    //add to the layer manager
    layerMgr.append(playerSprite);
    layerMgr.append(flarbSprite);
```

```
canvas_.addCommand(quitCommand_);
canvas_.addCommand(pauseCommand_);

display_.setCurrent(canvas_);
canvas_.setCommandListener(this);

canvas_.repaint();
canvas_.serviceRepaints();
}
```

Here, we clear out the score and initialize the number of lives and speed of the enemy as well as clear out the level member and reset the paused state. We nullify the list_ too; this way the garbage collector can reclaim the main menu class. Then we set up the initial positions of the player and enemy sprites, as well as add them to the LayerManager object. We then add the appropriate commands to our game screen and redraw the whole thing. Note the call to serviceRepaints to ensure that nothing else happens until the screen is drawn.

Getting back to the commandAction code, we see that after we initialize the game, we start the background music loop with our Player object. This Player was initialized in the constructor with a MIDI file streamed from the JAR.

The next case is setting the mode to GAME_MODE_MAIN-MENU. Here, we need to clean up the game resources just in case we are coming back from a game after a game over or manually quitting with the cleanUpGame method:

Listing 12-16: Cleaning up the mess our game makes

```
public void cleanUpGame()
{
    layerMgr.remove(playerSprite);
    layerMgr.remove(flarbSprite);
    layerMgr.remove(bulletSprite);

    canvas_.removeCommand(quitCommand_);
    canvas_.removeCommand(pauseCommand_);
    canvas_.removeCommand(resumeCommand_);
}
```

This method simply removes all the Sprites from the GameCanvas as well as the commands. These are re-added when we start the game again in the previously described initializeGame method.

Following the call to cleanUpGame is buildMainMenu.

Listing 12-17: Building the main menu screen

```
public void buildMainMenu()
{
    list_ = null;   //to help out the garbage collector

    //build the main menu
    list_ = new List("ATTACK OF THE FLARB", List.IMPLICIT);
    list_.insert(MENU_START, "Start Game", null);
    list_.insert(MENU_SCORES, "High Scores", null);
    list_.insert(MENU_EXIT, "Exit", null);

    list_.addCommand(exitCommand_);
    list_.addCommand(selectCommand_);

    display_.setCurrent(list_);
    list_.setCommandListener(this);
}
```

We first null out the list_ just in case an old one is still hanging around. Then, we create a new one and add each element to it. Finally, we set it as the currently displayed Screen and make the MIDlet its commandListener for selection events and soft buttons.

Our buildForm method is called when we set the GAME_MODE_SCORES state.

Listing 12-18: Building the high score form

```
public void buildForm()
{
    form_ = null;
    ScoreCompare scoreCompare = new ScoreCompare();

    //create the form
    form_ = new Form("HIGH SCORES!");

    //create the items
    StringItem stringItem = null;

    try
    {
        RecordStore recordStore = RecordStore.openRecordStore("scores", false);

        if (recordStore != null)
        {
            byte[] recordBytes;
```

```
                String scoreString;
                String nameString;
                RecordEnumeration recordEnumeration = recordStore.enumerateRecords
                        (null, scoreCompare, false);

            if (recordEnumeration != null)
            {
                for (int i = 0; i < recordEnumeration.numRecords(); i++)
                {
                    int recordId = recordEnumeration.nextRecordId();

                    recordBytes = recordStore.getRecord(recordId);
                    scoreString = new String(recordBytes);

                    stringItem = new StringItem(("SCORE: " + (i + 1) + "\n"),
                            scoreString);
                        form_.append(stringItem);
                }

                recordStore.closeRecordStore();
            }
        }
    }
    catch (RecordStoreException e)
    {
        e.printStackTrace();
    }

    form_.addCommand(backCommand_);

    display_.setCurrent(form_);
    form_.setCommandListener(this);
}
```

Here, we create a RecordEnumerator to traverse our high score RecordStore in descending order. We build a Form out of StringItems — one for each score. The layout directives aren't very useful in the emulator, so I put a linefeed at the end to force the next StringItem to be placed on the next row in the Form.

Finally, we deal with the GAME_MODE_OVER state. The first thing we do here is check if we have a high score using the checkHighScore method:

Listing 12-19: Checking for high scores

```
public void checkHighScore(int score)
{
    int scoreCompareVal;
    String scoreString;
    ScoreCompare scoreCompare = new ScoreCompare();
    byte recordBytes[];

    try
    {
        RecordStore recordStore = RecordStore.openRecordStore("scores", true);
        RecordEnumeration recordEnumeration = recordStore.enumerateRecords(null,
                scoreCompare, false);

        if (recordEnumeration != null)
        {
            for (int i = 0; i < recordEnumeration.numRecords(); i++)
            {
                int recordId = recordEnumeration.nextRecordId();

                recordBytes = recordStore.getRecord(recordId);
                scoreString = new String(recordBytes);
                scoreCompareVal = Integer.parseInt(scoreString);

                if (score > scoreCompareVal)
                {
                    int delRecordId = recordId;

                    String outString = Integer.toString(score);

                    if (i != (recordEnumeration.numRecords() - 1))
                    {
                        //we've got to delete the last one and
                        //add a new one
                        for (int x = i; x < recordEnumeration.numRecords(); x++)
                        {
                            if (x == (recordEnumeration.numRecords() - 1))
                            {
                                recordStore.deleteRecord(delRecordId);
                            }
                            else
                                delRecordId = recordEnumeration.nextRecordId();
                        }

                        //now add the new one
                            recordStore.addRecord(outString.getBytes(), 0,
                                    outString.length());
                            recordStore.closeRecordStore();
```

```
                            return;
                        }
                        else
                        {
                            recordStore.setRecord(recordId, outString.getBytes(), 0,
                                    outString.length());
                            recordStore.closeRecordStore();
                            return;
                        }
                    }
                }
            }

        recordStore.closeRecordStore();

    }
    catch (RecordStoreException e)
    {
        e.printStackTrace();
    }
}
```

This rather convoluted function uses a RecordEnumerator to traverse the high score table in descending order. If we find a score that's less than the current one, we then delete the lowest score and append the current one to the RecordStore. If the score in question is the last score in the RecordEnumerator, we just replace it. That's a lot of code for a seemingly simple operation — such is the case with RecordStores.

Updating the Game

Now that we've gotten most of the interface and housekeeping code out of the way, it's time to look at the heart of the MIDlet, update.

Listing 12-20: Updating the game state

```
public void update()
    {
        if ((!suspended_) && (!paused_) && (gameMode != GAME_MODE_OVER))
        {
            canvas_.update();

            updateBullet();

            if (updateFlarb())
```

```
    {
        //game over
        setGameMode(GAME_MODE_OVER);
    }

    if (checkBulletCollision())
    {
        score += (FLARB_POINTS * (1 + level_));
        resetFlarb();

        //remove bullet
        bulletInPlay_ = false;
        layerMgr.remove(bulletSprite);
    }
}

canvas_.repaint();
}
```

First off, we only do any processing if the MIDlet isn't suspended, paused, or in the GAME_MODE_OVER state. Next, we call our GameCanvas' update method, which we described when going over the AttackOfTheFlarbCanvas class. The GameCanvas' update performs the player movement in response to the keys, as well as launching the bullet. While we're on the subject, we might as well take a brief detour and have a look.

Listing 12-21: Bustin' a cap

```
public void fireBullet()
{
    if (!bulletInPlay_)
    {
        bulletInPlay_ = true;

        bulletSprite.setPosition(playerSprite.getX() - (bulletSprite.getWidth() / 2)
                + (playerSprite.getWidth() / 2), playerSprite.getY()
                - bulletSprite.getHeight() - 2);
        layerMgr.append(bulletSprite);
    }
}
```

This method sets the bullet Sprite according to the player's location, and adds it to the LayerManager. This happens only if there isn't another bullet, as indicated by bulletInPlay_, of course.

Now, getting back to our MIDlet's update method, we call updateBullet. This moves the bullet up the screen and checks to see if we've gone off the top of the screen with it.

Listing 12-22: Updating the bullet's movement and state

```
public void updateBullet()
{
    if (bulletInPlay_)
    {
        bulletSprite.setPosition(bulletSprite.getX(), bulletSprite.getY()
            - BULLET_SPEED);

        int bulletY = bulletSprite.getY();

        //the bullet has gone off the top of the screen
        if (bulletY < -bulletSprite.getHeight())
        {
            bulletInPlay_ = false;
            layerMgr.remove(bulletSprite);
        }
    }
}
```

As you can see, we decrease the y coordinate of the bullet by the BULLET_SPEED constant. If the bullet has gone past the top of the screen, we remove it from the LayerManager and notify that no bullet is in play by setting bulletInPlay_ to false.

We then call updateFlarb, which is responsible for moving the enemy ship.

Listing 12-23: Updating the menacing Flarb alien ship

```
public boolean updateFlarb()
{
    flarbSprite.setPosition(flarbSprite.getX() + moveSpeed_, flarbSprite.getY());

    int flarbX = flarbSprite.getX();

    if (flarbX >= canvas_.getWidth())
    {
        flarbSprite.setPosition(-flarbSprite.getWidth() , flarbSprite.getY()
            + flarbSprite.getHeight());

        int flarbY = flarbSprite.getY();

        //we've hit the ground
```

```
        if (flarbY >= (canvas_.getHeight() - flarbSprite.getHeight()))
        {
            return(true);
        }
    }

    return(false);
}
```

This method first sets the Flarb ship's position over to the right by the number of pixels specified in the moveSpeed_ member. We then check if it has gone off the right edge of the screen. If so, we move the Flarb down one row. If the end result of this move down is a collision with the bottom of the screen, we return true to indicate a game over situation; otherwise, we return false. Upon returning from this method call, we set the game mode to GAME_MODE_OVER if there has been a collision with the bottom of the screen.

Nearing the end of this method, we check to see if the bullet has collided with the Flarb ship. This is a simple process of using the Sprite's pixel-accurate collision methods.

Listing 12-24: Checking to see if a Flarb caught a bad one

```
public boolean checkBulletCollision()
{
    if (bulletInPlay_)
    {
        if (bulletSprite.collidesWith(flarbSprite, true))
        {
            return(true);
        }
    }

    return false;
}
```

If there is a bullet in play, we use collidesWidth to see if the bullet has collided with the Flarb Sprite. If so, we return true; otherwise, we return false. Once this method has returned, we add to the score in the update method, move the Flarb ship back up to the top of the screen, and increase his speed. To move the Flarb back, we use the resetFlarb method.

Listing 12-25: Resetting the Flarb invasion force

```
public void resetFlarb()
{
    ++level_;

    flarbSprite.setPosition(-flarbSprite.getWidth() , START_Y);
    moveSpeed_ += 2;
}
```

This simple method increases the current level, moves the Flarb Sprite back to its starting position, and boosts the movement speed by two pixels per frame. The end result is a faster, deadlier Flarb ship. Every time you destroy the Flarb, the relentless onslaught continues. Resistance is futile.

Figure 12-2: The same lousy Flarb game, new platform: J2ME

Running on Hardware

Now that you have a completed game up and running, how do you test this on a phone? Good question. The fact is, there is no one way to do it. It may sound like a cop-out, but you really have to check your developer documentation for the target handset to see how this is done. In many cases, the handset manufacturer will have a special application loader for developers. These application loaders, such as Motorola's iDEN Java Application Loader, may use a cable that connects to your PC's serial or USB port to the phone. Others, such as Nokia's Developer Suite or Sony Ericsson's loader tools, use Bluetooth or IrDA to upload JARs to the handset. It is also possible to use a web server to deploy MIDlets for over-the-air provisioning. See Chapter 16, "MIDlet Distribution," for more information on how this is done.

One thing you must note is that some handsets are very picky about the contents of the JAD file. For instance, some Motorola handsets don't like it when there are letters in the version number (e.g., "1.0A"). Some other handsets don't like spaces in certain fields or have further restrictions on the kinds of characters you can use in the JAD. The problem is, the vast majority of loader tools or handset error messages won't tell you specifically what's wrong with the JAD and instead will simply tell you there has been an "installation error" or "application error" when you try to upload or install a MIDlet on your device. A good place to keep track of these handset-specific issues is on the MicroDevNet at www.microdevnet.com. Aside from being an excellent resource of articles on J2ME development, the site also has numerous PDF files that detail the capabilities of many popular J2ME handsets. These documents may prove invaluable when catering your build to a specific device.

Note   In addition to various JAD requirements, many handsets have strict JAR size restrictions. For instance, on Nokia Series 40 devices, the JAR cannot exceed 64K. Some developers have gotten around these limitations by downloading additional content once the MIDlet has started. When using this technique, you can also run into RecordStore space restrictions.

In short, your best bet is to check the device manufacturer's development site. Table 12-1 lists a few of the popular sites to get you started.

Table 12-1: Manufacturer and carrier-specific developer sites

Name	Web site
Sony Ericsson	www.sonyericsson.com/developer
Nokia	forum.nokia.com
Siemens	www.siemens-mobile.com/developer
Motorola	www.motocoder.com
Motorola/iDEN	www.idendev.com
SprintPCS	developer.sprintpcs.com

The Sony Ericsson Device Explorer

For the sake of completeness, I'll give an example of one OEM's application loader. In this case, we'll look at the Sony Ericsson Device Explorer. This handy tool is available with Sony Ericsson's own J2ME SDK for their line of devices, which can be freely downloaded from their web site.

Connecting to the Phone

Sony Ericsson devices usually have at least three flavors of connections: serial, IrDA, and Bluetooth. In this case, I have attached an IrDA communicator to one of my host PC's USB ports. In order to get the device to communicate using IrDA, you need to turn on this feature in the phone's own menu. Every handset may have different settings, but on my K700 this is found in Connectivity/Infrared Port. Under this menu, you have three options: On, Off, and 10 Minutes. Click On, and your handset is ready to communicate.

The IR port on the K700 is the black strip on the top of the device. Place this end facing your IR device attached to the host PC, and Windows should detect another device nearby. If not, double-check the handset and make sure you have your IrDA transmitter installed correctly on your PC.

Using Device Explorer

Now that the phone is set up and connected, start the Sony Ericsson Device Explorer application. You should see a window that looks like Figure 12-3. After starting the application, the Device Explorer will attempt to connect to the handset. You should see a small dialog pop up in the corner like in Figure 12-4.

Now, all you need to do is click **File ▸ Install** and you will be brought to a dialog like Figure 12-5. Here you can select a JAD or JAR to upload to the device. Click **Install**, and the file will be sent to the target device. After a successful upload, dismiss the dialog and you should see a new folder in your Device Explorer window. It's really that simple.

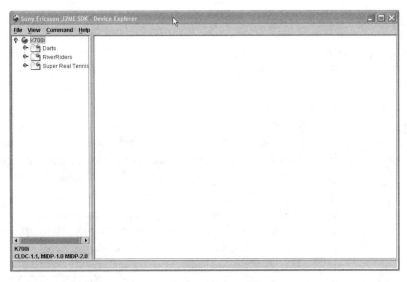

Figure 12-3: The Sony Ericsson Device Explorer in action

Figure 12-4: Connecting to the handset

Figure 12-5: Uploading the JAR

Debugging on Hardware

You may find that when you try to run your MIDlets on different devices they will not work as they do in the emulator. In fact, I can almost guarantee this. The emulator bears almost no resemblance to the way most J2ME devices perform in the wild. Thus, there is no substitute for running your code on a real device. But how exactly do you debug code that runs on a handset?

This is a very good question. And as with the previous section, it really depends on the manufacturer. The best-case situation is some Sony Ericsson phones, such as the Z1010, which can work with Borland JBuilder's debugger and allow you to step trace your code as it runs on the actual handset. Unfortunately, this is a rare exception.

In other cases, such as with some Motorola iDEN handsets, you can issue an AT command to the handset with a terminal program and read the output from your println commands as well as errors and exceptions. However, many handsets don't have even this feature. Thus you're back to stone-age debugging techniques such as ringing the phone when you get into a suspect function, or just compiling the code and praying that it works without a hitch. The fact is, J2ME hardware debugging is a nightmare.

Conclusion

So, now you have a completed game. Granted, this is a really basic MIDlet. Depending on the phone, you may find that it is not optimized for real handset use. We will discuss optimizations and running MIDlets on hardware in a later chapter.

Also, the game itself is very simple. You can use this framework to add any game enhancements you want. Try adding different enemies, weapons, and power-ups. The possibilities are endless. I hope that the end result of this chapter is a simple game framework that gives you an extremely basic applet structure to use for most any game.

You will find that this not only barely scratches the surface of MIDP 2.0 game programming, but also hardly touches on game programming in general. I suggest reading books on general game development and attempting to apply them to MIDP 2.0. For instance, elements of AI, graphics techniques, collision, and other basic game programming techniques are directly applicable to MIDP 2.0 game programming. You just have to make sure you can apply these techniques in an efficient and compact manner.

Chapter 13

Wireless Networking with HTTP

Introduction

Okay, we've gone through graphics, sound, GUI, and plenty of other facets of game programming that aren't necessarily unique to mobile devices. Since MIDP 2.0 is primarily designed for cell phones, we have one unique characteristic: Wherever we have phone service, we have a wireless Internet connection. This chapter will explain the basics of wireless transmission technology and show you how to use the HTTP protocol to connect to the Internet. Most of the hard technical facts in this chapter come from Andy Dornan's absolutely excellent book, *The Essential Guide to Wireless Communications Applications* (Prentice Hall, ISBN 0-13-031716-0). I give this book my absolute highest recommendation if you are really interested in the nuts and bolts of wireless networks and technology.

The Wireless Network

When reading about wireless phone networks you quickly become awash with strange acronyms and unfamiliar jargon. GSM, CDMA, 1XRTT, and other scary-looking terms leap from the page. Yes, there is a wide variety of different standards and technologies mobile phones use for communication. The good thing is, you really do not need to know much about them. It doesn't hurt to be familiar with the underlying technologies behind the scenes though.

Bandwidth

Bandwidth is a term frequently used to determine the speed of an Internet connection; or perhaps more specifically, the amount of data your connection can accommodate. The bandwidth refers to the capacity of the Internet connection, or how "fat" the "pipe" that carries your data is. For instance, if you have a cable modem, your bandwidth is much larger than that of an ordinary dial-up modem connection. More data can reach your system per second via cable than dial-up.

There typically are two different bandwidth figures: one that measures your transfer capacity for sending information (uplink) and another for receiving information (downlink). In the case of the average cable modem, downlink bandwidth usually ranges somewhere between 1 and 3 megabits per second. The uplink bandwidth usually ranges somewhere from 500 kilobits to 2.5 megabits per second.

To give you a little perspective, a megabit is 2^{20}, or 1048576, bits. A byte is 8 bits. There are 1024 bytes in a kilobyte. Therefore one megabit is equal to 128 kilobytes. If you compare these figures to a typical local area network that uses 10- or 100-megabit hardware, you can see that these figures are significant but have a way to go until they reach the responsiveness we are used to from using our own LANs.

Frequencies

In the case of digital wireless phone networks, the bandwidth usually refers to the range of radio frequencies on which the signals travel. This range of frequencies is often referred to as spectrum. The wider the frequency range, the more data the signals can carry. Well, sort of.

The range of frequencies available to wireless phone carriers depends on the country in which they are operating. Governmental organizations such as the Federal Communications Commission (FCC) in the United States or the International Telecommunication Union (ITU) in Europe determine which frequency ranges are available to private industry. They then determine how to auction, sell, or otherwise give away chunks of this spectrum to different private interests. This is one of the reasons why phones bought in the United States usually don't work on European networks. The frequency range used for many mobile phones in Europe is reserved in the United States for military use. Therefore, even if an American mobile phone network uses the same transmission technology as European carriers, the phones that the American carrier uses will most likely remain incompatible with European systems as it communicates on an entirely different frequency range. There are global phones that are able to operate on multiple frequencies as well as satellite systems to address this problem.

Multiplexing

Now that a carrier has a chunk of spectrum to play with, which technologies it uses to deploy mobile phone service determines how many customers it can support and what kinds of data transfer speeds users can expect. This is where all the acronyms come in.

The first principle is that most mobile phone networks are indeed cellular. Although the term "cellular" is typically used in reference to old analog networks, even new digital networks use cell architecture to provide service. What this means is a wireless carrier has a series of base stations, or cells, which receive transmissions from customers inside a certain radius. There are a number of different types of cells that vary in the area of coverage they provide. The way these cells communicate with the customers and the network as a whole vary depending on the type of technology used, yet the basic concept remains the same.

The number of customers each cell can serve is largely dependent on the type of multiplexing technology the carrier uses. Multiplexing slices up the wireless spectrum a carrier owns into "sub-bands" to address multiple customers. Each of these sub-bands can then be accessed by multiple users. The two major competing multiplexing techniques are Time Division Multiple Access (TDMA) and Code Division Multiple Access (CDMA).

TDMA multiplexes a sub-band so that up to three users share the same frequency. It does this by allowing each user a small amount of time to use the sub-band. Once the user's time is up, control is released and another user can access the same sub-band. These time slice interruptions are so small that they are imperceptible to the user. Voice conversations continue seamlessly despite all of these tiny interruptions.

CDMA is what is called a spread-spectrum system. That is, a CDMA phone sends the same signal on multiple sub-bands. However, each signal is encoded differently. The individual cell can pick out which signal is encoded for it to understand. The San Diego-based telecommunications giant QUALCOMM is the inventor and holder of the patents to CDMA. There are various flavors of CDMA (such as W-CDMA) that feature different proportions of QUALCOMM-patented technology.

Current Digital Wireless Phone Services

Digital wireless phone services are typically referred to as Personal Communication Services, or PCS. These PCS services are based upon TDMA or CDMA technology. The big three these days are Global System for Mobile Communications (GSM), General Packet Radio Service (GPRS), and cdmaOne.

GSM has been in use throughout Europe for quite some time. This is because the governments in Europe made it a standard early on. The United States took a free-market approach and allowed the market to find its own standard, with the decision ultimately being chosen by customers' wallets. GSM is based on

TDMA technology and allows up to 14.4 kilobits per second transfer rates for data traffic in modern implementations.

The cdmaOne standard is, as you can probably guess, based on QUALCOMM's CDMA technology. Transmission speeds on cdmaOne can reach 14.4 kilobits per second. This is comparable to GSM and most GPRS systems in action today.

GPRS is an upgrade to existing GSM networks and can yield data rates from 14.4 kilobits per second up to 115.2 kilobits per second on the upstream or downstream connection. The actual bit rates depend on the type of GPRS network implemented and the higher speeds are rather uncommon. Generally, the upstream connection is the same or higher in speed than the downstream link.

The major change in GPRS is the fact that it is a packet-switched network. Both GSM and cdmaOne are circuit-switched. The term "circuit-switched" means that each user maintains an open communications stream, using resources even when there is no data transferring. Packet-switched networks send voice and data in little chunks, called packets. This is how the Internet works via the TCP/IP protocol. What this means is if there is a period of silence in a conversation, or no data being sent through a socket, there are no packets being transmitted. This allows many more users to use the same sub-bands since they can take advantage of gaps in the packet flow. Because of the fact that both voice and data are just packets, more advanced GPRS implementations promise the ability to make voice calls while simultaneously maintaining a data connection. This means you can surf the web and talk simultaneously.

Packet switching also means that carriers can charge data access by the packet instead of the minute. With existing circuit-switched networks you are charged by time. If you stare at the same WAP page for an hour, you get charged for an hour's worth of access. With a packet-switched system you are only charged for the kilobytes downloaded in the transmission of that WAP page. This also has far-reaching implications for game developers as the amount of data you are transferring in multiplayer games affects the consumer's billing.

The Future of Wireless: 3G

All of the digital wireless systems mentioned in the previous section are known as second generation, or 2G, systems. This is in contrast to first generation, or 1G, which is composed of the stone-age analog systems of the '80s and early '90s. As for current 2G systems, GPRS is actually commonly referred to as 2.5G. Because of its ability to potentially deliver higher speed access, it is sort of in limbo between the slower second generation networks of today and the third generation, or 3G, networks of the future.

3G networks are supposed to give the average user 144 kilobits per second transfer rates at minimum levels of service. They can provide up to 2 megabits per second under optimal conditions. Naturally, there are a number of different competing 3G standards. Of course, QUALCOMM has their own standard, CDMA2000, which is a clear upgrade path for their current cdmaOne carriers.

CDMA2000 has three phases of deployment. In the first phase, you get the baseline 144 kilobits per second transfer rate as required by the basic 3G definition. By the time you get to the third phase of CDMA2000 implementation, you have up to 2 megabits per second and simultaneous voice and data transfers. The three phases of CDMA2000 installation provide existing cdmaOne carriers with a simple and inexpensive upgrade path to 3G.

Other competing standards include Enhanced Data for Global Evolution (EDGE). This is an upgrade path for existing GSM carriers to provide 3G services with up to 384 kilobits per second transfer rates. EDGE is a TDMA-based system that is noted for its conservative use of bandwidth. Most likely, EDGE is the path that current GSM and GPRS carriers will go when moving into 3G. AT&T Wireless has made several announcements to this effect.

Wideband Code Division Multiple Access (W-CDMA) is another 3G CDMA scheme that can provide up to 4 megabits per second speeds using a wider frequency band. QUALCOMM has developed a fourth phase of CDMA2000 that can accommodate these higher speeds using the same small amount of bandwidth it already consumes.

Japan has seen one of the earliest rollouts of W-CDMA technology: the Japanese 3G standard from the creator of the amazingly successful iMode service, NTT DoCoMo. Freedom of Mobility multimedia Access (FOMA) from NTT DoCoMo is currently providing users with up to 384 kilobits per second transfer speeds with up to 2 megabits promised in the future. Customers have had many complaints of spotty service, defective handsets, and expensive fees, not to mention the handset recalls and other issues that have done much to tarnish NTT DoCoMo's sterling reputation in Japan. It is impressive that NTT DoCoMo has managed to install a small yet growing 3G network way ahead of the competition. Naturally, there are a number of other 3G standards, but a description of all of them is beyond the scope of this book.

Although 3G networks appear to be the wave of the future, it seems the current trend in the United States is to go with 2.5G solutions — even if many of them are dubbed "3G." This includes rollouts of CDMA2000 phase 1 or enhanced GPRS networks. Spectrum is scarce as well as investment capital these days, so carriers are being far more conservative with their technology plans as opposed to the glory days of the dot com boom. Considering the diminutive size of most game applets and the meager capabilities of current handsets, 384 kilobits per second is more than enough to download a simple 50-kilobyte sized game applet. Until full 3G we may not get Dick Tracy-style video conferencing and other perks, but the mobile gaming industry can survive with a middle-of-the-road solution for now.

Note Many European wireless phone carriers have been saddled with massive amounts of debt because of the huge fees paid to buy 3G spectrum. Revenue generated from games and other data services are being looked to as a way to make their money back.

So Who Cares?

You may be trying to wrap your brain around that whirlwind tour of buzzwords and raw statistics. Because MIDP handsets are available from a wide variety of carriers all over the planet, there's a good chance that your target handset could be running on GPRS, CDMA, or even EDGE or W-CDMA networks. As a programmer, this doesn't matter much since the programmer is isolated from the nuts and bolts via MIDP 2.0's Generic Connection Framework. The only relevant information may be the latency and bandwidth afforded by the given network technology. These features must be taken into account when deciding what kinds of applications you want to develop and how they will use the network. Obviously, on 3G systems you will have way more freedom to throw large chunks of data around — but will your users want to pay for it?

Hypertext Transfer Protocol

Before we get into the nitty-gritty of socket programming, we'll dip our toe into the pool of networking by using the simple HTTP protocol to download information off the Internet. Although HTTP is easy to use, it isn't exactly the most efficient way to transfer data. However, for many simple tasks such as downloading a file or interacting with servlets and other web technologies, MIDP 2.0's HTTP features are invaluable.

What Is HTTP?

For the uninitiated, HTTP stands for Hypertext Transfer Protocol. A *protocol* is a set of rules used to communicate between machines, programs, or even people. When two programs are using an agreed-upon set of standards, they can then freely exchange information. There are plenty of network protocols in the computer world — you may have heard of some of them such as IPX, TCP, and PPP. HTTP is unique in that it is an open standard application layer protocol created in 1990 for transferring files on the World Wide Web.

HTTP brings along with it many concepts you should be familiar with from using the web, such as the URL, or Uniform

Resource Locator. This is the address of an object on the web. For instance, it could be a site such as http://www.flarb.com or an individual file such as http://www.flarb.com/index.html. There are many features in HTTP that facilitate the transfer of images, text, sound, and other media on the web. You can read the latest details on HTTP at http://www.w3.org/Protocols/. The latest version of HTTP is version 1.1. MIDP 2.0 supports both HTTP 1.0 and 1.1, as many servers still use HTTP 1.0 despite 1.1's ratification in the late 1990s.

The Generic Connection Framework

So, now that you know a little about HTTP and what it is, how do you use it in MIDP? HTTP is very easy to use in MIDP 2.0, and Sun has provided a robust set of objects for easy transmission and retrieval of data on the web. In order to do any network communication, we must use the Generic Connection Framework.

Because of the massive size of J2SE's networking classes, Sun chose to replace java.net and java.io classes with what is called the Generic Connection Framework. This is a system that provides easy support for the protocols required in MIDP 2.0, as well as any other communications features a particular handset or OS vendor would wish to add. In fact, although MIDP 1.0 only required HTTP support, many handset manufacturers added socket functionality to the GCF on certain devices where low-level network access was needed.

The Connector

Enough with the preamble — now it's time to actually start communicating on the web with MIDP. The first class we need to know about is the Connector object. This class is a factory that creates Connection objects. We need to use Connection objects to access the network. Fortunately, Connector is very easy to use. Remember that you have to catch an exception when using these as they throw IOException when connections can't be made, resources aren't available, and such.

Creating a Connection

To create a Connection object, we use the open method in the Connection class:

```
static Connection open(String name)
```

The sole argument, name, is a string containing the URL of the object to which we want to connect. The Connector will parse this URL and determine, based on the contents (such as the "http:" string), what kind of Connection object to return. In the case of HTTP, the open method will return a StreamConnection object. We have to cast the result like this:

```
StreamConnection con = (StreamConnection)Connection.open("http://www.flarb.com");
```

Here you can see that we pass the URL of the Flarb web site as the name, and we cast the result to a StreamConnection object. Now that we have this stream connection, we can read and write to it. To read and write with a StreamConnection, we need to use the InputStream and OutputStream classes.

The InputStream

The InputStream is used to read data coming in from a network connection. To acquire an InputStream, we need to get one from our previously created StreamConnection. We do this via StreamConnection's openInputStream method:

```
InputStream openInputStream()
```

This method is fairly self-explanatory. Let's say we want to get an InputStream from our currently open StreamConnection:

```
InputStream in = con.openInputStream();
```

Now we're in business. To read a character from this InputStream, we use the read method:

```
int read()
```

When read is called, it returns an integer from 0 to 255, representing the character just read. If the end of the stream is reached, then –1 is returned instead. So, let's read a single byte from our stream. The code looks something like this:

```
int char = in.read();
```

Just as long as char isn't –1, you've got a valid character. It's that easy. There are a few other ways to read data from a stream if you want a little more flexibility. For instance, if you want to read a series of bytes in a row and store them in an array, you can use this version of read:

```
int read(byte[] b)
```

Here we pass in an array of bytes. The method will try to fill the array with bytes. It returns the number of bytes read as an integer so you know how far it got. If the end of the stream is reached, then –1 is returned. Otherwise, it will tell you how many bytes it put in the array. Of course, if you pass it a null reference to an array, an exception will be thrown. If the array is zero length, then zero bytes will be read (and will be reflected in the return value).

An even more flexible version of read is this one:

```
int read(byte[] b, int off, int len)
```

Here we pass the array first, but we then pass an integer offset into the array where we want to start placing the read data, and finally an integer that says how many bytes we want to read. As with the other versions of read, this returns an integer that tells how many bytes have been read. If we have reached the end of the stream, –1 is returned. Both of these advanced versions of read call the first version multiple times. So there isn't any magic here — just be aware of this.

If you would like to skip ahead in the stream to read another portion of it, you can use the skip method:

```
long skip(long n)
```

The sole argument, n, is how many characters in the stream you want to skip. The actual number of bytes skipped during this operation is returned as a long. In some cases, you may not be able to skip ahead as many bytes as you want because not enough data has been read in, or the data stream just isn't long enough. So, in some cases, the amount of bytes skipped can actually be 0.

Finally, to close the stream, simply use the close method:

```
void close()
```

This will close the stream and release the resources associated with it. Remember, memory and processing power are at a premium in mobile devices — so clean up after yourself.

The OutputStream

Okay, now we know how to read data to the web. In some cases, we might want to write data. Perhaps we want to send information via a form using GET or POST. These are both decent ways to do things like interactive high-score lists and other community features. We get an OutputStream largely the same way we got our InputStream, by asking the StreamConnection for it:

```
OutputStream openOutputStream()
```

So, the resultant code would look something like this:

```
OutputStream in = con.openOutputStream();
```

Now we have our OutputStream. From here we can write bytes to the stream and send it through the connection. The easiest way to do this is with the first version of the write method:

```
void write(int b)
```

This method will write the first byte stored in the integer argument, b, to the OutputStream. This first byte is stored in the 8 low-order bits of b. The rest of the integer is ignored. If you want to write an array of values, you can use the second version:

```
void write(byte[]b)
```

This writes the entire array to the OutputStream. You can also use the offset and length version, which works in a similar manner to InputStream's advanced write method:

```
void write(byte[] b, int off, int len)
```

Here we pass the array, and then pass an offset with which to start writing data (off) and the number of bytes to write (len). Exceptions will be thrown if the array is null or the connection is closed.

The underlying hardware may buffer writes to the stream. So sometimes when you do a write, that byte may not have actually been transmitted over the network to its destination. If you want to make sure your data makes it out, you need to call the flush method:

```
void flush()
```

This will send the buffered bytes to their destination immediately.
To close the OuptutStream, use the close method:

```
void close()
```

This will close the stream and release the associated resources.

A Simple Example

Now that we know the ins and outs of using streams with HTTP, we will create a simple MIDlet that reads high scores from a text file stored on a web server. In this case, the web server will be your own machine. By installing a web server on your machine, and using the URL http://127.0.0.1, you can connect to your own PC in the same fashion as any web site.

Installing the Web Server

I'm not going to go into detail on how to set up a web server, as there are entire books written on that subject. However, for the purposes of this example I will give you a few pointers. If you don't already have one installed, I suggest using Apache. It's free, and (last time I checked) it's the dominant server platform with an estimated 64% market share of all the web servers in operation on the net. To download Apache, go to http://httpd.apache.org. Here you can download various versions of the server for various platforms including Linux and Windows. Once you have gone through the installation process, open the httpd.conf file. This contains settings governing the operation of the Apache web server. Look for the setting "DocumentRoot." If you haven't touched anything, most likely it looks like this:

```
DocumentRoot "C:/Program Files/Apache Group/Apache/htdocs"
```

That path is the actual location of the web site. So if you put a file called index.html in that folder, you would be able to access it with the URL http://127.0.0.1/index.html. This is where we will put the file we are going to access in this example. If you look in the companion files, you will find a file called scores.txt. Put this file in the directory specified by the DocumentRoot configuration property. Now, before you run the MIDlet, make sure Apache (or whatever web server you happen to be using) is running.

The MIDlet

Now that we've got the web server out of the way, let's go on to the MIDlet. Note the packages that we include.

Listing 13-1: Our includes

```
import javax.microedition.midlet.*;
import javax.microedition.lcdui.*;
import javax.microedition.io.*;
import java.io.*;
import java.util.*;
```

We need to include both javax.microedition.io and java.io for our stream communication.

Also, before we get to the MIDlet class, we have a simple class we use to store the score.

Listing 13-2: The ScoreData class

```
class ScoreData
{
    String name;
    String score;
}
```

This has a string for the name and score, and that's all. We needed a convenient way to store the name and score in an object so that we could stuff them all in a vector for safekeeping.

We also have created a custom Canvas object used to draw each name and score as shown in Listing 13-3.

Listing 13-3: Our custom Canvas

```
class ScoreCanvas extends Canvas
{
    private HTTPScores app_;

    public ScoreCanvas(HTTPScores app)
    {
        app_ = app;
```

```
    }

    public void paint(Graphics g)
    {
        Font font = g.getFont();
        int fontHeight = 0;
        int y = 0;
        int x = 0;

        g.setColor(255, 255, 255);
        g.fillRect(0, 0, getWidth(), getHeight());
        g.setColor(0, 0, 0);

        //now go through the vector and draw the name and score...
        for (int i = 0; i < app_.scoreVector.size(); i++)
        {
            g.drawString(((ScoreData)(app_.scoreVector.elementAt(i))).name, x, y,
                    Graphics.LEFT | Graphics.TOP);

            x += 5 + font.stringWidth(((ScoreData)(app_.scoreVector.elementAt
                    (i))).name);

            g.drawString(((ScoreData)(app_.scoreVector.elementAt(i))).score, x, y,
                    Graphics.LEFT | Graphics.TOP);

            x = 0;
            y += font.getHeight();
        }
    }
}
```

Nothing really groundbreaking here. We just maintain a reference to the MIDlet with app_, and then access the vector inside the MIDlet to draw each score and name inside the paint method. The paint method just uses the font height and string width to manually draw each text string progressively down the screen.

Now, on to the MIDlet itself.

Listing 13-4: Our HTTPScores MIDlet class

```
public class HTTPScores extends MIDlet
{
    private ScoreCanvas canvas_;
    private Display display_;

    public Vector scoreVector;

    public HTTPScores()
```

```
    {
        canvas_ = new ScoreCanvas(this);

        scoreVector = new Vector();
    }

    public void startApp()
    {
        display_ = Display.getDisplay(this);
        display_.setCurrent(canvas_);

        getScores("http://127.0.0.1/scores.txt");

        canvas_.repaint();
    }

    public void getScores(String url)
    {
        ScoreData scoreTemp = null;
        StreamConnection streamCon = null;
        InputStream inStream = null;
        StringBuffer buf = new StringBuffer();

        scoreTemp = new ScoreData();

        try
        {
            //open URL to our file
            streamCon = (StreamConnection)Connector.open(url);

            inStream = streamCon.openInputStream();

            int character;

            while ((character = inStream.read()) != -1)
            {
                if (character != '\n')
                {
                    //the file is tab delimited
                    if (character != '\t')
                    {
                        buf.append((char)character);
                    }
                    else
                    {
                        scoreTemp.name = buf.toString();

                        //clear our data
                        buf = new StringBuffer();
```

```
                    }
                }
                else
                {
                    scoreTemp.score = buf.toString();

                    //add our score data to the vector
                    scoreVector.addElement(scoreTemp);

                    //now destroy this object and make a new one
                    scoreTemp = null;
                    scoreTemp = new ScoreData();
                    buf = new StringBuffer();
                }
            }

            //close our connection
            if (inStream != null)
                inStream.close();
        }
        catch (IOException e)
        {
            System.err.println("Connection error.");
        }
    }

    public void pauseApp()
    {
    }

    public void destroyApp(boolean unconditional)
    {
    }
}
```

First, we have three members: our custom canvas, the display object needed to draw anything, and of course the vector we will use to store the scores.

```
private ScoreCanvas canvas_;
private Display display_;

public Vector scoreVector;
```

The constructor simply creates our custom Canvas and vector.

```
public HTTPScores()
{
    canvas_ = new ScoreCanvas(this);

    scoreVector = new Vector();
}
```

Our startApp method is where it all begins:

```
public void startApp()
    {
        display_ = Display.getDisplay(this);
        display_.setCurrent(canvas_);

        getScores("http://127.0.0.1/scores.txt");

        canvas_.repaint();
    }
```

Here we create our display and set it as the current one. Then we call getScores and repaint. The getScores method is where we access the text file containing our scores (scores.txt) on the web, or in this case, our local machine. Let's look at getScores:

```
public void getScores(String url)
    {
        ScoreData scoreTemp = null;
        StreamConnection streamCon = null;
        InputStream inStream = null;
        StringBuffer buf = new StringBuffer();

        scoreTemp = new ScoreData();

        try
        {
            //open URL to our file
            streamCon = (StreamConnection)Connector.open(url);

            inStream = streamCon.openInputStream();

            int character;

            while ((character = inStream.read()) != -1)
            {
                if (character != '\n')
                {
                    //the file is tab-delimited
                    if (character != '\t')
                    {
```

```
                buf.append((char)character);
            }
            else
            {
                scoreTemp.name = buf.toString();

                //clear our data
                buf = new StringBuffer();
            }
        }
        else
        {
            scoreTemp.score = buf.toString();

            //add our score data to the vector
            scoreVector.addElement(scoreTemp);

            //now destroy this object and make a new one
            scoreTemp = null;
            scoreTemp = new ScoreData();
            buf = new StringBuffer();
        }
    }

    //close our connection
    if (inStream != null)
        inStream.close();
}
catch (IOException e)
{
    System.err.println("Connection error.");
}
}
```

Before we do anything in the getScores method, we declare and create several objects:

```
ScoreData scoreTemp = null;
StreamConnection streamCon = null;
InputStream inStream = null;
StringBuffer buf = new StringBuffer();

scoreTemp = new ScoreData();
```

We declare our scoreTemp object that will be used to store the score information we will place in the vector later. We also have our StreamConnection and InputStream, and a StringBuffer into which the data from the stream will be read. Now we venture into the try/catch block for the real heavy lifting of this method.

The first thing we do is get our streams going and declare an integer into which we will read our data:

```
streamCon = (StreamConnection)Connector.open(url);

inStream = streamCon.openInputStream();

int character;
```

We should all be familiar with this from the discussion of InputStreams earlier in this chapter. Now that we have our InputStream, we enter a loop where we read each byte and start parsing the data. Before we get into this, it's worth discussing the format of the actual scores.txt file.

The scores.txt file is plain text that is in Microsoft Excel's tab-delimited format. If you open up the file, it looks like Listing 13-5:

Listing 13-5: The hall of fame

```
Extra-P       20000
K-Cut         20000
Sir Scratch   1500
Neek          500
Mikey D       10
```

This has the name of the player with some space after it, and then a numerical score. This space is actually a tab — this is how Excel exports its data into a text file. Using Excel or Excel-compatible spreadsheet programs is a good idea for files like these because it allows for the easy editing and analysis of data files. Although you can't see it in a regular text editor, each line is punctuated with a carriage return. So, when parsing the file, we will read up until the tab character ('\t') for the name, and then read up until the carriage return ('\n') for the score until the end of the file is reached. With this in mind, now we can look at the reading loop of getScores:

```
while ((character = inStream.read()) != -1)
{
    if (character != '\n')
    {
        //the file is tab delimited
        if (character != '\t')
        {
            buf.append((char)character);
        }
        else
        {
            scoreTemp.name = buf.toString();
            //clear our data
            buf = new StringBuffer();
        }
    }
    else
    {
        scoreTemp.score = buf.toString();

        //add our score data to the vector
        scoreVector.addElement(scoreTemp);

        //now destroy this object and make a new one
        scoreTemp = null;
        scoreTemp = new ScoreData();
        buf = new StringBuffer();
    }
}
```

Here you can see that we keep reading until read() returns –1. That signifies the end of the file has been reached. If we haven't reached a carriage return ('\n') yet, we know we are reading the name. Thus, if the character read isn't a tab ('\t'), then we know we have a valid character of data. So we append our StringBuffer with this new character stored in the character variable. Otherwise, if it is a tab, we know we are done reading the name, so we convert the StringBuffer to a String and store it in the name member of our ScoreData object.

Now if we have read a carriage return, we know we are at the end of the line, and thus we have read in the score. So we convert the StringBuffer to a String and store it in the name member of our ScoreData object. We then add this object to the vector, and create a new StringBuffer and ScoreData to start with the new entry. Once we have –1 returned from read(), we have hit the end of the file and we're done reading. This is when we close the stream and wrap things up.

Going back to startApp, after we get the scores, we repaint the screen to display the contents of the score file we just read. When you first run this MIDlet, you will be presented with a Form that asks you if you want to communicate with the network, as seen in Figure 13-1. This is put up to alert users that they may be consuming minutes and/or incurring airtime charges by running this MIDlet. Click the first option and you can proceed with the MIDlet's execution. After this, if scores.txt is running in the root of your web server, the result should look like Figure 13-2.

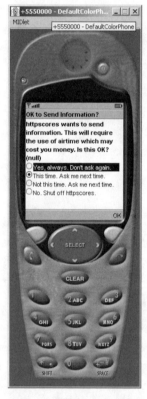

Figure 13-1: Alert message

Figure 13-2: Scores on display

Conclusion

Now you know how to interact with the World Wide Web using MIDP 2.0. A more advanced version of this MIDlet might actually use an InputStream and a servlet or cgi-script to allow the MIDlet to send a high score to the server via GET or POST and then update the list for future retrieval. We have covered the basics of HTTP communication — now it's time to get into sockets.

Chapter 14

Wireless Networking with TCP/IP

Introduction

In the previous chapter we went over the basics of wireless networking concepts and developed a MIDlet that used HTTP to read high scores from a web site. HTTP is fine for things like file retrieval and interacting with web back ends, but for actual wireless multiplayer games you need to use something lower level for less overhead for high-speed communication. This is where sockets come in.

Internet Game Programming

Programming multiplayer games that use the Internet is a rich subject, worthy of its own book. The basic concept is that you have two basic elements: the client and the server. The client is the game itself. This is the program that runs on your handset (or PC, console, or whatever) that takes your input and acts upon it like any other game. Except in this case, the client sends the results of your input through the network to a server. The server takes your input, along with that of other players connected through their own clients, and sends back its own data. This data could be the new positions of all the other players in the game world or perhaps information telling the client that you have been defeated by an opponent.

Another network architecture for online games is peer-to-peer communication. Peer to peer (P2P) gained popularity as a buzz-word in the glory days of Napster. Napster was a P2P network in that there was no central server handing out MP3 files to every-one. Instead, you connected directly to another user's computer and pulled files off it. That other user is considered a peer.

The concept of P2P is perhaps as old as network gaming itself. Some of the earliest multiplayer games on PCs required you to dial up your opponent directly with a modem for a head-to-head challenge. This directly contrasts with a client-server game such as Quake, where every player is connected to a single server that takes the player's moves and spits out the state of the game world to all attached clients.

Regardless of the method you choose for your game, you need to use the TCP/IP protocol to communicate over the Internet, and thus reach other MIDP handset users. And to do this you need sockets.

Sockets

For TCP/IP communication, MIDP 2.0 uses what are called sock-ets. Sockets have been around since the land before time known as the early '80s. Sockets were added to the Unix operating sys-tem in the form of the Berkeley Sockets Interface as a way to communicate over networks with various protocols.

What Is a Socket?

A socket can be thought of as a standard telephone jack, or socket. Through this socket you can communicate with another terminal (phone) in a bidirectional manner. That is, you can send data (talk) and receive data (listen). When you create a socket using MIDP 2.0's GCF, you are essentially creating one of these connections between your applet (the client) and a process running on another machine (the server). This process can be another mobile phone or an actual server machine listening for your phone's connection attempt.

Different Kinds of Sockets

There are two different kinds of sockets: streams and datagrams. Each type uses a different protocol to communicate. A stream socket uses TCP, which is a connection-oriented protocol. This means that you have an open connection that is maintained by the program to send and receive data. This connection is closed when the server or client explicitly closes the socket. Stream sockets have very much the same behavior as circuit-switched wireless network protocols, as discussed in the previous chapter.

Stream communication means that you receive the data sequentially in the order you sent it. Because a stream is continuous, the order of your data is guaranteed. This is also known as a reliable protocol. This may seem like a fairly basic operation, but the fact is the Internet is a very complicated web of nodes and networks. Packets sent out through a socket oftentimes arrive at their destination out of order. There is a lot of work going on behind the scenes to make sure that the packets are arranged in the order you sent them. This overhead, and the fact that you must wait for missing packets to arrive in your stream before accessing them, means that TCP is not the fastest way to send data over the Internet.

The second kind of a socket is a datagram socket. Datagram sockets use the UDP protocol, which is a record-oriented system instead of connection-oriented like streams. Datagrams are individual chunks of data, not continuous streams. This means that the packets sent will not necessarily be received by the server in the order you sent them. In fact, some packets may be duplicated and others may simply not arrive at all. This is otherwise known as an unreliable protocol.

"Why should I use something considered unreliable in my program?" you may ask. The issue here is speed. UDP packets require much less overhead and do not have to worry about being ordered sequentially upon arrival. Therefore they can be sent and received much quicker than data through a stream. The problem is that it is up to your application to deal with the fact that the data is potentially arriving out of sequence or not at all. This may involve sending acknowledgment messages, embedding a time stamp inside your data to order it yourself, and using various client prediction schemes to make educated guesses about what information the user may be sending if there is a gap in the packet transmissions.

Note   Even though UDP is faster, networking is one of the more problematic features on most handsets. On some devices, even with the networking code put in another thread, the entire MIDlet will halt until the transmission is complete. So, UDP or no, you'll still have some performance issues aside from the inherent flakiness of the network. Network communication is definitely a feature that requires a lot of handset testing.

Sockets and the GCF

Datagram and stream socket support is brand new for MIDP 2.0. Although TCP/IP is not mandatory in the MIDP 2.0 specification, it has been formally laid out and offered as a common feature to any J2ME vendor. I suspect sockets will be pretty much standard on any MIDP 2.0 device — but there are always exceptions. Make sure to check the developer documentation for your target device to make sure TCP/IP is an option.

The SocketConnection

Support for both stream (TCP) and datagram (UDP) sockets is provided through the SocketConnection class. Much like the StreamConnection, you request one of these from the Connector factory class. In this case, the protocol used (TCP or UDP) is specified in the protocol portion of the URL passed to Connector's open method. Previously, we used http:// to specify a web address. In this case we use either socket:// for TCP or datagram:// for UDP. So, let's say we want to get a TCP connection to our host PC. The code might look something like this:

```
SocketConnection sc = (SocketConnection)Connector.open("socket://127.0.0.1:5000");
```

At the end of the IP address (127.0.0.1), we specify a port number after the colon. This is optional. If you don't specify a port number, then MIDP will attempt to connect to the address on a random port. If everything goes well, the result of this call is a TCP socket connection to your own host machine. Getting a UDP connection works in a similar manner:

```
SocketConnection sc = (SocketConnection)Connector.open("datagram://127.0.0.1:5000");
```

The only difference here is that we use the protocol specifier datagram:// to tell MIDP that we want a UDP socket. After this, both socket or datagram connections use the same interface via SocketConnection. The only thing you have to be aware of is that with a TCP socket all packets are guaranteed to arrive in order, whereas UDP is connectionless and thus you may not get your packets in order, or even receive them at all.

Getting Information about the Connection

Now that you have a SocketConnection, you can use the SocketConnection class to get information about the connection and also set various options. For instance, if you want to know the address to which this SocketConnection is connected, use the getAddress method:

```
String getAddress()
```

This method returns a string that contains the address (or IP address) to which the connection is bound.

If you want to know to which port you are currently connected, use the getPort method:

```
int getPort();
```

This is as simple as it gets — the return value is the port to which the socket is connected.

You can also set various SocketConnection options with the setSocketOption method:

```
void setSocketOption(byte option, int value)
```

This method is used to tell the low-level networking code on the handset about the behavior of your application. The first argument, option, is a byte value that identifies the option we are setting. These options are fields inside the SocketConnection class: KEEPALIVE, LINGER, SNDBUF, RCVBUF, or DELAY. The second argument, value, is the value to which we are setting this option.

In most cases, these are merely hints to the low-level networking layer and aren't necessarily adhered to. For instance, you can set the size of the send buffer by using the SNDBUF option:

```
sc.setSocketOption(SNDBUF, 100);
```

This code tells the system to set the send buffer to be 100 bytes. We don't actually know if this happened, however, because the networking subsystem pretty much does what it wants. You can use these settings in an attempt to optimize the way the networking system works for the way your application behaves.

If you want to see the current values for any of these options, use the getSocketOption method:

```
int getSocketOption(byte option)
```

As you can see here, we merely pass one of the option types, and the method returns an integer with the value of that option. If the option isn't available, the return value will be –1.

Writing and Reading with Sockets

Because SocketConnection is derived from Connection, just like InputConnection and OutputConnection, we read and write data the same way we did in our HTTP example. Except in this case we are transmitting binary data instead of plain text HTTP data. To read data, just get an InputStream from your SocketConnection like this:

```
InputStream is = sc.openInputStream();
```

To get an output stream for writing, use openOutputStream:

```
OutputStream os = sc.openOutputStream();
```

You already know how to read and write from InputStream and OutputStream objects if you have read Chapter 13, "Wireless Networking with HTTP."

A Simple Example

The socket example in this chapter is actually two different programs: a MIDP 2.0 client and a Windows server. The end result is a simple tic-tac-toe game that gets the computer's move from a remote server on the Internet. Although the server itself generates its own move, theoretically it could be receiving move information from another player and passing it on to the MIDP 2.0 client. Although this is not a book about Windows network programming, we will delve into the Windows server briefly so you know what the MIDP 2.0 client is dealing with later on. The code for both the client and server projects is found in the chap14 folder in the companion files.

Figure 14-1: The tic-tac-toe client running in the emulator

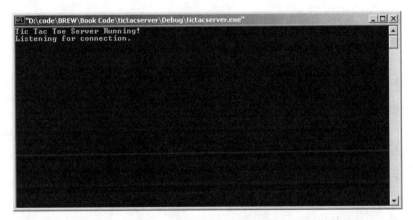

Figure 14-2: The tic-tac-toe Win32 client running in the console window

The Server

The Windows socket API is known as Winsock. This is very similar to the Berkeley Sockets Interface with a few extras unique to Windows. We will not deal with any of the Windows minutiae at the moment; that is a topic for a whole other book. If you want a great explanation of Winsock, check out James A. Frost's excellent paper at world.std.com/~jimf/papers/sockets/winsock.html. That page contains skeleton code for both a client and server. The latter is used as a basis for the tic-tac-toe Winsock server application.

The only source file of the server is tictacserver.cpp. At the start of the file there are a few global variables and definitions. Yeah, I know — but I said this was quick and dirty.

Listing 14-1: Definitions

```
#define CONDITION_WIN    255
#define CONDITION_LOST   254
#define CONDITION_DRAW   253

#define PORTNUM 50000

unsigned char g_pnGameBoard[9];
int g_nWinner;
```

The first three defines are special codes that will be sent to the server to signify a win, loss, or draw. Next, we have the port definition. Port 50000 is just an arbitrary number; chances are, nobody is using it. Feel free to change it if you like.

Finally, we have the global variables. The array of nine characters, g_pnGameBoard, is used to hold the contents of the tic-tac-toe game board. The g_nWinner variable is used to signal if someone won. If it is set to 0, then nobody has won yet. If it is set to 1, then the client has won. If it is set to 2, then the server has won.

Here is something we have not seen in a while, a main loop. Here is the server's main:

Listing 14-2: Main server loop

```
int main(int argc, char* argv[])
{
    SOCKET sockHandle;
    bool bBreakOut = FALSE;
```

```
printf("Tic Tac Toe Server Running!\n");

//Start up winsock
WSADATA info;
if (WSAStartup(MAKEWORD(2,0), &info) != 0)
{
    printf("Cannot startup winsock!\n");
    WSACleanup();
    exit(1);
}

ResetGame();

//Open socket on our port
if ((sockHandle = CreateStreamSocket(PORTNUM)) == INVALID_SOCKET)
{
    printf("Cannot create socket!\n");
    WSACleanup();
    exit(1);
}

//Infinite read/write loop
while (1)
{
    bBreakOut = false;
    printf( "Listening for connection.\n");

    //Wait for client to connect
    SOCKET newSocket = accept(sockHandle, NULL, NULL);

    if (sockHandle == INVALID_SOCKET)
    {
        printf( "Connection error!\n");
        WSACleanup();
        exit(1);
    }

    //While the game is in progress, run turns
    while (!bBreakOut)
    {
        bBreakOut = DoMove(newSocket);
    }

    closesocket(newSocket);
}

WSACleanup();
return (0);
}
```

The first thing we do is declare a few variables. First, a SOCKET, sockHandle, is declared. Then our global Boolean, bBreakout, is declared right below. The socket is obviously used for communication while the bool is used to tell the server to break out of its infinite loop of waiting for player communication when the game has ended.

Before we do any socket operations, we have to initialize the Winsock subsystem. We do this with a call to WSAStartup. With this call we tell Winsock which version we want to use. In this case we specify Winsock 2.0.

Next, we initialize the global game variables with ResetGame.

Listing 14-3: Resetting the game

```
void ResetGame()
{
    //no winner
    g_nWinner = 0;

    //seed randomizer
    srand(GetTickCount());

    //clear the game board
    memset(g_pnGameBoard, 0, sizeof(char) * 9);
}
```

This is all very self-explanatory.

We next create a stream socket using our custom function, CreateStreamSocket:

Listing 14-4: Creating the server-side socket

```
SOCKET CreateStreamSocket(unsigned short nPortnum)
{
    char    pszHostName[256];
    SOCKET sockHandle;
    sockaddr_in sa;
    hostent *hp;

    gethostname(pszHostName, sizeof(pszHostName));
    hp = gethostbyname(pszHostName);

    if (hp == NULL)
        return(INVALID_SOCKET);

    memset(&sa, 0, sizeof(sockaddr_in));
```

```
sa.sin_family = hp->h_addrtype;
sa.sin_port = htons(nPortnum);

sockHandle = socket(AF_INET, SOCK_STREAM, 0);

if (sockHandle == INVALID_SOCKET)
    return INVALID_SOCKET;

if (bind(sockHandle, (sockaddr *)&sa, sizeof(sockaddr_in)) ==
    SOCKET_ERROR)
{
        closesocket(sockHandle);
        return(INVALID_SOCKET);
}

listen(sockHandle, 3);
return(sockHandle);
}
```

This is all basic Winsock stuff. We get our host name by calling
gethostname. We then take our socketaddr_in structure and fill it
with the appropriate settings including our port number, which is
passed in the short integer argument nPortnum. We convert that
port number to network byte order using htons. Then, using the
socket function, we create a stream socket. Because we are going
to use listen we also have to use the bind function. This associates
the socket with the port and other attributes we set in the
sockaddr_in structure. Finally, we set the socket to listen on the
socket for any incoming connection. We pass 3 as the argument to
tell Winsock that we want a maximum of three waiting connections in queue.

Now, back to the main loop. After creating the stream socket,
we enter our infinite loop of waiting for connections and send-
ing/receiving stream data:

```
while (1)
{
    bBreakOut = false;
    printf( "Listening for connection.\n");

    //Wait for client to connect
    SOCKET newSocket = accept(sockHandle, NULL, NULL);

    if (sockHandle == INVALID_SOCKET)
    {
        printf( "Connection error!\n");
```

```
        WSACleanup();
        exit(1);
}

//While the game is in progress, run turns
while (!bBreakOut)
{
    bBreakOut = DoMove(newSocket);
}

closesocket(newSocket);
}
```

The first thing we do is call accept. What this does is block until we receive a socket connection. Once the connection is made, we then call DoMove in an infinite loop until the bool, bBreakOut, is flagged as true. Once bBreakOut is flagged, we close the socket and return to the top of the loop where we wait for another connection. DoMove is where all the magic happens.

Listing 14-5: Performing a move on the server

```
bool DoMove(SOCKET sock)
{
    //Read the socket to get the move
    unsigned char nCell;
    int nBytesRead = 0;
    int nTotalBytes = 0;
    int nBytesSent = 0;
    int nTotalBytesSent = 0;
    bool bFinished = false;

    char buf[32];

    printf("Got connection..attempting to read data.\n");

    //Read move data in from client
    while (nTotalBytes < sizeof(char))
    {
        nBytesRead = recv(sock, buf, sizeof(buf), 0);

        if (nBytesRead < 0)
        {
            int nErr = WSAGetLastError();
            ResetGame();
            return TRUE;
        }
        else
```

```
            nTotalBytes += nBytesRead;
     }

     //Copy the data into our integer
     memcpy(&nCell, buf, sizeof(char));

     printf( "Read data from client...cell %d...continuing...\n", nCell);

     //If there is a win condition, the game is over
     if (nCell == CONDITION_WIN)
     {
          ResetGame();
          printf("Server lost! Resetting server!\n");
          return TRUE;
     }
     else if (nCell == CONDITION_LOST)
     {
          ResetGame();
          printf("Server won!  Resetting server!\n");
          return TRUE;
     }
     else if (nCell == CONDITION_DRAW)
     {
          ResetGame();
          printf("Draw!  Resetting server!\n");
          return TRUE;
     }

     //Fill in the cell if it is unoccupied
     if (!g_pnGameBoard[nCell])
     {
          g_pnGameBoard[nCell] = 1;
     }
     else //Otherwise, something bad is going on
     {
          printf("Someone is cheating! Exiting!\n");
          WSACleanup();
          exit(1);
     }

     //Now do alleged AI (random placement)
     while (!bFinished)
     {
          //Keep generating cell positions until we get a good one
          nCell = rand()%9;

          //If the cell isn't occupied, fill it and send it
          if (!g_pnGameBoard[nCell])
          {
```

```
            g_pnGameBoard[nCell] = 2;

            printf( "Sending move data out to client cell %d...\n", nCell);

            //Send this cell ID out
            while (nTotalBytesSent < sizeof(char))
            {
                nBytesSent = send(sock, (const char*)&nCell, sizeof(char), 0);

                if (nBytesSent <= 0)
                {
                    int nErr = WSAGetLastError();
                    ResetGame();
                    return TRUE;
                }
                else
                    nTotalBytesSent += nBytesSent;
            }

            bFinished = true;
        }

        printf( "Sent move data...returning to accept.\n");
    }

    return FALSE;
}
```

This may seem like a large function, but it is actually very simple. Overall, this gets the turn information from the client in the form of a single byte. This byte tells the server where the client placed its O. If the client sends a message signifying a win, loss, or draw, we terminate the game. Otherwise, we then pick a random cell to put the server's X and send that out to the client.

First we declare and initialize a bunch of variables. The first, nCell, is used to hold which cell on the game board we are receiving a move for or placing the server's X in. Although we are only going to send and receive a single byte for each turn, we use the variable nBytesRead to determine if we have read or sent enough bytes with our socket calls. The nTotalBytesSent variable is used to determine how many bytes we have sent, while nTotalBytes is used to determine how many bytes we have received. As mentioned before, these should both equal 1 if we have successfully sent or received a move. Finally, buf is a general-purpose buffer we use to place the data we are sending or receiving.

After the variable declaration, we wait in a loop calling recv to take in any socket communication from the client. Notice we always check to see if the socket call has returned an error by returning a number of bytes read equal to or less than zero. If so, we just bail. Sure, that is not very robust, but this is not a commercial-grade application anyway. We use this behavior for all socket errors in the server.

Next, we check the win conditions. If the game is over, we reset the game and return false from the function. This tells the main loop to break out and listen for a new client socket connection.

We then fill in the cell in the game board sent in from the client. If there is already something in that cell, then something is amiss. In this case, we bail once again. Perhaps someone is cheating with a hacked client. Perhaps I am just being a little paranoid. There is nothing wrong with a little defensive programming, however.

Now it is time for our astounding artificial intelligence. Well, not really. What we do is stay in a loop, generating random cell positions until we find one that is empty. Once we get a valid cell, we send this move out to the client as a single byte by using the send function. We loop until we have sent out all the bytes, and of course, bail upon any socket error.

That is about it. The server is exceedingly simple. You can use this code as a framework for a more complicated game server. In most cases, game servers are attached to player and world databases sometimes using SQL and other database systems. Also, they may match up players with others who would like to play and broker games between them. Obviously, this simple game of tic-tac-toe is a far cry from the advanced commercial game servers of most real wireless multiplayer games. But it serves our purpose of getting to know the MIDP 2.0 socket APIs.

The Client

Now, on to the game client. This is a traditional game MIDlet, involving graphics, user input, and now socket communication. It is a simple game of tic-tac-toe, but instead of playing against a computer AI embedded into the MIDlet, the moves are coming from the computer player residing on the server. For the sake of testing, the server and the client will reside on the same machine. That is, we will use the special IP address that actually always refers to the host machine, 127.0.0.1, to connect to the server.

The Constants

There are three constants we use in our TicTacClient MIDlet that mirror those defines we used in the Win32 server code:

```
interface Constants
{
    public static final int CONDITION_WIN  = 255;
    public static final int CONDITION_LOST = 254;
    public static final int CONDITION_DRAW = 253;
}
```

Here we have a constant for each final game result: win, lose, or draw. This value will be sent to the server if we cause a game over state with a move, or the server will send one to use if the server logic ends the game.

The TicTacClient MIDlet

Before we get into the Canvas, which handles the drawing and input logic, we will discuss the actual MIDlet class. This is where all the heavy lifting is done in regard to game logic and managing the socket connections. The first thing that we do in our MIDlet is declare a bunch of members:

```
private int move_;
private TicTacCanvas canvas_;
private Display display_;

private SocketConnection sc_;
private InputStream is_;
private OutputStream os_;
```

```
public int[] gameBoard;
public int winner;
```

Here we have a bunch of private members, which are used internally by our MIDlet, and a few public ones, which will be accessed by the Canvas later on. First we have the integer, move_, which is used to represent the cell in our tic-tac-toe grid in which we are placing our X. Secondly we have the canvas_ and display_ members, which are obviously used for the graphics and key input as in most of our other MIDlets in the book. We also have our Socket-Connection, InputStream, and OutputStream members. These will be used to maintain a TCP connection with the Win32 server running on our local machine. Finally we have the integer array, gameBoard, which will be a nine-element array with an integer for each cell of the tic-tac-toe grid. We also have the integer member winner, which is used to represent the win condition status: win, lose, or draw.

The Constructor

The constructor doesn't do much; it just creates some of the basic objects and clears out the initial values.

Listing 14-6: The TicTacClient constructor

```
public TicTacClient()
{
    winner = 0;

    canvas_ = new TicTacCanvas(this);

    gameBoard = new int[9];

    for (int i = 0; i < 9; i++)
    {
        gameBoard[i] = 0;
    }
}
```

We initialize our connections in the startApp method:

Listing 14-7: The startApp method

```
public void startApp()
{
    openConnection();

    display_ = Display.getDisplay(this);
    display_.setCurrent(canvas_);
    canvas_.repaint();
}
```

The canvas and display code here is fairly mundane, but it's the mysterious call to openConnection that interests us. Let's look at that method in detail:

Listing 14-8: Opening the socket connection

```
void openConnection()
{
    try
    {
        sc_ = (SocketConnection)Connector.open("socket://127.0.0.1:50000");
        is_ = sc_.openInputStream();
        os_ = sc_.openOutputStream();
    }
    catch(IOException e)
    {
        Alert a = new Alert("TicTacClient", "Open Connection: connection failed...",
                null, AlertType.ERROR);
        a.setTimeout(Alert.FOREVER);
        display_.setCurrent(a);
    }
}
```

Inside the try/catch block we create our socket connection by using the URL socket://127.0.0.1:50000. This URL will open a TCP socket connection to our local machine on port 50000. Obviously, our client has to be running or this will fail. If the connection fails, I decided to be nice and bring up an alert to notify the user. Granted, the rest of this MIDlet deals rather poorly with errors — but I saw it in some Sun sample code and it seemed like a good idea at the time. Note that we are creating an InputStream and OutputStream at the same time. These will be used to read data to and write data from the server. However, some devices may not be able to handle both an InputStream and OutputStream open at the same time. You'll have to experiment with your hardware to find out. In the emulator it works fine — but as most anyone who has done any real mobile development will tell you, the emulator is almost meaningless when it comes to real-world device behavior.

Reading and Writing the Move

Speaking of InputStream and OutputStream, let's look at the writeMove and readMove methods. First, writeMove:

Listing 14-9: Writing a move to the server

```
boolean writeMove(int movedata)
{
    move_ = (char)movedata;

    try
    {
        os_.write(move_);
    }
    catch(IOException e)
    {
        Alert a = new Alert("TicTacClient", "Write Move: Connection failed...", null,
                AlertType.ERROR);
        a.setTimeout(Alert.FOREVER);
        display_.setCurrent(a);
        return false;
    }

    if (move_ >= CONDITION_DRAW)
    {
        //game over
        closeConnection();
    }

    return true;
}
```

Here we take a single integer argument, movedata. This will be filled with the number of the cell in which we are placing an X. We simply call the write method of our OutputStream to send this information to the server. If the information we are sending to the server is the win condition (CONDITION_DRAW, CONDITION_WIN, CONDITION_LOSE), we shut down the connection. Also, we catch any possible IOException and throw up an alert if something wrong has happened with the network communication.

To read a move, we use the readMove member:

Listing 14-10: Reading a move from the server

```
boolean readMove()
{
    try
    {
        //we only want to read one byte
        int move_ = 0;
        move_ = is_.read();

        if (move_ >= 0)
        {
            gameBoard[move_] = 2;

            winner = checkWin();

            if (winner > 0)
            {
            if (winner == 1)
                {
                    writeMove(CONDITION_WIN);
                }
                else if (winner == 2)
                {
                    writeMove(CONDITION_LOST);
                }
                else
                {
                    writeMove(CONDITION_DRAW);
                }

                closeConnection();

                return (false);
            }
            else
                return (true);
        }
    }
    catch(IOException e)
    {
        Alert a = new Alert("TicTacClient", "ReadMove: " + e, null, AlertType.ERROR);
            a.setTimeout(Alert.FOREVER);
        display_.setCurrent(a);
```

```
    }
  return (false);
}
```

This is a little more complicated. Here, we read the move from the server by calling the read member in our InputStream. The result is put in our move_ member. If we actually have some valid data, we place a 2 in the appropriate game board cell. The value of 2 in a gameBoard cell represents a O, whereas 1 is an X, and 0 means it's blank. Then, we check for a win condition. If we have won, we send this information to the server via a call to writeMove and subsequently close the connection. As with other similar methods, we throw up an alert if something has gone wrong with the connection.

Game Logic

The checkWin method is a simple method we use to determine if the game is over. It looks like this:

Listing 14-11: Checking for a win condition

```
int checkWin()
{
    if (scanBoard(1))
        return 1;

    if (scanBoard(2))
        return 2;

    if (scanBoard(3))
        return 3;

    return 0;
}
```

We simply call scanBoard three times — once to check if the X's (us) have won, next to see if the computer has won, and finally to see if we have a draw. Let's look at that method.

Listing 14-12: Scanning the board for patterns

```
boolean scanBoard(int player)
{
    int i;

    //Scan for a draw
    if (player == 3)
    {
        for (i = 0; i < 9; i++)
        {
            if (gameBoard[i] == 0)
                return false;
        }
            return true;
    }

    //Check horizontals and verticals
    for (i = 0; i < 3; i++)
    {
        if ( (gameBoard[(i * 3)] == player) &&
            (gameBoard[(i * 3) + 1] == player) &&
            (gameBoard[(i * 3) + 2] == player) )
        {
            return true;
        }

        if ( (gameBoard[i] == player) &&
            (gameBoard[(1 * 3) + i] == player) &&
            (gameBoard[(2 * 3) + i] == player) )
        {
            return true;
        }

    }

    //Check diagonals
    if ( (gameBoard[0] == player) &&
        (gameBoard[1 + 3] == player) &&
        (gameBoard[2 + 6] == player) )
    {
        return true;
    }

    if ( (gameBoard[2] == player) &&
        (gameBoard[1 + 3] == player) &&
        (gameBoard[6] == player) )
    {
        return true;
```

```
        }

        return false;
}
```

The sole argument, player, is used to check the win condition we are looking for. If player is 1, we are looking to see if player 1 (us) has won. If player is set to 2, we are looking to see if the server has won. If player is 3, we are checking for a draw.

So, you can see that first we check for a draw if player is set to 3. We do this by seeing if every cell in the gameBoard array is filled. If there is a single 0 cell, we know that there is at least one empty space and thus we don't have a draw.

After looking for a draw, we check to see if either we or the server has Xs or Os in any of the winning layouts. It may look a little peculiar, but we are using a single-dimensional array to represent the 3 x 3 tic-tac-toe grid. First we check to see if there is a win horizontally or vertically by looking through each row and column. Then we check the two possible diagonal winning layouts. If there are three Xs or Os in any of these configurations, there is a winner and we return true. Otherwise, we return false.

The final two methods of note are related to closing the connection.

Cleaning Up

The closeConnection method has been seen in a few previous methods. Here it is in detail:

Listing 14-13: Closing the connection

```
void closeConnection()
{
    try
    {
        is_.close();
        os_.close();
        sc_.close();
    }
    catch(IOException e)
    {
        Alert a = new Alert("TicTacClient", "Close Connection: connection failed...",
                null, AlertType.ERROR);
        a.setTimeout(Alert.FOREVER);
```

```
    display_.setCurrent(a);
  }
}
```

We simply call the close method on the InputStream, Output-Stream, and StreamConnection objects.

Finally, our destroyApp method calls this just to make sure things are cleaned up:

Listing 14-14: destroyApp

```
public void destroyApp(boolean unconditional)
{
    closeConnection();
}
```

The Canvas

The last thing to discuss here is our custom Canvas subclass, TicTacCanvas. The only member of TicTacCanvas is a reference to our MIDlet class:

```
private TicTacClient app_;
```

This will be used to reference members and methods while drawing and processing game input. Input is handled via the keyPressed method:

Listing 14-15: Keypress actions

```
public void keyPressed(int keyCode)
{
    int cell = -1;

    //no input if winner
    if (app_.winner != 0)
        return;

    switch (keyCode)
    {
        case KEY_NUM1:
        cell = 0;
        break;

        case KEY_NUM2:
        cell = 1;
        break;
```

```
        case KEY_NUM3:
        cell = 2;
        break;

        case KEY_NUM4:
        cell = 3;
        break;

        case KEY_NUM5:
        cell = 4;
        break;

        case KEY_NUM6:
        cell = 5;
        break;

        case KEY_NUM7:
        cell = 6;
        break;

        case KEY_NUM8:
        cell = 7;
        break;

        case KEY_NUM9:
        cell = 8;
        break;
    }

    if (cell < 0)
        return;

    //If the cell is clear, fill it in
    if (app_.gameBoard[cell] == 0)
    {
        app_.gameBoard[cell] = 1;
        app_.winner = app_.checkWin();

        if (app_.winner == 0)
        {
            //Send move to server, receive server's move
            if (app_.writeMove(cell))
            {
                app_.readMove();
            }
        }
        else    //Send win condition to server
        {
```

```
            if (app_.winner == 1)
                app_.writeMove(CONDITION_WIN);
            else if (app_.winner == 2)
                app_.writeMove(CONDITION_LOST);
            else
                app_.writeMove(CONDITION_DRAW);
        }
    }

    repaint();
    serviceRepaints();
}
```

This method may look long, but it's fairly simple. First off, if there is a win condition, then the game is over. So if the winner member of our MIDlet class is anything but 0, we just bail out of this method as there is nothing left to do. Next, we determine which cell in our tic-tac-toe grid we are going fill in by looking at which key is pressed. Luckily, there are nine cells and nine number keys (excluding the 0). Tic-tac-toe was seemingly meant for cell phones, as we simply need to associate each key with a position in the grid. Note that your number pad layout is actually vertically flipped from the layout on the handset. So if you are using the keypad instead of the emulator's graphical representation of the phone's number pad, you may be a little confused at the correspondence between the number and the cell.

Next up, if we have a valid cell in which to place our X, we go ahead and drop it in the array. After performing our move, we see if we have ended the game. If so, we send this information to the server via writeMove. Otherwise, we send the move over to the server with writeMove. Finally, repaint the screen again.

This brings us to the second method of our TicTacToeCanvas, paint.

Listing 14-16: The paint method

```
public void paint(Graphics g)
{
    int linesx, linesy, lineex, lineey;
    int circlecx, circlecy, circler;

    g.setColor(255, 255, 255);
    g.fillRect(0, 0, getWidth(), getHeight());
    g.setColor(0, 0, 0);
```

```
//g.drawString("Hello World!", 0, 0, Graphics.LEFT | Graphics.TOP);

int i, j, contents;
int skipX, skipY;

g.setColor(0, 0, 0);

//Draw lines of tic tac toe board
skipX = getWidth() / 3;
skipY = getHeight() / 3;

//Draw game board lines
for (i = 1; i < 3; i++)
{
    linesx = i * skipX;
    linesy = 0;

    lineex = i * skipX;
    lineey = getHeight();

    g.drawLine(linesx, linesy, lineex, lineey);

    for (j = 1; j < 3; j++)
    {
        linesx = 0;
        linesy = j * skipY;

        lineex = getWidth();
        lineey = j * skipY;

        g.drawLine(linesx, linesy, lineex, lineey);
    }
}

//Draw Xs and Os
for (i = 0; i < 3; i++)
{
    for (j = 0; j < 3; j++)
    {
        contents = app_.gameBoard[(j * 3) + i];

        if (contents == 1)
        {
            //Draw blue X
            g.setColor(0, 0, 255);

            linesx = (i * skipX) + 2;
            linesy = (j * skipY) + 2;
```

```
              lineex = ((i + 1) * skipX) - 2;
              lineey = ((j + 1) * skipY) - 2;

              g.drawLine(linesx, linesy, lineex, lineey);

              linesx = ((i + 1) * skipX) - 2;
              linesy = (j * skipY) + 2;

              lineex = (i * skipX) + 2;
              lineey = ((j + 1) * skipY) - 2;

              g.drawLine(linesx, linesy, lineex, lineey);
          }
          else if (contents == 2)
          {
              //Draw red 0
              g.setColor(255, 0, 0);

              circlecx = (i * skipX) + (skipX / 2) + 1;
              circlecy = (j * skipY) + (skipY / 2);

              if (skipX < skipY)
                  circler = skipX / 2;
              else
                  circler = skipY / 2;

              circler -= 3;

              //note the ridiculous gymnastics we have to do to draw a simple circle
              g.drawArc(circlecx - (circler), circlecy - (circler), circler * 2,
                      circler * 2, 0, 360);
          }
      }
  }
}

//If we are waiting for something, notify user
if (app_.winner != 0)
{
    g.setColor(0, 0, 0);

    if (app_.winner == 1)
    {
        g.drawString("You Win!", getWidth() / 2, getHeight() / 2, Graphics.HCENTER
                | Graphics.BASELINE);
    }
    else if (app_.winner == 2)
    {
```

```
        g.drawString("You Lose!", getWidth() / 2, getHeight() / 2, Graphics.HCENTER
            | Graphics.BASELINE);
    }
    else
    {
        g.drawString("Draw!", getWidth() / 2, getHeight() / 2, Graphics.HCENTER |
            Graphics.BASELINE);
    }
  }
}
```

Okay, this one is a little long, but all it really does is draw a bunch of lines, Xs, Os, and maybe a game over message. First we clear the screen with a white rectangle. Then, we figure out how much of a gap between lines we need to draw a grid centered on the screen. Note that we use the width and height of the Canvas to dynamically create this board. This particular paint function is a good example of making a game that rescales itself to any reasonable screen size. Techniques like this can help you make games that require minimal modifications when bringing them over to different devices.

Anyway, we then draw our grid, based off of metrics we calculated in our skipX and skipY variables. We then go through each cell in the MIDlet class's gameBoard array and draw an X, O, or nothing at all for each one. Note that to draw a circle we actually have to draw a 360-degree arc. I really wish Sun would just make a drawCircle method. Come on, guys, I know you can do it! Finally, if there is a win condition we draw either a win, lose, or draw text message in the center of the screen. It's not pretty, but it's functional.

Note   Of course I got your hopes up through this entire chapter, but for some handsets, socket usage requires the MIDP 2.0 MIDlet to be a trusted app that is digitally signed with a special certificate. Getting this certificate is a mess, which means you might have to resort to HTTP not because the handset can't do it, but because of brain-dead handset manufacturers and carriers.

Conclusion

Now you know the basics of socket communication. Note that this is hardly a real commercially viable MIDlet. In a real commercial game you have to handle disconnected sockets, massive latencies, and the MIDlet being suspended and resumed at any time. This will require closing and reopening SocketConnections as well as InputStream and OutputStreams. Not to mention modifying the server code to handle resumed sessions with clients. Also, playing against a computer AI on a remote server is hardly a real multiplayer game. As an exercise for yourself, you might want to modify the server so that it accepts input from two clients and lets them play against each other. However, for the purposes of this chapter, a client vs. AI provides a much simpler example to guide you through.

Chapter 15

Optimizing Your Game

Introduction

Now that we have gotten our code up and running on a real handset, you may have noticed that some devices aren't as fast as we'd like. Or maybe you just want to trick out your code to be as fast as possible. This chapter focuses on a few tricks you can use to optimize for speed, memory usage, and file space. All three are important factors to consider when launching your game commercially. Keep in mind that despite the new tuning options, the performance of the emulator is not related to that of the handset itself. This means you're going to have to try these tricks on a real handset.

How to Time Your Code

The basic tool you need to measure performance is one that will allow you to time your functions. For J2SE and other platforms there are programs called profilers that will provide detailed analysis of your code's executions; things like how much time is spent in each function, which functions take up the most execution time per run, and other information can be used to tune and tweak your code for maximum performance.

I have yet to see a decent profiling tool for J2ME. However, you can time the execution of your method calls by using the currentTimeMillis method:

Listing 15-1: Timing code

```
long time1 = System.currentTimeMillis();
methodWeTime();
long time2 = System.currentTimeMillis();
System.out.println(time2 - time1);
```

As you can see from this code snippet, we first get the current time, then call our method, and then get the time again. We print out the difference between these two times, which will tell us how long, in milliseconds, it took for the method to execute. If you do not have a data cable and terminal access to your phone, you could write these values out to a file and analyze it later. It may be worthwhile to hold the values in memory and then write out to a file in the destroyApp method, as file system access can be excruciatingly slow and thus throw off your timing readings.

Basic Tips

There are a few general tips you can apply to the design of your MIDlet that can improve performance and memory usage. Some have already been discussed in previous chapters, but it is worth reviewing them here. Some of these may depend on the platform you're running, so some performance tuning may have to be done on a per-handset basis.

Note Each device is different. On some handsets you may notice that certain optimizations don't appear to do much, while on others you may have radical performance increases.

Avoid Redundant Computations

Many accessor methods may seem simple enough, but behind the scenes a lot of computation is done when they are called. For this reason, it's a good idea to store frequently used values in variables returned by these methods instead of constantly calling the accessor. For instance, you may think the Image class' getWidth and getHeight methods are simply returning the value of their respective internal members. However, I have found saving these values out in an array and using it instead of calling the accessors will result in a significant performance gain on some handsets.

This also goes for things like string lengths, getting the current time, and other member calls. At the very least you are avoiding the overhead of calling a method and at most you are cutting out some significant redundant processing.

Keep Classes and Interfaces to a Minimum

Each class, public or otherwise, ends up being a separate file that must be loaded at run time. If you have a zillion classes everywhere, the initial loading and setup time of your MIDlet can be quite long. Also, each class takes up memory — so with the addition of each class you are eating up precious RAM and JAR space. Granted, these are both less of an issue on modern phones, but it still is advised to be cautious with how many classes you use.

For instance, if you have a large number of interfaces with different groups of constants in them, you might as well merge them together into one. Look for other opportunities for merging or eliminating unnecessary classes. Interfaces in general are often unnecessary and only serve as a handy way to make code more usable in most cases. If you can do without pseudo multiple inheritance and the other benefits of interfaces, go without. Sometimes, you have to abandon all good Java coding practices to get your code to fit in restrictive JAR size limitations.

Eliminate Unnecessary Methods

Each method takes up precious memory and JAR space. Sure, it may be nothing compared to a large PNG, but it pays to economize your methods. Probably the biggest area for this is in accessor methods. I suggest simply having public members you can modify instead of having an accessor method for each one. Sure, this isn't the Java way — but when you're trying to squeeze your game into a 64K JAR size, you need to nip and tuck anywhere you can.

Minimize the Number of PNG Files

The same rule applies to PNGs. The time it takes to load and
unpack a PNG file can be quite long on some handsets. Therefore,
if you store each frame of animation as a separate file, the load
time for your game can increase dramatically. Also, each PNG file
has added information that is redundant across multiple PNGs —
such as palettes, transparency chunks, and other data that is common to each frame of a given animation. By consolidating images
into one larger bitmap (perhaps via UV mapping) and then using
clip rectangles, Sprites, or regions to draw smaller sections of the
bitmap to the screen, you can save RAM and JAR space.

Crush Your PNGs

PNGs can contain a lot of superfluous information. Also, there are
a number of different ways to compress a PNG — some more efficient than others. Your favorite paint program may not do a
particularly good job of making sure your PNGs are the smallest
size possible.

The most obvious size conservation technique is to use the
fewest number of colors possible. Reduce your color depth to 4-bit
(16 color) if you are only using that many. As long as your bitmap
is paletted, most programs will reduce the palette down to the
fewest colors. However, it may be a good idea to help it along by
changing the bit depth to the lowest possible.

There is also an open-source tool, Pngcrush, that can be used
on the command line to minimize the size of your PNGs. Pngcrush
can be downloaded at pmt.sourceforge.net/pngcrush. What this
tool will do is remove unnecessary chunks, as well as try a number of different compression schemes on the image, in order to
create the smallest possible PNG file.

Optimize MIDI Files

Despite their generally diminutive size, it is still possible to have a
bloated MIDI file. There are a number of simple guidelines to creating slim and trim MIDIs. This includes removing author name,
copyright info, and any other header details. These are stored as
plain text inside the MIDI file and are totally unnecessary to the

playback of the tune. Keep the number of instruments and tracks to an absolute minimum. Also, avoid expensive effects such as pitch bends that generate a large number of MIDI instructions.

Static Initialization Can Be Bad

If you have a static initialized array, you may be getting more than you bargained for. Let's say you have an array like this in your class definition:

```
static char[] array = {(char)1, (char)2};
```

You may think that you are only taking up 2 bytes of memory. However, unlike C/C++, this is not simply placing values in a static memory segment for use at run time. Instead, this is actually generating instructions that will load each value into its respective array cell when the class is loaded. Instead of each element taking up a byte, the data and associated instructions will take up 4 bytes per entry. The workaround to this if you have large arrays (such as a tile map) is to read them in from a resource stream at run time.

Taming the Garbage Collector

One of the nice features of the Java platform is garbage collection. Unlike C/C++, where you have to manage your own memory allocations, Java will clean up after you — essentially deleting objects when you aren't using them. The problem is the process of deleting objects and reorganizing memory can cause a major hit in performance. Even worse is that you never quite know when the garbage collector is running or what it is doing. A lot of times you may be unknowingly calling methods that actually create new objects and discard old ones to the garbage collector.

These problems usually happen with immutable objects such as Strings. When using a String, many seemingly mundane operations actually create a new copy of the String and discard the old object. When manipulating text, it is advised to use StringBuffers instead — these are mutable Strings that can be modified without creating new copies and garbage objects.

With this said, you should also be sure to delete unused objects as soon as possible. This usually means setting the reference to null as soon as you are done using it. This goes for member references inside the object as well. You might go as far as writing a method for each class that goes through and nullifies each reference member. This would be called before nullifying the object reference itself to give the garbage collector more of an idea of what to throw out.

The garbage collector is a low-priority thread that runs when the MIDlet is idling or you finally run out of memory. Because of this, the garbage collector will not be called immediately after nullifying an object. Eventually, the garbage collector will reclaim this memory and dispose of the object once the reference is nullified. In some cases, you may have to ensure deletion by manually calling the garbage collector via the System.gc() method; but this is just a suggestion. The documentation states that the JVM will make a "best effort" to reclaim memory upon calling this method. Your guess is as good as mine as to what that actually entails.

Object Reuse

Somewhat related to our memory discussion is the reuse of objects. To avoid memory fragmentation, unnecessary garbage collection, and redundant object creation, it's a good idea to reuse objects when you can. For instance, instead of dynamically allocating objects to be added into a vector or other linked-list class, you might allocate an array of these objects at run time and manage their usage yourself. This means you have to track which ones are in use and which ones are free, but by writing your own managed object class you can be sure that you are reusing objects instead of allocating new ones all the time.

On these small devices it is a good idea to avoid dynamic memory allocation at all costs — using managed object pools can give the flexibility of acquiring and releasing objects without the overhead of memory allocation and garbage collection. Although object pooling may not give you a performance increase for small arrays (in fact, some have suggested it is just the opposite), it will reduce memory fragmentation over long execution periods. Object pools limit the garbage collector's actions because your object pool should be persistent through your MIDlet's execution — or at least be more persistent than dynamically allocated objects. Hence the potential performance boost.

Obfuscation

One of the most popular ways to shrink the size of your JARs is to use what is called an obfuscator. Obfuscators were originally intended to jumble around your classes so that they were hard to read when decompiled. This protected your code from being reverse-engineered and potentially stolen by some unscrupulous programmer and used in a rival's commercial program. Okay, not exactly the hacker ethic and all, but those days are over.

One of the ways code is obfuscated is by changing classes and variables to have unreadable names like "a," "b," "ab," etc. It also may remove unused fields, classes, debugging information, and even methods. A side effect of this process is that your variable and class names are shorter, hence a potential shrinking of your code size. For this reason, obfuscation became a popular way to minimize JAR size in MIDP development. Now, obfuscators not only advertise their security features but also their "code shrinking" ability.

Installing ProGuard

Most J2ME IDEs, as well as Sun's own KToolbar, allow for the easy integration of third-party obfuscators. In the case of KToolbar, the natively supported one is the open-source ProGuard. ProGuard is a free obfuscator that drops right into KToolbar's environment. To install ProGuard, simply download the proguard.jar file from proguard.sourceforge.net and copy it to your WTK20/bin folder. Now, the menu option **Project ▸ Package ▸ Create Obfuscated Package** should be available. This will create a JAR containing an obfuscated version of the code.

The Results

Let's take one of our sample programs and see how much space we save. If we look at the unobfuscated JAR file generated by WTK20 for our geometry MIDlet, we see that it is 2,623 bytes. Now, if we obfuscate it, the end result is a 2,204-byte JAR. That's an almost 20% reduction in size. Not gigantic, but not insignificant either. Your results may vary depending on the project.

Controlling Obfuscation

In some cases, you may need some classes to remain unobfuscated. For instance, you may have a public interface to a library JAR that you want others to use. In this case, you have to mark specific classes as unobfuscated so that ProGuard knows to leave these untouched. Unfortunately, KToolbar does not have built-in support for obfuscation scripts; however, it is possible to do this via the command line or in other IDEs. If you look at the ProGuard documentation, you see that there is a command line option, "-keep," which will allow you to specify class names that will not be obfuscated. There are a number of different command-line directives that can be used to affect how ProGuard obfuscates and what it chooses to preserve.

Basic Graphics Optimizations

There are a few common techniques used in game programming that can speed up your game's performance. One of the most basic of tips is to limit how much of the screen you actually draw. For instance, in Attack of the FLARB, the background is largely white, with a few moving Sprites. So, what you really need to do is clear out the previous positions of the changed Sprites with a white rectangle and draw the new positions every frame. If you have a bitmap background, you can clear out the background by drawing the chunks of the bitmap that were behind the objects in the previous frame.

When you get into double buffering situations, this may lose some of its appeal since most hardware is actually copying over the entire back buffer Image every frame. This operation dwarfs any savings you may make in bitmap drawing optimizations. Still, it may be worth it to keep track of two frames' worth of positions and update the changed sections of every back buffer.

As far as conserving memory by restricting color usage goes, this may work on some devices but not on others. The fact is, most hardware converts paletted PNGs (such as 16- or 256-color images) to the bit depth of the screen. So, if you have a phone with a 16-bit screen, that tiny 4-bit image is going to get blown up by four times to 16 bit. Still, using paletted images can crunch down the file size of the PNGs and thus have a much better time fitting in a tiny JAR.

Conclusion

In this chapter you've learned a little bit about how to optimize J2ME code in various ways. Optimization is an art unto itself, and entire books have been written on the subject, including various tomes on high-performance Java. I suggest reading some of those books if you are really interested in fully optimizing your code. Remember that each handset is different, so if you go crazy optimizing for one phone, you may find the performance gain does not cross over to every device.

Chapter 16

MIDlet Distribution

Introduction

Now that you know how to actually develop your own wireless game using MIDP 2.0, how do you get it out to market? This chapter will focus on the basics of getting your games in the hands of paying customers. The industry is always shifting and changing, so a lot of this information may seem vague and incomplete because, well, there is no one solid business model. A lot of this you are going to have to figure out on your own, bub.

Via the Web

The simplest way to distribute your MIDlets is by publishing them yourself. If you do a Google search for MIDlets, you'll find a lot of web sites that offer MIDlets for downloading. How is this done? The first thing you need is a valid JAD file. The JAD was discussed early in the book — it is a file that describes the MIDlet with such properties as its name, description, size, and other criteria. Once you have a JAD, you can place the JAD and the JAR, which contains the MIDlet, on a web server. Both the JAD and JAR have to be in the same directory. Also, the JAD's MIDlet-Jar-URL property has to be set to the URL at which you are placing the JAR and JAD file. So if I had put the HelloWorld MIDlet on Wordware's server, the MIDlet-Jar-URL property would look like this:

```
MIDlet-Jar-URL: http://www.wordware.com/HelloWorld.jar
```

The next step is configuring the server with the proper MIME types. There are two types you need to install:

```
.jad    text/vnd.sun.j2me.app-descriptor
.jar    application/java-archive
```

Once you have these two associations for the JAR and JAR file types, you can then point your phone's browser to the appropriate URL and it will download and install the JAR on the handset. You can test this by using your PC's web browser; if everything is correct, Sun's Wireless Toolkit emulator should allow you to install and run the JAR.

How do you actually make money from this method? Good question. Unless you set up some kind of shopping cart or PayPal scheme, web distribution like this is usually only good for free games and demos. However, in Japan there is a somewhat thriving market of off-menu web-based content providers. It may be worth a shot, but I probably would recommend other routes or at least not using web distribution exclusively.

Commercial Web Portals

There are a number of web portals that have popped up over the years that specialize in selling applications that run on various portable devices including J2ME handsets. Perhaps the most popular is Handango (www.handango.com). Here you can browse through thousands of applications for all sorts of handheld devices including numerous J2ME handsets from manufactures like Nokia, Motorola, and Sony Ericsson.

Getting your MIDlets distributed on Handango is a snap. Simply sign up for the partner program and you can register yourself or your company's products in the Handango catalog. Handango has various restrictions on the kinds of applications they allow in the catalog, including a restriction on all adult content. Regardless, they offer a wide variety of applications for sale including a large number of games.

Figure 16-1: An example Handango catalog page for a J2ME app.

Once you are a partner, you can determine the price of your games and enter a description as well as screen shots and various other marketing materials to be listed in the web catalog. Handango's custom Commerce Engine is flexible enough to allow you to place buttons on your own company web site that will allow buyers to purchase your games directly from Handango's store. Handango also has branded stores on other company sites that may drive more traffic toward your games. For each sale, Handango takes a 30% chunk out of the retail price. You get the rest. You can constantly monitor the sales of your games via your own partner account on the Handango site.

How people actually get games on their handsets varies depending on the device. Some devices require Handango to send an SMS message with a URL linking to the JAR, others use the WAP browser to install off the web, while still others need a data cable or Bluetooth hookup to your PC. Handango provides clear instructions on how to download games for each supported device.

There are other web portals that are focused on J2ME and mobile software distribution. Some of the more popular for J2ME distribution are www.zingy.com and www.microjava.com. Some of these portal services also have positions on carrier decks such as at AT&T and Nextel. Although web portals are an increasingly popular way to distribute and market MIDlets, the real deal is over-the-air distribution with a carrier.

Note   Most web portal sales figures in the U.S. are less than impressive. However, developers have had some decent success with European web sites such as Jamba! and others. Many web portal services (including domestic ones) also provide content to carriers — and thus can be an alternate way of getting on a carrier as well.

Retail

Retail distribution of MIDlets is a fairly new concept that was first pioneered in Europe as a mass-market distribution technique appealing to the average consumer. Here in the U.S., a company called PlayPhone (www.play-phone.com) has been selling games at retail in a few stores such as Fry's, EB Games, and Safeway.

In the store, what you buy is a DVD case containing a code and instructions on how to download the game onto your phone. There is no actual physical media involved. Instead, you use the unlock code to access a WAP site that will give you a URL used to install the game over the air. Getting your own games into retail will involve becoming a content partner with PlayPhone. Check the web site for the proper corporate contacts.

Over the Air

Web and retail distribution is nice, but what you really want to be able to do is allow your customers to use their own mobile device to browse through games, pick the one they like, buy it, and then have the fee charged to their phone bill as it installs wirelessly over the carrier network to the device. This is called over-the-air distribution. In a way, we have previously discussed this, as in many cases Handango or doing your own web MIDlet download will work over the air. In fact, MIDP 2.0 formally details over-the-air distribution in the specification — meaning every MIDP 2.0 device will be able to download MIDlets off of the web as described earlier in this chapter.

What I'm really talking about here is getting placed on the carrier's list of games that any user can download. Having to type in a URL with a fumbly phone keypad and look for your game is not going to get you many customers. But getting on a central list of games that every user can access with a few clicks on her phone is how you really pull in customers.

Becoming directly available on a carrier's wireless portal is a lot of work. It involves getting distribution deals with carriers as well as navigating their testing and submission process. Some carriers are easier to approach than others, but as the industry widens, the big publishers seem to be shutting the door on the little guys. This means you may have to go through a third party, such as a wireless game publisher, instead of leaping straight to the carrier itself.

When we talk about J2ME carriers in the United States, we mean Sprint, AT&T Wireless, Cingular, Nextel, and T-Mobile. Each one of these carriers has its own J2ME distribution scheme — some more restrictive than others. Here I'll give you a brief rundown of every major J2ME carrier's distribution programs. Note that Handango has begun to provide content for both AT&T Wireless and T-Mobile through their catalog. So, going direct may not be necessary, or even possible, in a few cases.

Note   Although Cingular has purchased AT&T Wireless, the merger will take a while to complete. For now, they still have separate content publishing schemes.

- **Sprint PCS:** Sprint PCS is the most restrictive of all carriers. They rarely let any new companies provide games directly, and instead encourage you to go through existing publishers to distribute your games on Sprint PCS. Sprint's developer site can give you more information and tools to get going. They even have their own custom SDK with Sprint-specific extensions necessary for supporting their platform. Sprint has also teamed up with Handango for the new Content Connection service for further distribution opportunities. Go to http://developer.sprintpcs.com to see what it's all about.

- **Cingular:** Cingular has their own developer site at http://alliance.cingularinteractive.com/. Here you can get information on developing and distributing applications for Cingular's handsets. This not only includes J2ME, but also RIM, PocketPC, and WAP applications as well. Cingular has a new DirectBill service, which allows you to charge users directly to their phone bill for applications. Cingular takes a 35% cut of the fee, leaving the developer with a healthy 65% of the retail price. Cingular does charge a setup fee for this service, which is good for up to 15 applications. If you wish to provide more than 15 applications, you need to pay to serve another 15.

- **T-Mobile:** T-Mobile's developer site is located at http://developer.t-mobile.com/tmobile/. Here you can download tools and get information on developing for T-Mobile. T-Mobile requires content partnerships to provide applications directly to the wireless consumer.

- **Nextel:** Nextel was the first carrier in the U.S. to provide MIDP support on mobile phone handsets. Nextel uses a Motorola-developed technology called iDEN instead of CDMA, GSM, or GPRS. As a result, Nextel only stocks Motorola-made iDEN handsets that aren't available anywhere else. These are sturdy, well-built models that now include a few popular color models suitable for games. This includes one of the earliest MIDP 2.0 devices on the U.S. market — the i730. Motorola's iDEN developer community site can be found at

http://idenphones.motorola.com/iden/developer/developer_
home.jsp. Here you can download tools and SDKs for their
iDEN handsets as well as find information on distribution.
Nextel also has their own developer site at http://devel-
oper.nextel.com. Recently, Nextel has begun using a partner
program where they only accept MIDlets from officially recognized publishers. Check out both the iDEN and Nextel site for
more information.

- **AT&T Wireless:** AT&T Wireless has been offering MIDP
  downloads for a while now, including many popular exclusive
  games with their mMode service. The site can be found at
  http://www.attwireless.com/developer/. AT&T has various
  tools and SDKs, but also gives live video conferences to
  registered developers, which keep you up to date on new technologies and developments in the wireless world. Getting on
  AT&T's mMode deck requires being accepted as a content
  provider. As you can probably guess, this involves your standard array of Machiavellian political maneuvering and
  schmoozing.

Publishers and Aggregators

From reading the previous section, you may gather that many carriers have closed up the retail channel and only offer access to a
select few publishers and content providers. This can be both a
blessing and a curse, as these middlemen often can give you wide
access to huge markets with little effort. But they also can take
unfairly enormous revenue cuts for doing very little work — not
to mention act in various shady and nefarious ways when it comes
to actually paying you. There are two kinds of content providers in
the gaming world — publishers and aggregators — although the
line between these two types of providers is blurring.

Publishers

A publisher is typically a company that will pay for the development of a game, test it, and then publish and market the product to
consumers. In some cases, a publisher may have some licensed
intellectual property such as the rights to a movie or popular

console video game title that they want to turn into a wireless game. In other cases, a publisher may give you an advance on royalties (or just an advance) to develop an original title that they will distribute.

Note Read any publishing or distribution contract carefully. As many record industry veterans will tell you, make sure you know about "recoupment" before you start counting those potential royalty dollars. Publishers have many ways to account for costs associated with a game's production that will ensure you never see a penny above the initial advance even if your game generates piles of revenue worldwide.

In the wireless world, things can be a little informal — especially with the payment part. A lot of wireless publishers aren't paying anything for development, and instead are taking enormous chunks of revenue for simply allowing you to use their carrier relationship to get your game out. Oftentimes this means you have to test and even localize your own game for foreign markets. However, the more work you do on your side, the more leverage you have to negotiate a better royalty rate. Examples of wireless publishers include newcomers such as MFORMA, Airborne Wireless, and Mobliss, along with traditional console and PC game heavy-hitters like THQ, Activision, and NAMCO.

Note It's not uncommon for a major publisher to pay millions of dollars for a movie license but try to get the game developed for free or at cost.

Aggregators

So what's an aggregator? Good question. The truth is, they aren't much different from publishers. *Aggregators* are usually publishers that don't pay you in advance. The only reason they exist is because they convinced a carrier to give them access to the carrier's customer base and placement on the deck. Then, they prevent other companies from coming into the market, and instead force everyone to come through them for distribution. They take a huge chunk of your revenue in exchange for merely allowing you access to the carrier's customers. Most of the time they do absolutely no marketing or promotion, and usually won't even test or localize your game.

Sometimes, I think many aggregators (and publishers, for that matter) should wear a ski mask and point a sawed-off shotgun at your head when drawing up a contract. Still, I do find aggregators useful for accessing foreign markets where it just isn't worth spending lots of time doing my own localization and distribution.

Don't think that all of these organizations are staffed by total creeps. Believe it or not, I've found some aggregators and even publishers that do a fantastic job of localization, distribution, and even sending the checks out. Also, aggregators that know the local culture may do a better job at modifying your game to appeal to local tastes than you — that is, if they even bother. I've had some success with some aggregators that have made major changes to my games in an attempt to appeal to the local market. Your mileage may vary — but be sure to thoroughly research any aggregators you may be thinking of using.

Note　If you're serious about making money in this space, get a lawyer. Or at the very least read your contracts very thoroughly. If you're getting a contract from an aggregator or publisher, chances are it's written to favor them — not you.

The lines blur here because a lot of aggregators have realized that they can't compete with no-budget games, and have begun to transform themselves into traditional full-service publishers. Otherwise, you might think of an aggregator as a simple distributor; in fact, many publishers use aggregators to distribute their content in regions where they don't have direct carrier relationships (which is yet another bite out of your revenue stream). Also, some carriers that previously worked exclusively with one or a few aggregators are opening up to publishers and other content providers. This may greatly diminish the role of the so-called aggregator.

Conclusion

Details are thin on the ground here, but the fact is there are no hard-and-fast rules for MIDlet distribution. Obviously, the most cash is in getting a direct carrier relationship. However, a lot of the time that simply isn't possible because publishers and aggregators have locked up the retail channel. The good news is, you can slap a free MIDlet on your own web site and have people playing it today. The bad news is that if you actually want to make money at this, the path isn't as clear.

Appendix A

JBuilder Mobile Edition

Introduction

Throughout this book we assume the reader is using Sun's free J2ME IDE, KToolbar. While KToolbar is a competent tool for some tasks, when it comes to developing commercial-quality mobile games you'll probably reach for something more complete. There are a number of IDE products out there that work with J2ME — many of them J2SE tools that include J2ME features. Borland's JBuilder Mobile Edition sort of falls in this category. It is a low-cost J2ME version of their familiar J2SE development environment, JBuilder. This appendix will give you a brief rundown of the product and show how you can get some of the examples in this book working as a JBuilder project.

Installation

Installing JBuilder Mobile Edition is simple. For those who have not purchased the full version, simply go to www.borland.com/ mobile and download the free demo. (This demo package includes other stuff such as their C++ Mobile Edition as well.) You must submit your email address to Borland's web site. Shortly after this process, Borland will automatically email you a registration code that will allow you to use JBuilder Mobile Edition for a limited time. When you install JBuilder, it will ask for the registration file or code it emailed to you. This trial period should be long enough for you to determine whether you want to make the full purchase.

Your First JBuilder Project

Let's take the first HelloWorld MIDlet we developed way at the beginning of this book and bring it into JBuilder. This should give you a good idea of how to use JBuilder with this project and any other future project you may embark on.

Creating a Project

First, we need to create a project. To do this, click on **File ▸ New Project**. You will then be presented with the Project Wizard. This wizard will help you set up your project, pick the JVM, and control other project properties before creating the JPX file. The first of the three wizard dialogs is shown in Figure A-1.

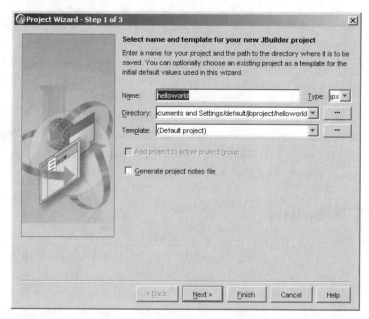

Figure A-1: The first screen of the Project Wizard

You can type whatever you want here, but to keep it simple, fill out the dialog as shown in Figure A-1. The project name actually ends up being the package name, as you can have multiple packages per project. None of our example source uses packages, but it is good practice. We will have to perform a slight modification to our source in order to get it to comply with JBuilder's insistence on packages. (The modification is merely adding the statement package helloworld; in the first line of HelloWorld.java.)

Click **Next** to proceed to the next screen of the wizard, as shown in Figure A-2. Here you can set all kinds of properties relating to paths and additional classes, including the JVM itself. As you can see in the JDK option, the JVM is set to the J2SE VM. We need to select the MIDP 2.0 VM in order to make a MIDlet. To do this, click the button to the right of the JDK text box. The Select a JDK dialog will appear as shown in Figure A-3. Depending on the JDKs you have installed on your development machine, you may see some slightly different options. According to ours, we need to click the last option, **J2ME Wireless Toolkit 2.0_01**. After doing this, leave everything else as is and click **Next**.

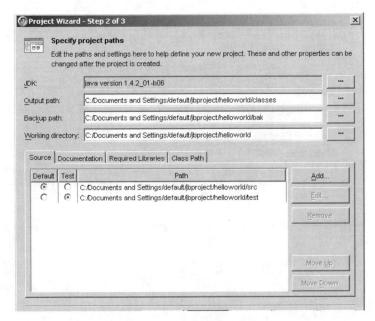

Figure A-2: The second screen of the Project Wizard

Figure A-3: The Select a JDK screen

Now the final step. The third screen, as shown in Figure A-4, needs no changes. Here you can set various Javadoc properties and such, but this is of no interest to us at the moment. Click **Finish**.

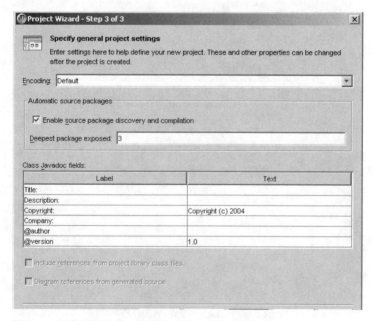

Figure A-4: The final screen of the Project Wizard

Creating a MIDlet

Now that we have created a project, we have to add the HelloWorld source. However, the project itself isn't enough to begin coding. We have to add a MIDlet to the project before we can do anything. To do this, click **File ▸ New**. You will be presented with the Object Gallery window as shown in Figure A-5. Click on the **Micro** option on the left, and then the MIDlet icon in the right panel. This will bring us to the MIDlet Wizard.

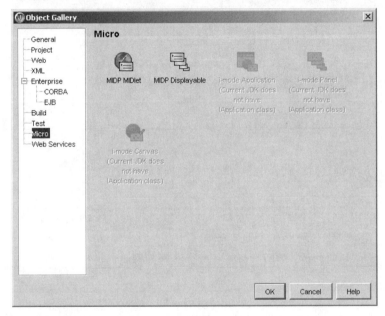

Figure A-5: The Object Gallery

The first screen of the MIDlet Wizard is as shown in Figure A-6. Here we need to type in the name of our main class. Make sure you use the proper capitalization, and type **HelloWorld**. This is the class name of our MIDlet in the HelloWorld example, and thus the name of our main class here. Click **Next**.

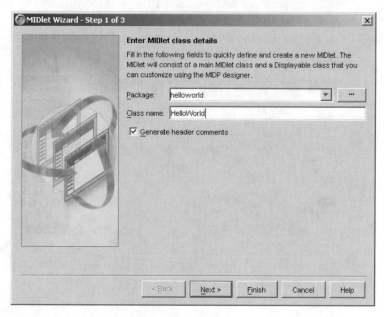

Figure A-6: The first screen of the MIDlet Wizard

The second screen contains the Displayable properties, as shown in Figure A-7. By default, JBuilder creates a MIDlet class and a Displayable class for the interface. We could work with this architecture, but if you just want to get the old code running, ignore this and click **Next**. We'll have to remove this class from the project later.

The final screen of the MIDlet Wizard, as shown in Figure A-8, allows us to name the runtime configuration. This is the configuration we use to apply settings to the emulator. Fill it out as seen in Figure A-8 and click **Finish**.

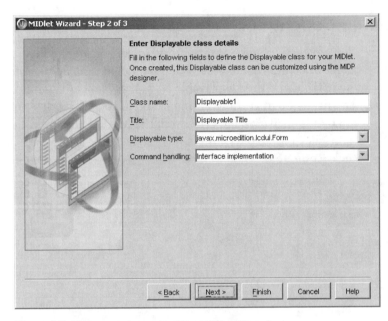

Figure A-7: The second screen of the MIDlet Wizard

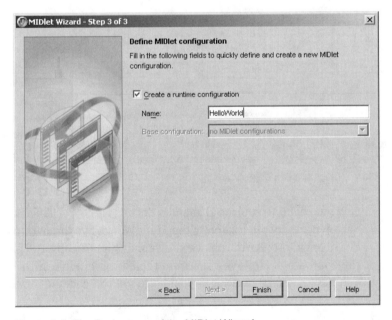

Figure A-8: The final screen of the MIDlet Wizard

Adding Code to the Project

Now you should have a project that looks sort of like Figure A-9.
JBuilder creates some stub code that includes default classes for
the MIDlet and the Displayable as well as standard comments.
The first step in getting our old example code to work is to
remove the Displayable class from the MIDlet. To do this, simply
right-click on **Displayable** in the Project panel on the left and
click **Remove**.

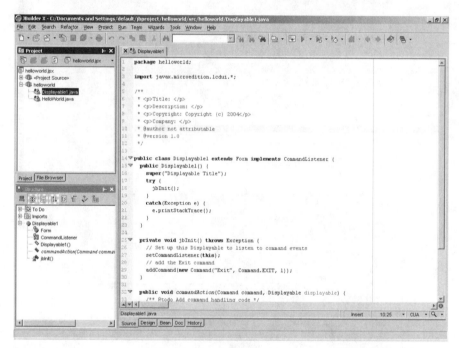

Figure A-9: Our project in the JBuilder IDE

Now, we need to replace Borland's default HelloWorld class with
our own. You could just copy the HelloWorld.java file over from
our original project to replace the default file, or copy and paste
the contents of HelloWorld.java to the editor window. Either way,
you have to make one slight change to get the code to compile.

JBuilder encapsulates our classes in packages. As mentioned earlier, HelloWorld is now included in the helloworld package. Thus, add this code to the first line of the project:

```
package helloworld;
```

Now, to compile this project, click on **Project ▸ Make Project**. A tone should sound, signifying the project has compiled with no problems. To run HelloWorld in the emulator, click on **Run ▸ Run Project**. The end result should be familiar, as shown in Figure A-10.

Figure A-10: HelloWorld running in the emulator

Conclusion

Obviously, this appendix just barely scratches the surface of what can be done with JBuilder. Explore the documentation and see what you can do. JBuilder features a robust debugger, lots of editing features, integrated source control, and support for custom SDKs from Sony Ericsson, Nokia, Motorola, and more. This is a full-featured and inexpensive IDE that should be seriously considered by any J2ME developer.

Appendix B

J2ME vs. BREW

Introduction

Sun's J2ME and QUALCOMM's Binary Runtime Environment for Wireless (BREW) standard are the two hot platforms in the U.S. wireless market. My previous book, *Wireless Game Development in C/C++ with BREW* (ISBN 1-55622-905-4) focused exclusively on QUALCOMM's technology. In that book, I provided a short primer on J2ME and a comparison between the two platforms. This appendix serves the same purpose, from the other side of the fence.

What Is BREW?

BREW is QUALCOMM's answer to J2ME as a wireless applications platform. Handsets that support QUALCOMM's BREW include many from such familiar manufacturers as Nokia, Motorola, LG, and more. In fact, you might notice that many of these handsets are exactly the same as their counterpart, except they have a different model number and run BREW instead of Java. Although BREW carriers exist all over the world, the largest concentration of customers is in the United States and South Korea. Having invented the CDMA standard that is used heavily in these regions, QUALCOMM has not managed to bring the BREW platform to GSM carriers in Europe yet — despite some interest from European handset manufacturers such as Sony Ericsson and Nokia.

BREW is a platform that runs native code written in C, C++, or even Assembly Language. This is the main difference between the two — with J2ME being an interpreted platform-independent language, some hardware details are glossed over for you. Also, Java's sandbox security model largely prevents you from accessing the low-level functions of the device (MIDP 2.0's signed MIDlets not included). With BREW you are given free reign over the file system, memory, and other features. For this reason, BREW applications must go through a lengthy testing and certification process before being distributed to carriers.

BREW also includes one crucial element missing from Java — distribution. Using QUALCOMM's Brew Distribution System, certified BREW applications are distributed to carriers all over the world. Although content providers still need individual carrier relationships, QUALCOMM handles the billing and distributes your royalties directly after taking their 20% cut. However, because of the use of this BDS, your application distribution options are limited to carriers. If you can't get on a carrier, there currently is no alternative — no retail distribution, no web portal distribution, and no self-distribution.

In the case of J2ME, you have many different distribution options, as discussed in this book. However, you must manage your own billing relationships with each carrier and portal. With the hundreds of operators and portals all over the world, this can be a formidable task. But, with both systems, getting those crucial business relationships is equally difficult.

The Tools

With J2ME, you don't have to spend a dime on tools. Sun's Wireless Toolkit is free, and all you need to get started is a simple text editor to write code. This is not so with BREW; QUALCOMM's platform relies on many expensive and proprietary tools, which raises the barrier for entry quite a bit.

To write code for QUALCOMM's BREW emulator you need to use Microsoft Visual C++. A non-academic version of this IDE can run you several hundred dollars, depending on which version you get. The BREW SDK itself can be downloaded for free from QUALCOMM's web site at www.qualcomm.com/brew. To compile native code, you need to either purchase ARM's compiler suite for $1,500 or use the free GCC compiler for ARM. However, in order to get the crucial files to properly set up the GCC compiler, or get other mandatory tools such as the AppSigner and AppLoader, you need an account on QUALCOMM's exclusive developer Extranet. This Extranet access is only granted after acquiring a Verisign account to digitally sign and authenticate your BREW application. This service runs about $400 a year for 100 signatures.

The final step in developing BREW content is to get the application True BREW certified. This is an expensive process that involves spending around $1,000 per handset to have the application tested at an external QA lab. The application is tested for memory leaks, interface issues, and to otherwise see if it blows up the phone or not. If it passes, you are then able to politic the carriers for distribution. If not, you have to spend $1,000 on another run.

The Platforms

The major differences between the platforms have already been illustrated. J2ME is a high-level platform-independent wireless applications platform with wide support from both free and commercial tools. BREW is a lower-level technology relying on a mix of commercial and free tools, as well as a robust distribution and billing solution.

Both platforms include support for various image formats, sprites, tiles, MIDI music and other media formats, both HTTP and TCP/IP networking, GUI controls, and other standard features. BREW has a lot of other features as well, many of which can be found in handset-specific extensions to MIDP created by the hardware manufacturers or carriers.

Moving from J2ME to BREW

You might be interested in bringing your existing Java content to BREW. If so, what's the easiest way to convert your J2ME code to BREW? Well, this is more of an art than a science really, as every developer has his or her own methods. If you keep your code clean and abstract both platforms' particulars into higher-level code, the process can be made much easier.

If you are a total BREW neophyte, I would suggest getting a copy of my previous book. This book is very similar to it — in fact you might think of this as a port of my original BREW book to Java. You can see how the techniques you learned in this book work in BREW. Secondly, I suggest you write your BREW code in C++. By using C++ you can mimic J2ME's object-oriented structure to make porting as easy as possible.

Also, keep in mind that there are different restrictions and device capabilities on BREW handsets. For instance, the way BREW implements sprites and tiles is quite different from MIDP 2.0. Also, most versions of BREW do not support threads, which may cause some major headaches when porting over MIDP code to the platform. There are also some file format differences, with BMP being the most common image format on BREW devices.

Conclusion

Both BREW and J2ME offer similar capabilities in graphics, networking, sound, and other areas. It's worth building your own tools and techniques for easy conversion between J2ME and BREW if you want to address the U.S. market. And for the third time, I'll plug my first book, *Wireless Game Development in C/C++ with BREW* (ISBN 1-55622-905-4), for a good primer on QUALCOMM's platform.

Index

Don't make last year's game!

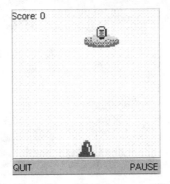

Multiplayer games are easier to publish, faster selling, and more fun.

And they are fast and easy to make!

Entelepon has delivered turn-based and real-time massively multiplayer games, as well as scoreboards, contests, and downloadable assets.

Now our advanced multiplayer technology is ready to be plugged into your products. Whether you want a simple scoreboard or the whole enchilada, we'll provide you with a proven code base and host your game on our server farm. Opt into our marketing network to lower your costs and advertise your game directly to consumers.

It's easy; contact us today:
www.entelepon.com